Violence

For my colleagues and students
at the New School for Social Research

Violence
Thinking without Banisters

Richard J. Bernstein

Polity

First published in 2013 by Polity Press

Polity Press
65 Bridge Street
Cambridge CB2 1UR, UK

Polity Press
350 Main Street
Malden, MA 02148, USA

ISBN-13: 978-0-7456-7063-8
ISBN-13: 978-0-7456-7064-5(pb)

A catalogue record for this book is available from the
British Library.

Typeset in 11 on 12.5 pt Baskerville
by Toppan Best-set Premedia Limited
Printed and bound in Great Britain by
the MPG Printgroup

The publisher has used its best endeavors to ensure
that the URLs for external websites referred to in this
book are correct and active at the time of going to press.
However, the publisher has no responsibility for the
websites and can make no guarantee that a site will
remain live or that the content is or will remain
appropriate.

Every effort has been made to trace all copyright
holders, but if any have been inadvertently overlooked,
the publisher will be pleased to include any necessary
credits in any subsequent reprint or edition.

For further information on Polity, visit our website:
www.politybooks.com

Contents

Acknowledgments

I am grateful for permission to use revised versions of my previously published work. "The Aporias of Carl Schmitt," *Constellations*, 18/3 (2011); "Hannah Arendt's Reflections on Power and Violence," *Iris: European Journal of Philosophy and Public Debate*, 3/5 (2011); "Jan Assmann: The Mosaic Distinction and Religious Violence," *Graduate Faculty Philosophy Journal*, 32/1 (2011).

I completed this manuscript during the summer of 2012 when I was a Fellow at the *Forschungskolleg Humanwissenschaften* (Institute for Advanced Studies) in Bad Homburg. I want to thank Professor Rainer Forst for inviting me to be a Fellow of the Institute and the Alfons & Gertrude Kassel-Stiftung for supporting my visit. The entire staff of the Institute helped to make my stay extremely pleasant and productive. I also want to express my gratitude to my research assistant Santiago Rey who helped to edit the manuscript. I want to thank Jean van Altena for her meticulous and judicious editing. John Thompson, as always, has enthusiastically encouraged me in writing this book. I have had the good fortune to teach for the past two decades at the New School for Social Research. This book is the result of the lively critical conversations with my colleagues and students. It is dedicated to them.

Preface

I have entitled this work *Violence: Thinking without Banisters*. "Thinking without banisters" (*Denken ohne Geländer*) was one of the favorite expressions of Hannah Arendt – and it has a special meaning for her. Arendt was convinced that the eruption of twentieth-century totalitarianism meant a radical break with tradition. No longer could we rely on traditional political and moral categories to help us comprehend our times. If we are to engage in the activity of thinking after the break in tradition, then we can't rely on banisters or fixed points; we are compelled to forge new ways of thinking and new concepts. Thinking, which Arendt sharply distinguished from knowing, is primarily concerned with meaning – with making sense of the world in which we find ourselves. Thinking is not to be identified or confused with calculation, means–end rationality, or even scientific knowing. Thinking is an activity that must be *performed* over and over again in order to keep it alive. There is always a danger that thinking will disappear – to be replaced by some non-thinking substitute. For Arendt, keeping thinking alive has the utmost practical significance. In *The Life of the Mind* she raised the question: "Could the activity of thinking as such, the habit of examining whatever happens to come to pass or attract attention, regardless of results and specific content, could this activity be among the conditions that make men abstain from evil-doing or even 'condition' them against it?" (Arendt 1978: 5).

Although the experience that provoked her thinking was the horror of totalitarianism, her insights about thinking without banisters are part of a much larger sea change that has taken place. From a variety of philosophical orientations there has been a multifaceted critique of the appeal to any fixed metaphysical, epistemological, political, or moral foundations. A dominant metaphor suggested by Descartes no longer seems appropriate for characterizing thinking – the metaphor of a solid foundation upon which our thinking can rest. One of the reasons why the appeal to banisters and/or foundations has been so seductive is because of the fear that the only other alternative is some form of radical skepticism, self-defeating relativism, or nihilism. I once labeled this the "Cartesian Anxiety," and it has haunted us (and continues to do so) (see Bernstein 1983: 16–20). Thinking without banisters is the alternative to both foundationalism and nihilism. And this type of thinking is urgently needed to understand violence.

We live in a time when we are overwhelmed with talk, writing, and especially images of violence. Whether on television, the internet, smartphones, films, or the video screen, we can't escape representations of actual or fictional violence – so much so that we easily become numb and indifferent to still another report or depiction of violence – another suicide bombing, another assassination or violent rebellion in some remote part of the world, another report of domestic violence, another action movie or video game filled with all sorts of violence. The media typically have a field day when some deranged person unexpectedly starts killing in a high school, university, or movie theater. But after a few days of 24/7 reporting, these incidents pass into oblivion. Even a momentous event like 9/11 does not provoke much public *thinking* about violence. Our age may well be called "The Age of Violence" because representations of real or imagined violence (sometimes blurred and fused together) are inescapable. But this surfeit of images and talk of violence dulls and even inhibits thinking. What do we mean by violence? How are we to characterize the different types of violence, and how are they related to each other? What can violence achieve? Is there a type of creative violence that enhances life? What are the limits of violence? How is violence related to nonviolence? These are some of the questions that I will explore.

Philosophers have long been concerned with war. There isn't a major philosopher who hasn't directly or indirectly dealt with war. And insofar as war involves violent killing, it is, of course, closely associated with violence. But violence is a much broader category than war. Clearly, in the popular imagination, physical killing is still the paradigm of violence. But there can be all sorts of violence – legal violence, structural violence, linguistic violence, symbolic violence, even religious violence – that do not immediately involve physical killing. But what concerns me is how the different types of violence so easily turn into physical violence – bodily harm and ultimately physical killing.

Although there are many different ways of approaching violence, I focus on five thinkers who have engaged in a sustained reflection – thinking without banisters – about violence. And each of them has been extremely influential. They are Carl Schmitt, Walter Benjamin, Hannah Arendt, Frantz Fanon, and Jan Assmann. I approach them by asking what we can learn about violence from them. What are the strengths and weaknesses of their reflections on violence? In my concluding remarks I show how we can weave their contributions together into a nuanced dialectical understanding of the relationship of violence and nonviolence.

Introduction

There is a disturbing paradox about violence. We are overwhelmed by talk and images of violence, and there is now a vast literature on different types of violence, ranging from child abuse, domestic violence, rape, serial murder, and suicide bombing, to the new sophisticated robotic weapons of modern warfare. The issue of whether human beings in the course of history are becoming more or less violent (and by what criteria) is hotly debated. Different classifications of violence have been proposed, such as structural violence, symbolic violence, legal violence, etc. But there is no consensus about any classificatory schema or how different types of violence are related to each other. The paradox is that although (or perhaps because) there is so much discussion of violence, there is enormous confusion about what we even mean by violence. In the course of this study I will be dealing with different types of violence. I have decided to approach these issues by concentrating on the works of five thinkers who have thought deeply about the meaning of violence: Carl Schmitt, Walter Benjamin, Hannah Arendt, Frantz Fanon, and Jan Assmann. Each of them has been extremely controversial and provocative – and they have been immensely influential. I will also consider many other thinkers who have been influenced by them, including Jacques Derrida, Judith Butler, Simon Critchley, and Slavoj Žižek (among others). Of course, there are other important thinkers who have been concerned with violence, but I have three reasons for my selection. First, many more recent discussions of violence take their departure from the reflections of one or more of these five. Second, they represent widely different orientations and disciplinary approaches to the discussion of violence. Third, they deal with a great variety of different types of violence including political violence, colonial violence, structural violence, symbolic violence, legal violence, and religious violence. Of the five thinkers that I examine, four were born in Germany. This is not completely accidental. If one believes, as I do, that thinking is ultimately grounded in personal experience, then from the time of the First World War to the defeat of Hitler and the Nazis, Germany has been one of the most violent and murderous societies in history. The reflections of these four thinkers are deeply rooted in their personal experiences in Germany. Their lives span the twentieth and the beginning of the twenty-first centuries. The fifth thinker, Frantz Fanon, was born in Martinique, studied in France, and moved to Algeria to become the director of a French psychiatric hospital. He resigned from his position in 1956 and was deeply involved in the Algerian armed struggle to overthrow the French colonial system. Fanon, unlike the other four, was not only a writer and theoretician of violence; he was an active participant in the Algerian fight for liberation. *The Wretched of the Earth*, written during the last year of his life when he was dying of leukemia, has become a modern classic – one that justifies the necessity of violence in order to overthrow colonialism. It continues to inspire those fighting colonialism, neo-colonialism, and oppression throughout the world.

Carl Schmitt is the most controversial German thinker of the twentieth century. Even his most severe critics acknowledge that he was a brilliant, original thinker of legal, jurisprudential, and constitutional issues. In 1933 he joined the Nazi party, and he helped to formulate some of the most nefarious Nazi legal policies. The posthumous publications of his diaries reveal the depth of his anti-Semitism. So it is all too easy to dismiss him. But Schmitt can not be so easily dismissed. Many of the most important thinkers of the twentieth century have critically engaged with his writings. Two of his most famous and discussed books, *Political Theology* and *The Concept of the Political*, were written in the 1920s, before he had any association with the Nazis. In the past few decades there has been an enormous international renaissance of interest in Schmitt. Much of this new interest has been by thinkers and activists who think of themselves as on the political left. In my chapter on Schmitt I explore the reasons why Schmitt has been such an important and influential thinker. Let me indicate briefly some of the key reasons. Schmitt has been a relent-less critic of what he takes to be the failures of modern liberalism in all its forms – political, legal, economic, and cultural. Even if one rejects some of his extreme criticisms, he has a knack for putting his finger on knotty problems that any defender of liberalism must face. He is remarkably perspicacious about the changes in warfare that have taken place in recent history – a change from a time when war between states involved *defeating an enemy* to total war that involves the complete *annihilation of a foe*. Many of his admirers are impressed by his "realistic" sense of politics and his definition of "the political" as involving the antithesis of public friends and enemies. And the friend/enemy distinction also involves the real *possibility* of physical killing. Schmitt places the emphasis on the role of decision in politics and is skeptical about norms. One of his enormous appeals is the appar-ent clarity, crispness, and polemical force of his prose. I approach Schmitt with a single question in mind. What does Schmitt teach us about violence? I carefully analyze his most famous early (pre-Nazi) monograph, *The Concept of the Political*. I argue that a close reading of this text reveals a whole series of aporias in his thinking. The most fundamental aporia concerns his implicit normative-moral stance – the orientation that is the basis for his sharp critical judgments. On the one hand, he ridicules and scorns the appeal to legal and other norms in understanding "the political." "The political" has nothing to do with moral judgment or normative justification. But, on the other hand, he makes strong normative-moral judgments when he condemns liberalism, the dehumanization of absolute enmity, and the depoliticization of the world. He claims to be a tough-minded realistic analyst and theoretician. But I argue that Schmitt's analy-ses and judgments presuppose a normative-moral orientation that he never justifies and never makes fully explicit. What is worse, he undermines the very possibility of such a justification. Paradoxically, although Schmitt develops a sophisticated and nuanced understand-ing of how unlimited absolute enmity and violence has come to domi-nate the twentieth century, he doesn't provide us with the conceptual resources for judging and condemning *any* sort of violence. His talk about "dehumanization" turns out to be empty rhetoric.

When the 28-year-old Walter Benjamin wrote his essay "On the Critique of Violence" (which appeared *before* Schmitt's *Political Theology* and *The Concept of the Political*), he dealt with many of the same issues as were fundamental for Schmitt. Both were seeking to come to grips with the fragility of the Weimar Republic, the failures of the parliamentary system, and the outbursts of violence on the right and the left that followed Germany's defeat and collapse after the First World War. Benjamin seeks to comprehend revolutionary violence and its opposition to legal violence. He was inspired by Sorel's *Reflections on Violence*. Like Sorel, he claims that the aim of revolutionary violence is to destroy existing state power. When Benjamin's essay was first published in 1922, it was almost totally ignored (a great exception was Schmitt), but since the 1960s, when his work became better known, it has been extensively – almost obsessively – interpreted. Virtually every thinker since that time who has dealt with the meaning of violence has felt the need to comment on and interpret anew what Benjamin was saying in his cryptic and elusive essay. The most provocative notion in the essay is divine violence – and the contrast Benjamin draws between divine violence and mythic violence. The key to understanding what Benjamin is saying in his essay is crucially dependent on how one understands divine violence. In my chapter on Benjamin, I focus on what divine violence means and the role it plays in Benjamin's critique of violence. And I pursue the ways in which commentators have interpreted divine violence – including Herbert Marcuse, Jacques Derrida, Gillian Rose, Judith Butler, Simon Critchley, and Slavoj Žižek (among others).

One of the most interesting interpretations of divine violence is elaborated by Butler and Critchley. Although I raise doubts about whether Benjamin's text really warrants their interpretation of divine violence as a form of nonviolence, they nevertheless highlight something that is crucially important in Benjamin's essay – and important for understanding violence. They stress the way in which Benjamin's critique is played out against the background of his reflections on nonviolence. (Schmitt has very little to say about nonviolence; he was also completely scornful of pacifism.) Butler and Critchley emphasize that the commandment "Thou shalt not kill" is not to be read as a supreme categorial law that admits of no exceptions, but rather serves as a guideline for action (*Richtschnur des Handelns*). Benjamin, in a sentence that I will carefully analyze, writes: "[The commandment] exists not as a criterion of judgment, but as a guideline for the actions of persons or communities who have to wrestle with it in solitude and, in exceptional cases, to take on themselves the responsibility of ignoring it" (Benjamin 1996: 250). According to Butler and Critchley, the commandment not to kill is a guideline that allows for exceptions. In short, the commitment to nonviolence is compatible with the justification of violence in exceptional cases. Benjamin cites the Jewish rejection of the condemnation of self-defense as an example of such an exceptional case. I critically examine interpretations of Benjamin's essay, ranging from Marcuse's claim that Benjamin shows the historical necessity of revolution, to Derrida's uneasiness that Benjamin's essay allows for an interpretation that makes the bloodless gas chambers of the Holocaust an expiation of God's anger. I argue that – for all its thought-provoking quality – Benjamin's remarks about divine violence and its opposition to mythic violence are too condensed and cryptic to resolve the issue of the conflict of interpretations. More important, his essay does not provide an adequate basis for an understanding of violence and its interplay with nonviolence. The power of the essay – the reason why it has attracted so much commentary and creative interpretation – is because of the *questions* it raises about violence and nonviolence, not because of the answers it provides.

Hannah Arendt, although a close personal friend of Benjamin and the person responsible for introducing Benjamin to an American public, never discusses or even mentions Benjamin's essay. Arendt, however, was concerned with violence and nonviolence throughout her life. She argued that totalitarianism introduced a form of violence and terror into the world that was completely novel. She sought to comprehend the radical evil of totalitarianism. Violence also plays a significant role in her discussion of fabrication and *homo faber* in *The Human Condition*. In *On Revolution* she argues that when we properly understand the meaning of revolution, then we will see that it has nothing to do with violence. The end of revolutions is the achievement of public freedom. Violence cannot create this freedom; violence is instrumental and only destroys.

In the 1970s Arendt turned to a full-scale discussion of the meaning of violence and its relation to nonviolent political power. She was deeply disturbed by the rhetoric of violence, and occasional incidents of actual violence that were becoming increasingly manifest in the Black Power movement and in the more militant factions of the student movement. She was severely critical of those who "glorify" violence, who think that violence cleanses and transforms human beings. She condemns what she takes to be the irresponsible views of Sartre, who wrote an inflammatory preface to Fanon's *The Wretched of the Earth*. And although she indicates that Fanon's actual

understanding of violence is more nuanced than Sartre's, she criticizes the influence of his book for encouraging violence. I believe
that the popular rhetoric of violence in the 1960s touched a deep
emotional nerve that elicited memories of the Nazis.

Arendt criticizes a dominant way of thinking about power and
violence that dates back to ancient times. This is the conception of
power as "power over." Power is conceived of as basically the rule
of an individual or a group over other individuals or groups. If this
is the way in which we conceive of power, then C. Wright Mills is
correct when he declares: "All politics is a struggle for power: the
ultimate kind of power is violence" (Mills 1956: 171). But against
this dominant way of understanding the relation of power and violence, Arendt seeks to recover a conception of power as *empowerment*,
which is achieved when human beings act in concert together. The
emergence of this type of power involves acting together, persuasion,
deliberation, and the sharing and testing of opinions – not violence.
For Arendt, power and violence are *antithetical* concepts – even though
she knows that in the "real world" they rarely ever appear as separate.
I show that Arendt's distinctive understanding of power is related to
a network of concepts, including spontaneity, natality, action, public
space, isonomy, and public tangible freedom. Together, these concepts
articulate her vision of the meaning of politics.

I have characterized Arendt's thinking as an "exaggerated" thinking. She deliberately exaggerates the antithetical differences between
power and violence because she wants to recover something that we
are in danger of forgetting and losing – a sense of what political
power can be and what it can achieve. Another way of putting this is
to say that Arendt highlights those "privileged moments" in history
when the political power of the people as empowerment flourished.
Her analysis of power and politics provides a critical normative standard for judging and evaluating actual politics in the "real world."
Against the criticism that Arendt is nostalgic about an idealized
conception of the Greek polis that never really existed, I argue that
her understanding of nonviolent power and politics helps to illuminate and understand the effectiveness of many modern progressive
political movements, including the early civil rights movement in
the United States and the essentially nonviolent uprisings that led
to the overthrow of Communist regimes in Eastern Europe. Arendt's
views concerning power and violence culminate in her concept of
"the revolutionary spirit." She sees this emerging in the eighteenth

century, especially in the American Revolution, which she contrasts to the French Revolution. She declares that the history of revolutions from the eighteenth century until the present "politically spells the innermost story of the modern age" (Arendt 1977: 3). She draws a sharp distinction between rebellion and revolution. The end of rebellion is liberation from oppression, but the "end of revolution is the foundation of freedom" (Arendt 1965: 140). Violence may be necessary and justified in the rebellion against oppression, but it never founds public freedom. Arendt, like Benjamin, realizes that there are exceptional, limited circumstances when violence can be justified, but she never completely analyzes this. Her remarks about when violence can be justified are all too brief and sketchy. This is a serious lacuna in her thinking. Her own analysis demands that we face up to the issue of when and how violence can be justified. Just as she distinguishes between power and violence, revolution and rebellion, she also draws a sharp distinction between liberty and freedom. Liberty is always liberty *from* something – whether it is liberty *from* hunger and bodily needs or liberty *from* political oppression. Although liberty is not to be identified with freedom, it is a necessary condition for the realization of freedom. But liberation from oppressive rulers may require violent armed struggle. To make this point concrete, I refer to Arendt's favorite example of a revolution – the American Revolution. Employing her categories, the American Revolution was "preceded" by a war of liberation – an armed struggle that involved killing. The revolution itself, the creation of a *novus ordo saeculorum*, could only come into being after the success of the armed struggle against the British. Furthermore, at an earlier stage of her career, Arendt justified violence when she argued for the creation of an international Jewish army to fight Hitler and the Nazis.

When Arendt wrote her essay *On Violence*, she was reacting against the popularity of the rhetoric of violence that was, in part, attributed to Fanon's *The Wretched of the Earth*. Her essay has been read as an attack and refutation of Fanon – just as Fanon's book has been read as a celebration of violence. I argue that this is a profound (but all too common) misreading of Fanon. Fanon is engaged in a *critique* of violence. There are three aspects to this critique: (1) a deep understanding of the structure and dynamics of colonial violence, (2) a justification of the necessity of armed struggles to overthrow colonial violence, and (3) a critique that is intended to foster and orient revolutionary praxis – the achievement of what Fanon calls *libération*.

The violence that is Fanon's primary concern is *the violence of the colonial system* instituted and cultivated by the colonists. He analyzes the political, economic, cultural, and socio-psychological dimension of this system – a system that instigates murder, massacres, and torture. The colonized subject is *created* and constituted by the colonial system – a system instituted and reified by the colonizers. The rage and violence that spontaneously erupts among the colonized – especially the rural population – is a dialectical consequence of the violence of the colonists. If this spontaneous violence remains unchecked and unlimited, it will destroy the revolutionary movement. This spontaneous violence must be limited and channeled into a disciplined armed struggle by political leaders who are responsive to the needs and demands of the people. Fanon's dominant concern is *libération*, not *violence*. Or rather, by analyzing the structure and dynamics of colonial violence, he seeks to show why armed struggle is required to destroy the colonial system – including *both the colonists and the colonized* – in order to achieve *libération*. *Libération* is not to be identified with achieving national independence – although independence is a necessary condition for the realization of *libération*. Although Fanon barely indicates what he means by *libération*, his brief remarks about active participation of the people suggest that it is close to what Arendt means by public freedom. Most of *The Wretched of the Earth* is *not* about the violence of the colonized; it is about the obstacles that stand in the way of achieving *libération*. And the greatest obstacles are internal ones. Fanon fears that a "colonial mentality" will survive national independence and undermine the goal of the revolutionary struggle. He is critical of native bourgeoisies and political leaders who are out of touch with the people. He condemns anti-racist racism and gratuitous brutal violence. He fears that in many post-colonial societies, indigenous leaders will engage in the same colonist practices of violence in order to secure their own power.

The relationship between Arendt and Fanon turns out to be very different from how it initially appears. *The Wretched of the Earth* is an argument showing why armed struggle is necessary to overthrow the colonial system. Benjamin and Arendt both indicate that there are circumstances when violence can be justified. And I argue that Fanon's book should be read as a sustained argument showing why overthrowing the colonial system (especially in Africa) constitutes one of those "exceptional cases" in which violence – directed armed struggle – is justified. Consequently, there is a productive tension between the views of Arendt and Fanon, rather than a stark incompatibility. Arendt is rightly critical of some of the rhetorical excesses of Fanon when he speaks about the cleansing and transforming power of violence. She helps to underscore Fanon's own awareness of the limits of violence – and of the danger of perpetuating the cycle of violence and counter-violence. She is extremely wary of the abuse of alleged "justifications" of violence. And she has an acute sense of the limits of violence. Violence by itself can never achieve what she calls public freedom and what Fanon calls *libération*. But there is a way in which Fanon compels us to take seriously that there are concrete, historically specific circumstances where armed struggle can be justified. Appealing to Arendt's own categories, we can say that there are times and circumstances where violent struggle is justified in order to liberate a people from oppressive (or totalitarian) rulers.

There is another extremely important respect in which Arendt helps us to appreciate the delicate dialectical balance between violence and nonviolence. I do not think that there are any fixed (effective) criteria for determining when violence is and is not justified. I am also skeptical that there can even be effective guidelines. Even the appeal to self-defense is not innocent. For all too frequently – in both individual cases and in the justification of military actions – the appeal to "self-defense" is used as a smokescreen to obscure nefarious motives and aims. We should always be skeptical about proposed justifications of violence – even claims of "self-defense." But here, Arendt's appeal to the creation of public spaces in which there is genuine debate and deliberation becomes vital and relevant. For it is only in such an open space of debate that there can be an assessment and check on the abuses of "justifications" of violence. I agree with Arendt that a persuasive argument can never be a definitive knockdown argument. There is no escape from risky political judgments. But with Benjamin, Arendt, and Fanon (as well as with Butler and Critchley), we can affirm that this doesn't rule out the possibility of exceptional circumstances in which violence *is* justified. Or, if we use Benjamin's phrasing, we have "to take on the responsibility for ignoring" the fundamental commitment to nonviolence. We cannot anticipate what will constitute "exceptional circumstances." Because there are no fixed criteria or guidelines that are ever completely adequate to determine when violence is (and is not) justified, thorough public debate is essential.

Initially, Jan Assmann's discourse seems quite different from that of Schmitt, Benjamin, Arendt, and Fanon. Each of these thinkers is directly concerned with the relation of violence and politics. But Assmann's dominant concern is that of religion and cultural memory. His analysis of what he calls revolutionary monotheism and the Mosaic distinction – there is only one true God and only one true religion – contains *potential* violence. Throughout history such exclusive monotheism has been employed to "justify" violence against those who are judged to be infidels. When Assmann first introduced the Mosaic distinction, he spoke of it as a "murderous distinction" – no gods but God! He seeks to trace the historical deconstruction of the Mosaic distinction. This is the significance of the idea of Moses the Egyptian. For in this Moses discourse, the stark opposition between Israel and Egypt (where Israel symbolizes the true religion and Egypt symbolizes false idolatry) is deconstructed. Assmann claims that the potential violence of the Mosaic distinction should not be confused with actual violence. When he analyzes key passages in the Hebrew Bible that deal with violence, he argues that these are intended to serve as a *symbolic* warning about slipping back into idolatry – slipping back into false religion. Although he insists that revolutionary monotheism introduces a new kind of religious violence, he wants to distinguish between religious violence and political violence. It is not monotheism, but the political abuse of monotheism, that leads to actual violence and physical killing in the name of the "true" God. But I argue that there is good reason to be skeptical about this distinction between religious and political violence, on both biblical textual and historical grounds.

There is another aspect of Assmann's reflections on cultural memory that has significant consequences for understanding the relation of violence to nonviolence. Given his understanding of cultural memory, we are always haunted by the past. There is also the possibility of a cultural return of the repressed after a period of latency. This means that we are always haunted by the potential violence of exclusive revolutionary monotheism. If we follow the logic of Assmann's reasoning, he challenges all those narratives of historical progress which suggest that with the "triumph" of reason and modernity we can finally overcome religious violence. This is a dangerous illusion because it underestimates the eruption of the severity of "monotheistic moments" that have occurred throughout history. And it is because of the potentiality of religious violence to take ever new actual forms that it becomes so urgent to deconstruct the Mosaic distinction.

In my critical discussion of these five thinkers – focusing on their insights and weaknesses – I seek to bring out the limits of violence. There are powerful ethical and political reasons to commit ourselves to nonviolence. But we are always haunted by the breaking out of new and unexpected forms of violence. That is why the task (*Aufgabe*) of opposing violence is an ongoing vigilant task. At the same time, we have to acknowledge that there are exceptional circumstances in which violence can be justified. I have indicated my doubts about the possibility of determining abstract fixed criteria or even significant guidelines for judging when violence is (and is not) justified. There is no criterion or guideline that cannot be twisted and abused. The only way to prevent such abuse is by cultivating publics in which there is a free and open discussion of the pros and cons of proposed justifications for the use of violence; publics in which individuals are committed to listening to each other, to sharing and testing their opinions – publics committed to rational persuasion. When engaged public debate and judgment withers – or is cynically distorted and manipulated – then there is nothing to prevent the triumph of murderous violence.

Chapter 1

The Aporias of Carl Schmitt

The Ambiguous Legacy of Carl Schmitt

In his 1991 book review of Bernd Rüthers, *Carl Schmitt in Dritten Reich*, William Scheuerman asked the question, "Why should anyone really care about right-wing legal thinker Carl Schmitt's activities during the dark days of Nazi dictatorship?" At the time, Schmitt was barely known in the United States, although there were signs of "the so-called Schmitt renaissance that has taken place both in North America and Western Europe during the last decade" (Scheuerman 1991: 71). Scheuerman was sharply critical of the new fascination with Schmitt and the "attempt to minimize Schmitt's complicity in the horrors of Nazi barbarism." He expressed the hope that Rüther's "refreshingly straightforward and fair study" of this dark and ugly phase of Schmitt's life would finally "discourage more scholars from rushing to hop on the Young Schmittian bandwagon" (Scheuerman 1991: 78).

But now, more than twenty years later, the "the so-called Schmitt renaissance" has turned into a veritable tsunami. Schmitt's work is actively and passionately discussed throughout the world. He has been hailed as the most incisive, relevant, and controversial political and legal theorist of the twentieth century – and the enthusiasm for Schmitt is shared by thinkers across the political spectrum from the extreme left to the extreme right. At the same time, we now have much more detailed knowledge of how quickly and actively Schmitt helped to implement Nazi policies, as well as the crudeness of his anti-Semitic slurs in both his public and his private writings.[1] How, then, are we to explain the current fascination with Schmitt? There are no simple explanations, but here are some of the strands that run through the current literature.

With the growing disillusionment with the varieties of "really exist-ing" liberal and neo-liberal democracies, Schmitt's early – and sus-tained – trenchant analysis of liberalism has been taken to be one of the most penetrating and devastating critiques of contemporary lib-eralism (in all its varieties). Even those who reject Schmitt's extreme diagnosis of contemporary liberalism concede that he locates some of its most serious weaknesses and problems. Schmitt reveals the deep tensions between democracy and liberalism with a greater sharp-ness than any other twentieth-century political thinker. And although Schmitt's early analysis of the crisis of parliamentary democracy was concerned primarily with the Weimar Republic, he had an insight into the problems that plague liberal democracies right up to the present. He exposed the hypocrisy of liberal humanism – a humanism that has become an ideological justification for a new, dangerous kind of war in which the aim is not simply to defeat, but totally to annihilate, the enemy. Those who approach Schmitt primarily as a legal and juridical thinker concede that he has revealed one of the most serious issues of legal jurisprudence – the "enigma of legal indeterminacy." Schmitt argues that, regardless of professed liberal claims that legal decisions should be based *solely* on the rule of law, in fact all legal norms are una-voidably open-ended and indeterminate. This means, as Scheuerman tells us, that "Every legal decision is a *hard* case. Liberal demands to clarify and codify law are inherently flawed because no system of legal norms can hope to guarantee even a minimal degree of regularity and determinacy within legal decision making" (Scheuerman 1999: 17). Even if one rejects Schmitt's extreme views about the relation between legal norms and actual juridical decisions, he opens up what has been, and continues to be, the most controversial issue in all defenses of the "rule of law": What are (and what ought to be) the limits of "discretion" in interpreting and applying the law?

Some political theorists find Schmitt's entire approach to politics refreshing and realistic. Schmitt avoids the "rationalism," "norma-tivism," and "moralism" that are presumed to plague so much of contemporary political theory. His famous (some would say infamous) pithy declarations that "the specific political distinction to which political actions and motives can be reduced is that between friend and enemy" and that "the distinction of friend and enemy denotes the utmost degree of intensity of a union or separation" have been interpreted as initiating a new, invigorating, realistic, and concrete approach to politics. Schmitt is the thinker who "tells it as it is" and doesn't pull any punches. Part of the attraction of Schmitt to left thinkers is that he provides sharp weapons for criticizing and exposing the normativism and rationalism of thinkers such as John Rawls and Jürgen Habermas.[2] He is an antidote to the "suffocating" Kantianism that dominates so much political theory and philosophy today. He exposes the inadequacies of theories of deliberative democracy, which overemphasize the role of deliberation and the appeal to reasons in making political decisions. Schmitt's defenders argue that the essence of real politics – even democratic politics – is not deliberation or seeking to achieve a "rational" consensus, but rather vigorous agonistic conflict and enmity. And Schmitt, so it is claimed, had the perspicacity to see that this is what is at the heart of "real politics."

The fecundity of Schmitt's thinking can be seen in other areas. Although a prolific writer, the two short texts that have been his most influential are *The Concept of the Political* and *Political Theology*. The latter begins with the dramatic claim: "Sovereign is he who decides on the exception," and declares that "all significant concepts of modern theory of the state are secularized theological concepts" (Schmitt 2005: 5, 36). There has been almost endless commentary on just these two claims. Prior to Schmitt, the expression "political theology," as he himself notes, was used primarily in the nineteenth century as a term of abuse. But today "political theology" has almost become a culture industry. Although there were other contemporaries of Schmitt – most notably Walter Benjamin – who were explicitly concerned with political theology, I think it is fair to say that Schmitt's work is the primary provocation for the extensive discussion of political theology today. The German political theorist Heinrich Meier argues that political theology stands at the very core of all of Schmitt's oeuvre; it is the key for understanding Schmitt. And Meier draws a strong contrast between political theology (Carl Schmitt) and political philosophy (Leo Strauss).

Finally, I want to mention still another approach to Schmitt's work. Andreas Kalyvas acknowledges that Schmitt's "enthusiastic support of the Nazi seizure of power in 1933, his infamous justification of Hitler's crimes, and his virulent anti-Semitism are more than enough to dissuade a discussion of Schmitt's views on democracy" (Kalyvas

2008: 80). Yet Kalyvas argues that a "selective critical reading" of Schmitt's major constitutional writings provides insights into the politics of the extraordinary that can be reconstructed to develop a theory of radical democracy. Kalyvas is perfectly aware that he is not only departing from Schmitt's explicit intentions but is using his "insights" to develop a theory of radical democracy that Schmitt would find repulsive. But Kalyvas exemplifies a characteristic of many of the new interpreters of Schmitt. Acknowledging Schmitt's Nazi complicity and the vulgarity of his anti-Semitic remarks, they focus on ways in which Schmitt's arguments and themes about law, constitutions, and politics can be appropriated and used for purposes that Schmitt never intended. And, of course, what so distresses some of Schmitt's harshest critics is that they see this selective use of Schmitt as ingenuous – a failure to realize that even his pre-Nazi Weimar writings are continuous with, and lay the groundwork for, his active Nazi complicity.

My purpose in this brief review of Schmittian themes is *not* to endorse any of them, but rather to indicate why we can't simply ignore Schmitt and the controversies surrounding his work. There are other reasons for taking Schmitt seriously. Debates about Schmitt's theses are not a new phenomenon. They began almost as soon as he started publishing, long before the Nazis came to power. Consider a partial list of some of the leading thinkers of the twentieth century who have seriously engaged with Schmitt. Among Schmitt's early contemporaries were Leo Strauss, Walter Benjamin, Martin Buber, Herbert Marcuse, Franz Neumann, Otto Kirschheimer, Karl Löwith, Hans Blumenberg, Alexandre Kojève, Hans Morgenthau, Joseph Schumpeter, and Friedrich Hayek. More recent discussants and critics include Jacob Taubes, Jürgen Habermas, Jacques Derrida, and Giorgio Agamben. One measure of any thinker's significance is the stature of those who feel the need to confront, discuss, and criticize his work. By this criterion no one can seriously doubt the importance of Schmitt (as distinguished from what sometimes seems like a faddish fascination).

The Political: The Friend/Enemy Distinction

My aim in this essay is to ask and answer a straightforward question: *What do we learn from Schmitt about enmity and violence?* I am not simply asking what he *explicitly* says about these concepts – although this is where we must begin. I want to see where his thinking leads – what is entailed by the trains of thought that he pursues. My question is direct, but answering it requires pursuing a number of byways. These include exploring (1) precisely how we determine *who* is the enemy and *who* is the friend; (2) how we are to understand decision and its relation to *political judgment* in concrete life; and (3) the aporetic character of Schmitt's "anti-humanism." I will focus primarily on *The Concept of the Political* – although probing Schmitt's claims will require ranging over his other writings published before and after this influential work. Schmitt tells us that "all political concepts, images, and terms have a polemical meaning" (Schmitt 1996a: 30). I agree with Schmitt, so I want to acknowledge from the outset that my discussion – insofar as it is political – has a polemical intent. But, as Schmitt also indicates, being polemical is not incompatible with being fair to one's adversary. I want to follow the hermeneutical principle of trying to give a fair account of Schmitt's views in order to have a serious encounter with his ideas.

So let's turn directly to the famous friend/enemy distinction as it is introduced in *The Concept of the Political*. This is not as straightforward as it seems. Like almost everything that one touches in dealing with Schmitt, this text raises complex contentious questions. Which edition are we to consider? *The Concept of the Political* was originally published as an essay in 1927, revised for publication as a short book in 1932 and revised again in 1933. Are we also to take into account his subsequent reflections on this famous text? Heinrich Meier has argued that the differences between the 1932 and the 1933 editions are crucial, because they reveal a "hidden dialogue" with Leo Strauss. Scheuerman thinks that Meier overemphasizes the role of political theology in Schmitt's jurisprudential and legal writings. He also claims that Meier "downplays the manner in which Strauss's antimodernism can be read as a frontal attack on the (for Strauss, inherently modernist) decisions embodied by Schmitt." But even more relevant, Scheuerman tell us:

> Because Meier is primarily concerned with chronicling Strauss's impact on Schmitt, he also clouds the fact that the truly important shifts in the basic argumentation of "the concept of the political" occurred between 1927 and 1932, *not* 1932 and 1933. Whereas the 1933 version of *The Concept of the Political* did include some changes probably encouraged by Strauss's 1932 essay, far more fundamental shifts in

Schmitt's thinking can be identified between 1927 and 1932 versions. (Scheuerman 1999: 227)

These "more fundamental shifts" are due to the influence of the young Hans Morgenthau.[3] I want to avoid getting entangled in these scholarly debates (except when I think they are relevant to my discussion) and I will focus on the canonical 1932 edition which has now been translated into English together with Leo Strauss's notes.[4]

Schmitt begins *The Concept of the Political* with a direct but consequential statement: "The concept of the state presupposes the concept of the political" (*Der Begriff des Staates setzt den Begriff des Politischen voraus*) (Schmitt 1996a: 19). The concept of the state not only presupposes the political; these two concepts are distinct and are not to be confused. This distinction is important, because when Schmitt defines the political, he leaves open the question of its application. "The political" may designate "entities" or groupings that are not states. And there may be "states" that are not truly political. Later in his essay, Schmitt indicates that the so-called liberal state is not really political when he emphatically declares: "There exists a liberal policy of trade, church, and education, but absolutely no liberal politics, only a liberal critique of politics" (Schmitt 1996a: 70).[5] Schmitt is not concerned with defining the state or characterizing its essence in this text. He does, however, mention some ways in which linguistic usage paraphrases what a state is. "The state is the political status of an organized people in an enclosed territorial unit," and "in its literal sense and in its historical appearance the state is a specific entity of a people" (Schmitt 1996a: 19). But identifying state and politics "becomes erroneous and deceptive at exactly the moment when state and society penetrate each other." When state and society become identical, when all "ostensibly neutral domains such as religion, culture, education, and the economy cease to be neutral," then the state becomes the "total state." "In such a state, therefore, everything is at least potentially political, and in referring to the state it is no longer possible to assert for it a specifically political characteristic" (Schmitt 1996a: 22). In short, if we restrict ourselves to trying to define the political by limiting ourselves to the concept of the state, we obscure the specific characteristic that makes something political. Let's follow closely how Schmitt introduces his definition of "the political."

A definition of the political can be obtained only by discovering and defining the specifically political categories. In contrast to the various relatively independent endeavors of human thought and action [*relativ selbstständigen Sachgebieten menschlichen Denkens und Handelns*], particularly the moral, aesthetic, and economic, the political has its own criteria which express themselves in a characteristic way. The political must therefore rest on its own ultimate distinction to which all action with a specifically political meaning can be traced. (Schmitt 1996a: 25–6)

Schmitt is making a key assumption here, which may initially seem quite innocent; but, as we shall see, it is not so innocent. He is assuming that there are categories and distinctions that are specifically political, and furthermore that we can sharply distinguish the political from other "endeavors" or spheres such as morality, esthetics, and economics. What is the warrant for this assumption? In part, in a tendentious manner, Schmitt is building upon the differentiation thesis associated with Max Weber. In the course of modern history different autonomous spheres emerge, each with its own distinctive criteria and logics. Without any further elaboration, Schmitt says: "Let us assume that in the realm of morality the final distinctions are between good and evil, in aesthetics beautiful and ugly, in economics profitable and unprofitable. The question then is whether there is also a special distinction which can serve as a simple criterion of the political and of what it consists. The nature of such a political distinction is surely different from that of those others. It is independent of them and as such can speak clearly for itself" (Schmitt 1996a: 26). I want to call attention to the rhetorical force of these claims. Not only does Schmitt *assume* the relative independence of these different realms, he suggests that there are simple (some might say simplistic) criteria for distinguishing them – "good and evil," "beautiful and ugly," "profitable and unprofitable." The distinctions in these different domains are *antitheses*. He thereby sets the stage for his definition of "the political."

The specific political distinction to which political actions and motives can be reduced is that between friend and enemy. This provides a definition in the sense of a criterion and not as an exhaustive definition or one indicative of substantial content. Insofar as it is not derived from other criteria, the antithesis of friend and enemy corresponds to the relatively independent criteria of other antitheses: good and evil in the moral sphere, beautiful and ugly in the aesthetic sphere, and so on. In any event it is independent, not in the sense of a distinct new domain, but in that it can neither be based on any one antithesis nor any combination of other antitheses. (Schmitt 1996a: 26)

But precisely how are we to understand the concepts of friend and enemy, and the relation between them? Schmitt's remarks are at once brief and cryptic. He writes: "The distinction of friend and enemy denotes the utmost degree of intensity of a union or separation, of an association or disassociation" (Schmitt 1996a: 26). This distinction can exist without drawing upon the antitheses that mark off the other endeavors or domains. The political enemy need not be morally evil or esthetically ugly. The friend/enemy concepts are to be understood "in their concrete and existential sense, not as metaphors and symbols" (Schmitt 1996a: 27). The friend/enemy antithesis is a *political* category; it is not to be taken in a "private-individualistic" sense. The enemy in the distinctively political sense need not be hated personally. "The enemy is not merely any competitor or just any partner in a conflict in general. He is also not the private adversary whom one hates. An enemy exists only when, at least potentially, one fighting collectivity of people confronts a similar collectivity" (Schmitt 1996a: 28). In short, Schmitt makes a sharp distinction between the political public friend/enemy distinction, where one fighting collectivity confronts another collectivity, and the private-individualistic animosity that I may bear to another individual (or group). Consequently, the enemy is a *public enemy*, not merely a private enemy. (And this is also true of the political friend.) We are told that friend and enemy concepts "are neither normative nor pure spiritual antitheses." The antithesis, Schmitt reiterates, is *concrete* and *existential*. And to emphasize this point, he writes: "The political is the most intense and extreme antagonism, and every concrete antagonism becomes that much more political the closer it approaches the most extreme point, that of the friend-enemy grouping" (Schmitt 1996a: 29). But how is one to determine who is a friend and who is an enemy? There is no neutral third party or general norm or standard to which we can appeal to distinguish friend and enemy. "Only the actual participants can correctly recognize, understand, and judge the concrete situation and settle the extreme case of conflict. Each participant is in a position to judge whether the adversary intends to negate his opponent's way of life and therefore must be repulsed or fought in order to preserve one's own form of existence" (Schmitt 1996a: 27). There is a crucial and consequential ambiguity in this claim, which is even clearer in the German original where Schmitt uses the phrase *"Die Möglichkeit richtigen Erkenntnis und Verstehens."* What counts as a *correct* (*richtig*) recognition, understanding, and judgment of the concrete situation – or to translate the German literally – "a correct knowledge and understanding" of the concrete situation? Can the actual participants misjudge the concrete situation, be mistaken about whom they take to be their real enemy? And if they can be mistaken, what criteria determine whether the participants incorrectly "recognize, understand, and judge"? The reason why this ambiguity is so crucial is because – in "the extreme case of conflict," the decision to go to war – the most fundamental political issue is whether or not the concrete situation has (or has not been) correctly recognized, understood, and judged. It doesn't help to say that – in the final analysis – only the participants can decide who is and who is not their enemy. This doesn't answer the question, but pushes it back, because we can ask again: Are there better and worse decisions? Are there decisions based upon a correct (or incorrect) knowledge and understanding of the concrete situation? (Think of the US intervention to overthrow Saddam Hussein.)

Even though the antithetical distinctions that mark off the different spheres are presumably "autonomous," nevertheless, there is a sense in which the political antithesis of friend/enemy can *trump* the other distinctions. "Emotionally the enemy is easily treated as being evil and ugly, because every distinction, most of all the political, *as the strongest and most intense of the distinctions and categorizations, draws upon other distinctions for support*" (Schmitt 1996a: 27, emphasis added). This, according to Schmitt, does not call into question the autonomy of the different spheres, but rather shows how the other antithetical distinctions can become subsumed under the political.

Both Meier and Scheuerman note an important shift between the original 1927 essay and the 1932 edition. In the original essay Schmitt writes as if "pure politics" is a separate domain, to be sharply distinguished from other domains such as morals, esthetics, and politics. But as Meier notes, "the conception of domains is replaced by a model of intensity" (Meier 1995: 22).[6] Scheuerman agrees with Meier about this shift.

Though the original 1927 essay occasionally seems to concede the oddity of the attempt to delineate politics clearly from other spheres of human activity, given the fact that political conflicts seem to relate inextricably to moral, economic, and even aesthetic differences, only in 1932 does Schmitt unambiguously acknowledge the inappropriateness of the attempt to conceptualize politics as something basically unrelated to other forms of human activity. Schmitt grasps that *"everything is potentially political"* and he notes that politics can emerge in every domain of human existence. (Scheuerman 1999: 229).[7]

The friend and enemy concepts are *concrete* and *existential*, but what does this mean, and how is this antithesis expressed? "For to the enemy concept belongs the ever present possibility of combat" (Schmitt 1996a: 32). Combat is to be understood in "its original existential sense." "The friend, enemy, and combat concepts receive their real meaning precisely because they refer to the real possibility of physical killing. War follows from enmity. War is the existential negation of the enemy" (Schmitt 1996a: 33). War is *not* "the continuation of politics by other means."[8] "War is neither the aim or the purpose nor even the very content of politics" (Schmitt 1996a: 34). But, as Schmitt insists, it is "an ever present possibility." We fail to do justice to the existential seriousness of politics unless we realize that it entails the real possibility (but not the necessity) of physical killing at those times when we believe that our very way of life, our existence, is threatened by an enemy. Schmitt introduces two other concepts that stand at the core of his thinking: *decision* and the *exception*. For, he tells us, "what always matters is the possibility of the extreme case taking place, the real war, and the *decision* whether this situation has or has not arrived." And he adds "that the extreme case appears to be an *exception* does not negate its *decisive* character but confirms it all the more" (Schmitt 1996a: 35, emphasis added).[9]

There is another important tension in Schmitt's reiterated insistence that "the friend and enemy concepts are to be understood in their concrete and existential sense" (Schmitt 1996a: 27). For these concepts – concrete and existential – pull in opposite directions. Typically, Schmitt uses the expression "concrete" to designate what is historically specific. If we are to understand the concrete meaning of the friend/enemy distinction, then we have to grasp the specific historical context and circumstances in which there are friends and enemies – otherwise we face the danger of meaningless abstractions. But "existential" is used to designate what is *always* characteristic of the political. In this sense, the existential transcends any historical context. Or, putting the point in another way, whenever we properly speak of the political (regardless of the historical period), we are speaking of friends and enemies in the "existential sense."[10]

Schmitt concedes that we can conceive of a world without the possibility of war, but that such a world would be "a world without the distinction of friend and enemy and hence a world without politics" (Schmitt 1996a: 35). Even though Schmitt says that in defining the political it is "irrelevant whether such a world without politics is desirable as an ideal situation" (Schmitt 1996a: 35), he doesn't hesitate to express his skepticism and contempt for such a world.

Political Enmity

For all its dramatic rhetoric, something fundamental still seems to be missing from this friend/enemy account of the political. After all, it is trivially true that throughout history there have been groupings of friends and enemies, and that all too frequently the hostility between them has led to war. And although there can be friends and enemies without actual war, there are times – especially when a group believes that its way of life is threatened – that a decision is made to go to war. If one wants to *stipulate* that the expression "the political" should be restricted and limited to this aspect of human existence (and ignore or denigrate so many of the other activities that we normally call "political" – e.g. elections, public policy debates), then it is difficult to see what is so illuminating about this approach or why it should be so controversial.[11] What is missing from our (and his account) thus far is a presupposition about human beings – what he calls "the pessimistic conception of man."[12] Schmitt was a great admirer of Hobbes – although, as we shall see, his relation to Hobbes is extremely complex. Later in his essay, Schmitt praises Hobbes in a passage that is revealing.

> Political thinkers such as Machiavelli, Hobbes, and often Fichte presuppose with their pessimism only the reality or possibility of the distinction of friend and enemy. For Hobbes, truly a powerful and systematic political thinker, the pessimistic conception of man is the elementary presupposition of a specific system of political thought. He also recognized correctly that the conviction of each side that it possesses the truth, the good, and the just bring about the worst enmities, finally the war of all against all. This fact is not the product of

a frightful and disquieting fantasy nor of a philosophy based on free competition by a bourgeois society in its first stage (Tönnies), but is the fundamental presupposition of a specific political philosophy. (Schmitt 1996a: 65)

Schmitt concludes this paragraph with the barbed remark: "The political adversaries of a clear political theory will, therefore, easily refute political phenomena and truths in the name of some autonomous discipline as amoral, uneconomical, unscientific, and above all declare this – and this is politically relevant – a devilry worthy of being combated" (Schmitt 1996a: 65–6). Clearly this remark is intended to anticipate and defend Schmitt from his potential adversaries. But as Leo Strauss points out, there is something extremely problematic about Schmitt's appeal to Hobbes – something that indicates an unresolved problem in Schmitt's use of the friend/enemy distinction.[13] It is certainly true that Hobbes tells us that "'the nature of war, consisteth *not in actual fighting;* but in the known *disposition* thereto' (*Leviathan* XIII). In Schmitt's terminology this statement means that the *status naturalis* is the *genuinely* political status; for, also according to Schmitt, 'the political' is found '*not in fighting itself* . . . but in a behavior that is determined by this real *possibility*'" (Schmitt 1996a: 90). When Hobbes speaks of the state of nature, he is clearly referring to *individuals,* not political groups. Furthermore, this characterization of the state of nature is fundamental for his political philosophy. But for Schmitt the political friend/enemy distinction is a *public* one; it refers to groupings – not isolated individuals. Within a political state, there may be *internal* dissension between friends and enemies. This is the condition of civil war. Both Schmitt and Hobbes are deeply concerned with avoiding civil war. But Strauss underscores the difference between Schmitt and Hobbes: "To be sure, the state of nature is defined by Schmitt in a fundamentally different fashion than it is by Hobbes. For Hobbes, it is the state of war of individuals; for Schmitt, it is the state of war of groups (especially of nations). For Hobbes, in the state of nature everyone is the enemy of everyone else; for Schmitt, all political behavior is oriented to *friend* and enemy" (Schmitt 1996a: 90).

The primary issue here is not simply to note the difference between Schmitt and Hobbes. Schmitt is aware of this difference. I want to highlight a gap in Schmitt's theory. What is the relation between individual enmity and public enmity? How are we to account for the genesis of public enmity?[14] How do we explain the transition from the existential threat experienced by an individual and the existential threat experienced by a group? When we speak of public enmity, to whom or what are we ascribing this enmity – the entire political group, its leaders, its sovereign? The gap between individual enmity and public enmity of a group is exacerbated because Schmitt says: "*Each participant* is in a position to judge whether the adversary intends to negate his opponent's way of life and therefore must be repulsed or fought in order to preserve one's own form of existence" (Schmitt 1996a: 27, emphasis added). This passage suggests that Schmitt is referring to each *individual* participant, but his political sense of friend and enemy requires that it is political *groups* that judge whether an adversary group intends to threaten their way of life. So it cannot be true that each participant, as *an individual*, is in a position to judge whether his adversary is threatening his way of life, for this would reduce public enmity to the private enmity of individual participants. If public political enmity is not to be identified with private enmity and is not simply the sum or aggregate of the enmity of individuals, then Schmitt's friend/enemy distinction demands some account of how public enmity arises – and who or what determines this public enmity. The comparison between Hobbes and Schmitt indicates an even deeper problem. Strauss brings this out when he writes: "This difference [between Hobbes and Schmitt] has its basis in the *polemical* intention of Hobbes's definition of the state of nature: for the fact that the state of nature is the state of war of all against all is supposed to motivate the abandonment of the state of nature. To this negation of the state of nature or of the political, Schmitt opposes the position of the political" (Schmitt 1996a: 90).

Hobbes's purpose in introducing the state of nature is to propose a *rational* solution to the problem posed by the war of all against all. It is the awareness and *fear* of the consequences of the state of nature that is the motivation for the "creation" of the Leviathan, the artificial mortal god that demands obligation in exchange for protection; that offers peace instead of war.[15] Perhaps it is more accurate to say that Hobbes seeks to *contain* enmity and thinks that this is possible only with a strong sovereign – but at times Hobbes expresses his doubts that the Leviathan can fully contain enmity. Even with a strong decisive sovereign there still remains the potential threat of civil war. But Schmitt is more emphatic in claiming that the enmity exhibited by the friend/enemy antithesis can *never* be fully contained; never completely eliminated by specious "rational" solutions. That would be the end of politics. This is why, despite Schmitt's claim to the contrary, he cannot – as Strauss himself notes – avoid the question of human nature.[16] The political friend/enemy distinction depends on an understanding of the nature and function of human enmity.[17] "Because the sphere of the political is in the final analysis determined by the real possibility of enmity, political conceptions and ideas cannot very well start with an anthropological optimism. *This would dissolve the possibility of enmity and, thereby, every specific political consequence*" (Schmitt 1996a: 64, emphasis added). No enmity, no friend/enemy, no politics!

Suppose we ask what is Schmitt's rationale or justification for his version of the pessimistic conception of man. Schmitt affirms that there is a close connection between theological dogmas of sin and the political conception of enmity. "The fundamental theological dogma of the evilness of the world and man leads, just as does the distinction of friend and enemy, to a categorization of men and makes impossible the undifferentiated optimism of a universal conception of man. In a good world among good people, only peace, security, and harmony prevail" (Schmitt 1996a: 65).

Politics as Destiny

In part, the attractiveness (perhaps one should say, the "seductive attractiveness") of Schmitt lies in his stark oppositions: friend/enemy; good/evil; beautiful/ugly; optimism/pessimism. There is sharpness, clarity, and decisiveness. Schmitt, with his polemical animus against anything that smacks of liberalism, cannot resist caricaturing all liberalism, as if all forms of liberalism presuppose a simplistic optimism about human nature and the goodness of human beings. *Either* one is naively optimistic about human beings, and consequently fails to grasp what is distinctive about the political, *or* one has a realistic concrete existential grasp of the real possibility of enmity.[18] There are those who affirm original sin and those who deny it (the naïve optimistic liberals). Schmitt emphatically declares: "The methodological connection of theological and political presuppositions is clear" (Schmitt 1996a: 65). Once again, we touch upon a fundamental tension and ambiguity. We can see this by examining more closely the connection that Schmitt draws between theological doctrines of sin and the political. Even though Schmitt concedes the possibility that some day there may be a completely depoliticized state of humanity, he thinks that it is a dishonest fiction to assume it to be at hand. But Strauss shows that, despite this caveat about the possibility of total depoliticization, Schmitt actually argues that "the political is a basic characteristic of human life; politics in this sense *is* destiny; therefore man cannot escape politics. . . . The inescapability of the political is displayed in the contradiction in which man necessarily becomes entangled if he attempts to eliminate the political" (Schmitt 1996a: 94).

> The political is thus not only possible but also real; and not only real but also necessary. It is necessary because it is given in human nature. Therefore the opposition between the negation and the position of the political can be traced back to a quarrel over human nature. The ultimate controversy is whether man is by nature good or evil. Here, however, "good" and "evil" are "not to be taken in a specifically moral or ethical sense"; rather "good" is understood as "undangerous," and "evil" as "dangerous." Thus the ultimate question is "whether man is a dangerous or an undangerous being, a perilous or a harmless, non-perilous being" (59) "All genuine political theories" presuppose man's dangerousness (61). Accordingly, the thesis of man's dangerousness is the ultimate presupposition of the position of the political. (Schmitt 1996a: 95)[19]

Strauss detects the ease with which Schmitt slides from value-laden concepts of good and evil to the more neutral concepts of dangerous and not dangerous (and the ease with which he moves from the idea of the pessimistic conception of man to original sin). When Schmitt first introduced his concept of the political by "defining the specifically political categories," he drew a sharp contrast between the moral antithesis of good and evil and the political contrast of friend and enemy. But now he doesn't hesitate to affirm that all political theories can be classified by whether they presuppose that man is by nature good or evil.

> One could test all theories of state and political ideas according to their anthropology and thereby classify these as to whether they consciously or unconsciously presuppose man to be by nature evil or by nature good. The distinction is to be taken here in a rather summary fashion and not in any specifically moral or ethical sense. The problematic or

unproblematic conception of man is decisive for the presupposition of every further political consideration, the answer to the question whether man is a dangerous being or not, a risky or a harmless creature [*ob der Mensch ein "gefährliches" oder ungefährliches, ein riskantes oder ein harmlos nicht-riskantes*]. (Schmitt 1996a: 58)

What does it mean to say "the distinction is to be taken here in a rather summary sense and not in any specifically moral or ethical sense"? Schmitt writes as if the *political* distinction of "good" and "evil" is the same as the distinction of dangerous and not dangerous. But then how are we to understand *this* antithesis? Strauss notes that there is a "double meaning" of evil – evil as *"human inferiority* or as *animal power."* He characterizes this latter "evil" as innocent evil. Contrasting Schmitt with Hobbes, Strauss says that "Hobbes had to understand evil as *innocent* 'evil' because he denied sin. . . . The opposition between evil and good loses its keen edge, it loses its very meaning, as soon as evil is understood as innocent 'evil' and thereby goodness is understood as an aspect of evil itself" (Schmitt 1996a: 99). Strauss makes these points in the context of arguing that Schmitt's critique of liberalism is still operating within the horizon of liberalism. And in doing so, he puts his finger on an aporia that stands at the center of Schmitt's critique.

> The task therefore arises – for the purposes of the radical critique of liberalism that Schmitt strives for – of nullifying the view of human evil as animal and thus innocent evil, and to return to the view of human evil as moral baseness; only in this way can Schmitt remain in harmony with himself if indeed "the core political idea" is "the *morally* demanding decision" (*Politische Theologie* 56). The correction that Schmitt undertakes in the view of evil held by Hobbes and his successors not only fails to meet the forgoing requirement but even contradicts it. Whereas in the case of Hobbes the natural and thus innocent "evil" is emphasized so that it can be *combated*, Schmitt speaks with an unmistakable *sympathy* of the "evil" that is not to be understood morally. (Schmitt 1996a: 99–100)

The more morally neutral distinction of dangerous and not dangerous is perfectly compatible with the liberalism that Schmitt wants to critique. Even the great Enlightenment thinker Kant, a major source for contemporary political liberalism, maintains that there is a propensity to evil in all human beings.

Schmitt's Aporia

There is a deep aporia that haunts *The Concept of the Political*. Indeed, it haunts much of Schmitt's work. Despite his frequent disclaimers, Schmitt clearly associates the political friend/enemy distinction with what Strauss calls the "human," i.e., the *moral* sense of good and evil.[20] And he associates the theological doctrine of original sin with the pessimistic conception of man and the enmity that is central for the political. This is the basis for those who, like Heinrich Meier, argue that political theology stands at the heart of Schmitt's thinking. Meier cites a decisive passage from *Political Theology*: "If the theological disappears, so does the moral; if the moral disappears, so does the political idea."[21] And there is plenty of evidence that Schmitt never really abandoned this early view expressed so forcefully in his *Political Theology* and reiterated in *The Concept of the Political*. "The fundamental theological dogma of the evilness of the world and man leads, just as does the distinction of friend and enemy, to a categorization of men and makes impossible the undifferentiated optimism of a universal conception of man" (Schmitt 1996a: 65). After asserting that the "methodological connection of the theological and political presuppositions is clear," Schmitt adds: "But theological interference generally confuses political concepts because it shifts the distinction usually into moral theology." Frankly (like Meier) I don't find this caveat convincing. It is difficult to resist the conclusion that this very confusion is at the heart of Schmitt's own thinking. There is a tension, then, between the strong connection between theology, morals, and politics that Schmitt explicitly affirms in his *Political Theology* and his claims about the autonomy of politics in *The Concept of the Political*.

Let's pursue the other side of this aporia – the one that asserts the autonomy of the political and its independence from the moral. When we use the concepts of good and evil in regard to politics, they presumably have their own distinctive (non-moral and non-theological) sense. What is this distinctive political meaning of evil? As we have seen, it amounts to the claim that man is dangerous. We don't need any political theology (as Hobbes, Machiavelli, Nietzsche, and Freud teach us) to know that man is dangerous. Furthermore, such a doctrine is compatible with both liberal and non-liberal doctrines.[22] One can even argue (contrary to Schmitt) that the very reason for the elaborate system of checks and balances in liberal constitutions is to restrict the dangerousness of human beings – especially the danger of their abusing political power.

Strauss accuses Schmitt of concealing his own "moralizing." Schmitt "affirms the political because he sees in the threatened status of the political a threat to the seriousness of human life. *The affirmation of the political is ultimately nothing other than the affirmations of the moral*" (Schmitt 1996a: 101, emphasis added). Strauss is absolutely right, and his point can be generalized. Schmitt's polemic, which begins by drawing the sharpest possible contrast between morals and politics, ends with a conception of politics that is intrinsically moral. Even if we bracket the issue of whether the moral itself is based on the theological, Schmitt's concept of the political disintegrates unless we understand that Schmitt is smuggling in a human, moral, conception of evil in his understanding of political enmity.

For all Schmitt's presumably tough-minded concrete existential political realism, he presupposes throughout *The Concept of the Political* a normative-moral perspective that he fails to make fully explicit and certainly does not attempt to justify.[23] Let's return to the beginning of his essay when he introduces the friend/enemy antithesis. He says that friend and enemy are "neither normative nor pure spiritual antitheses," and he affirms that his concern is "neither with abstractions nor with normative ideals, but with inherent reality and the real possibility of such a distinction" (Schmitt 1996a: 28). But this negative route – like negative theology – doesn't really tell us what is distinctive about the political friend/enemy distinction. And despite his initial denials, he appeals to normative-moral considerations when he critiques a pacifism that advocates a war to end all wars. "The war is then considered to constitute the absolute last war of humanity. Such a war is necessarily unusually intense and *inhuman* because, by transcending the limits of the political framework, it simultaneously *degrades* the enemy into moral and other categories and is forced to make him a *monster* that must not only be defeated but also utterly destroyed" (Schmitt 1996a: 36, emphasis added). When Schmitt uses expressions like "inhuman," "degrades," and "monster," he is not simply showing how such pacifism is self-contradictory. He is *morally* condemning what he takes to be *inhuman* and *degrading*. Strauss succinctly states this aporia.

> Now the polemic against morals – against "ideals" and "normative pre-scriptions" – does not prevent Schmitt from passing a *moral* judgment

on humanitarian morals, on the ideal of pacifism. Of course, he takes pains . . . to conceal this judgment. An *aporia* finds expression in this concealment: the threatened status of the political makes necessary an evaluative statement on the political; yet at the same time insight into the essence of the political arouses doubt about all evaluative statements on the political. (Schmitt 1996a: 104)

More generally, Schmitt is ruthlessly critical of what he takes to be the sheer hypocrisy of a liberal "ideological humanitarian conception of humanity" (Schmitt 1996a: 72).

Humanity as such cannot wage war because it has no enemy, at least not on this planet. The concept of humanity excludes the concept of the enemy, because the enemy does not cease to be a human being – and hence there is no specific differentiation in that concept. That wars are waged in the name of humanity is not a contradiction of this simple truth: quite the contrary, it has an especially intensive political meaning. When a state fights its political enemy in the name of humanity, it is not a war for the sake of humanity, but a war wherein a particular state seeks to usurp a universal concept against its military opponent. At the expense of its opponent, it tries to identify itself with humanity in the same way as one can misuse peace, justice, progress, and civilization in order to claim these as one's own and to deny the same to the enemy.

The concept of humanity is an especially useful ideological instrument of imperialist expansion, and its ethical-humanitarian form is a specific vehicle of economic imperialism. . . . To confiscate the word humanity, to invoke and monopolize such a term probably has certain incalculable effects, such as denying the enemy the quality of being human and declaring him to be an outlaw of humanity; and a war can thereby be driven to the most extreme inhumanity. (Schmitt 1996a: 54)

Suppose we analyze this passage with the same cool logic that Schmitt employs when he insists that the political can and *ought* to be radically separated from any normative-moral considerations. What is the basis for finding this ideological instrument of imperialist expansion objectionable? What is wrong with denying the humanity of the enemy? Historically, this has been a very effective weapon in intensifying enmity. Why should anyone object if the "inhuman" enemy is annihilated? What's wrong with wars being driven by the "most extreme inhumanity," even if we pretend that we are fighting the war for humanitarian purposes? If we are to be brutally realistic, then we have to acknowledge that humanitarian "ideological instruments" have been (and still are) extremely effective in whipping up the passions of a people to fight an enemy. Schmitt is not merely exposing what he takes to be inconsistencies in liberal humanitarianism; he is *condemning* it – but he is less than forthright in clarifying the basis of his condemnation. Ironically, we might even say that the basis for his sharp critique is his own version of a suppressed humanism. He condemns this abuse of the concept of humanity not simply because it is hypocritical and inconsistent, but because it leads to wars that are *driven to the most extreme inhumanity*.

In *The Concept of the Political* we are told over and over again that the friend/enemy distinction is existential. It has no normative meaning. But can the existential be separated from the normative as radically as Schmitt indicates? Let's analyze one of his most striking passages.

> War, the readiness of combatants to die, the physical killing of human beings who belong on the side of the enemy – all this has no normative meaning, but an existential meaning only, particularly in a real combat situation with a real enemy. There exists no rational purpose, no norm no matter how true, no program no matter how exemplary, no social ideal no matter how beautiful, no legitimacy nor legality which could justify men in killing each other for this reason. If such physical destruction of human life is not motivated by an existential threat to one's own way of life, then it cannot be justified. Just as little can war be justified by ethical and juristic norms. If there really are enemies in the existential sense as meant here, then it is justified, but only politically, to repel and fight them physically. (Schmitt 1996a: 48–9)

Despite Schmitt's dazzling polemic, for all his "negatives" in this passage, he asserts but doesn't justify his claims. Throughout history human beings have been prepared to die – and to kill if necessary – for some ideal to which they are passionately committed. If it is true that "only participants can correctly recognize, understand, and judge the concrete situation," then what is the basis for Schmitt telling us what can or cannot be *our* justification and decision for going to war? Who decides what counts as a proper justification: the actual participants or some third party? And if Schmitt admits that participants can be *mistaken* in what they take to be a justification for their actions, then he is obligated to provide some criteria for distinguishing what does and does not count as a justification. He might respond that any "justification" that is offered for going to war is effective *only* if it is "motivated by an existential threat to one's way of life." But does it even make sense to talk about "one's way of life" (*der eigenen Existenzform*) without taking account of the self-interpretations, ideals, values, and norms to which one is committed? On Schmitt's own account, the existential threat is not simply reducible to an overt physical attack, but rather the threat calls into question my *way of life*. I – or rather the "we" of a political grouping – have to believe and decide that our enemy is threatening our core convictions, what we stand for, our way of life. How can one possibly do this unless there is some sense of what we take to be fundamental to our way of life – what we most deeply value and cherish? What Schmitt calls an existential threat to a way of life makes sense only if we realize that a way of life – implicitly or explicitly – involves *our values and norms*. A "way of life" is not "bare life"! Contrary to Schmitt's claim that war and the readiness of combatants to die "has no normative meaning but an existential meaning only," what he actually shows is that what we take to be an existential threat is *dependent* on what we take to be the normative-moral meaning of our way of life.

Much later, in 1947, as Slomp points out, when Schmitt was in prison being interrogated about his Nazi past, he wrote *Ex captivitate salus*, where he raises the questions "Who is my enemy?", "Who can question me?", "Who is the Other"? And he answers by quoting Theodor Däuber's definition of the enemy: "He who questions our own *Gestalt*." And in his *Theory of the Partisan*, he elaborates this point: "The enemy is not something that for some reason we should do away with or destroy as if it had no value. . . . The enemy places himself on my own level. On this ground I must engage with the opposing enemy, in order to establish the very measure of myself, my own boundaries, my own *Gestalt*" (see Slomp 2009: 12–13).[24] But isn't this "*Gestalt*" just another expression referring to my "way of life"? On the one hand, Schmitt claims that existential confrontation between friend and enemy has no "normative meaning." But, on the other hand, the existential confrontation between friend and enemy only makes sense if we presuppose the intrinsic normative significance of the *Gestalt*, or way of life, of *both* friend and enemy. Indeed, the above passage adds a significant qualification – or at least a clarification – to the way the friend/enemy antithesis was introduced in *The Concept of the Political*. When Schmitt stated that "the distinction of friend and enemy denotes the utmost degree of intensity of a union or a separation," he did not indicate that the enemy has *value* and "places himself on my level." But now it becomes clear that both friend and enemy have *human value*. Consequently, I (we) *ought* not to treat the enemy as if the enemy were a brute animal, a subhuman, or a monster. Schmitt sounds almost Kantian when he says: "The enemy places himself on my own level" (*Der Feind steht auf meiner eigenen Ebene*). And we will see that if I treat my adversary as having no value, worth, or dignity – as something that can simply be annihilated – then I am *not* (strictly speaking) treating him as an enemy.[25]

Decision out of Nothingness?

This normative-moral meaning of our way of life has significant consequences for understanding the all-important concept of decision – and more generally, Schmitt's so-called decisionism. I have already referred to the context in which Schmitt introduces the concept of the decision and the exception in *The Concept of the Political*. Although the political always involves the real possibility of war, war *presupposes* "that the political decision has already been made as to who the enemy is" (Schmitt 1996a: 34). "What always matters is the possibility of the extreme case taking place, the real war, and the decision whether this situation has or has not arrived. That the extreme case appears to be an exception does not negate its decisive character but confirms it all the more" (Schmitt 1996a: 35). These remarks are made in the context of characterizing the concept of the political, but they echo his famous opening sentence of *Political Theology*: "Sovereign is he who decides on the exception." When Schmitt speaks about decision, he typically emphasizes the *event* or act of decision – an event that can never be deduced from any norm.

Let's consider the process by which participants make a decision about who is the enemy and when to go to war. The primary political issue for Schmitt is *who* makes the decision. But I want to probe *how* a decision is actually made in a concrete situation. *How* does one decide who is the enemy, and *how* does one decide whether the extreme case has arrived – when to go to war.[26] Schmitt is very effective in making the negative point that such a decision cannot be *deduced* from a norm. No norm entails a specific decision. There is always a gap or rupture between the event of a decision and any prior reasons that one gives for making a specific decision. This is true enough. But it ignores what is most vital in the process of decision making. Schmitt is not speaking about trivial decisions such as deciding what tie to wear on a given day, but momentous existential political decisions. Of course there is no algorithm – no explicit decision procedure – for making such a decision. In real politics, the actors who make these decisions are always exercising some *political judgment*. They don't arbitrarily decide who the enemy is and when to go to war. They may be badly informed, based on a mistaken view of the concrete situation and its consequences. Or they may be well informed, sensitive to the complexities of a concrete situation, and shrewd in appraising possible consequences. Actors make such decisions for *reasons* – whether these are good or bad reasons. The reasons *inform* (although they do not determine) decisions. Actors (including the sovereign) are always weighing and evaluating a great variety of factors in making the decision about who is the enemy and when the situation demands going to war. We do discriminate between actors who exhibit good and bad political judgment. By constantly emphasizing the disparity between norms and the decisional event, Schmitt actually neglects the crucial issue of *political judgment* – how actors evaluate the concrete situation, how they assess whether their "way of life" is existentially threatened, and whether this demands going to war. Political judgment is shaped by the normative-moral perspective of the actors making the decision. In short, if we want to understand political decisions, then we must consider the role of political judgment in making decisions. And if we want to understand political judgment, we cannot do this without an evaluation of the normative-moral orientations of friends *and* enemies.

Violence

As I have already indicated, my primary motive in approaching Schmitt is to pursue the consequences of his thinking for understanding violence – especially the violence that involves physical killing. Now his "official" position is that the friend/enemy distinction does not necessarily lead to violence. On the contrary, it can lead to the decision not to kill and not to go to war. It requires only the *real possibility* of physical violence. Furthermore, we have seen that although politics and enmity are not identical, the friend/enemy antithesis always involves enmity. Schmitt distinguishes different types of enmity, and he *condemns* the type of unlimited enmity of liberal humanitarianism that "justifies" the annihilation of the enemy. Gabriella Slomp puts the issue concisely when she declares that Schmitt's "friend/enemy principle is predicated on the notion of limited enmity." "The limitation on enmity imposed by *jus publicum europaeum* seemed to Schmitt anachronistic in the twentieth century. This motivated Schmitt's search for a new nomos that could attain in late modernity what *jus publicum europaeum* had achieved in early modernity, namely the containment of hostility" (Slomp 2009: 12). Slomp thinks that Schmitt's notion of limited enmity is "consistent and credible." But is it? Does Schmitt have the conceptual resources to distinguish limited from unlimited enmity, and to *condemn* the latter? Can he even make this distinction without presupposing a normative-moral orientation that would provide a justification for condemning unlimited enmity? I want to show why we have to answer these questions negatively.

Let's return to the question of Schmitt's "justification" of his pessimistic conception of man – the connection he draws between original sin and political enmity. In *Ex captivitate salus*, he cites the biblical story of Cain and Abel and comments: "The Other is my brother. The other reveals himself as my brother and the Brother, as my Enemy. Adam and Eve had two sons, Cain and Abel. Thus begins the history of mankind. This is the face of the father of all things. This is the dialectical relationship which keeps the history of the world going. And the history of the world is not over yet".[27] Commenting on this passage, Slomp writes:

> The story of Cain and Abel summarizes with pungency the consequences of Original Sin and provides Schmitt with a biblical explanation for violence's role as the underlying theme of human history. For if we try to overcome hostility and if we dream about a world in which harmony replaces dissonance, in which reconciliation replaces confrontation, and in which there exists perpetual peace, then we are avoiding the burden of responsibility bestowed upon us by Original Sin. It is not for man to unite that which God has divided as a punishment for the Original Sin. (Slomp 2009: 18)

But even if we accept Schmitt's interpretation of the story of Cain and Abel as the beginning of the "history of mankind," it doesn't really clarify the meaning of *political enmity* of friend and enemy. There is no "limited enmity" here – but the killing of a brother. The story of

Cain and Abel does not indicate why we must or *ought to* try to limit enmity.[28] So even if we grant that political enmity is unavoidable, what are the reasons for thinking that it ought to be limited?[29]

In *The Concept of the Political* Schmitt indicates that there are different degrees of enmity (*Feindschaft*), although he doesn't introduce any systematic typology of enmity. He speaks of the high points of politics when "the enemy is, in concrete clarity, recognized as the enemy." He cites several instances in modern times of the outbreak of such enmity. He refers to the *écrasez l'infame* of the eighteenth century; the fanatical hatred of Napoleon by the German barons, and Lenin's "annihilating sentences against bourgeois and western capitalism." These are all "surpassed by Cromwell's enmity towards papist Spain." Schmitt cites Cromwell's words: "'The Spaniard is your enemy,' his 'enmity is put into him by God.' He is 'the natural enemy, the providential enemy,' and he who considers him to be 'an accidental enemy' is 'not well acquainted with Scripture and the things of God,' who says: 'I will put enmity between your seed and her seed' (Gen. III:15)" (Schmitt 1996a: 68). In his 1963 Foreword to *The Concept of the Political* Schmitt criticizes the tendency to take the friend/enemy distinction as a slogan, and he chides those critics who claimed that he privileges the concept of the enemy over that of the friend. He does concede, however, that in his original book he did not distinguish "with sufficient clarity and precision" the different types of enemy: the conventional, real, or absolute (*konventioneller, wirklicher oder absoluter Feind*). In *Theory of the Partisan* Schmitt further develops his thinking about these three types of enemy and the corresponding types of enmity. This clarification (or revision) illuminates the way in which Schmitt employs the friend/enemy distinction. But at the same time it also strengthens my thesis that throughout his writings there is a misleading and deceptive fusion of descriptive categories and normative-moral categories.[30]

Conventional, Real, and Absolute Enmity

Schmitt links the conventional enemy and enmity with his understanding of the *jus publicum europaeum*, the system of law and the political practices that prevailed in Europe after the Westphalia Treaty. The central political unit became the sovereign state, and states had the right to wage war. In this type of war, uniformed armies fight each other. War is not a crime, and the enemy is not a criminal. The legitimate object of war is to defeat the enemy (not to annihilate the enemy). The enemy is a "conventional enemy." In the *jus publicum europaeum* there were relatively clear juridical distinctions between war and peace, combatants and noncombatants, legal soldiers and non-legal fighters. Between the Westphalia Treaty and the First World War, European jurisprudence regulated and humanized war.[31] When Schmitt initially introduced the friend/enemy distinction as the criterion of the political and sought to draw a rigid distinction between morals and politics, he had the *jus publicum europaeum* in mind as a model of political friends and enemies. And throughout his life he praised this way of conducting foreign policy and distinguishing political friends and enemies. But with the coming of the First World War, the *jus publicum europaeum* collapsed. The demand for concrete understanding requires us to grasp the new historical forms of the friend/enemy distinction – and the new historical forms of enmity.

Real enmity (*wirklicher Feindschaft*) (as distinguished from conventional enmity) becomes central for Schmitt in his historical and theoretical analysis of the partisan. He begins the *Theory of the Partisan* by declaring:

> The initial situation for our consideration of the problem of the partisan is the guerrilla war of the Spanish people waged against the army of a foreign conqueror from 1808 until 1813. In this war, a people – a pre-bourgeois, pre-industrial, pre-conventional nation – for the first time confronted a modern, well-organized, regular army that had evolved from the experiences of the French Revolution. Thereby, new horizons of war opened, new concepts of war developed, and a new theory of war and politics emerged. (Schmitt 2007: 3)

With the partisan arises a new type of friend/enemy distinction and a new type of enmity – real enmity. "The modern partisan expects neither law nor mercy from the enemy. He has moved away from the conventional enmity of controlled and bracketed war, and into the realm of another, real enmity, which intensifies through terror and counter-terror until it ends in extermination" (Schmitt 2007: 11). To clarify the meaning of this real enmity, Schmitt cites the Royal Prussian Edict of 1813 – the edict issued urging the Prussian population to fight Napoleon's invasion by every means possible. He calls this "the most astounding document in the whole history of partisan warfare" (Schmitt 2007: 42).

> Every citizen, according to the royal Prussian edict of April 1813, is
> obligated to resist the invading enemy with weapons of every type.
> Axes, pitchforks, scythes, and hammers are expressly recommended.
> Every Prussian is obligated to refuse to obey *any* enemy directive,
> and to injure the enemy with all available means. Also, if the enemy
> attempts to restore public order, no one should obey, because in so
> doing one would make the enemy's military operations easier. It is
> expressly stated that "intemperate, unrestrained mobs" are less dan-
> gerous than the situation whereby the enemy is free to make use of his
> troops. Reprisals and terror are recommended to protect the partisans
> and to menace the enemy. In short, this document is a Magna Carta
> for partisan warfare. (Schmitt 2007: 43)

This edict indicates a new way of thinking about the friend/enemy
distinction, and a new type of enmity. The opposing parties are not
two state armies. There is no recognition of the enemy's value or
humanity. The people are called upon to use all available means to
fight the enemy. The partisan blurs all the juridical distinctions that
were (in principle) central to the *jus publicum europaeum* – the distinction between military and civilian, between enemy and the criminal,
between war and peace. Slomp gives a succinct summary of the difference between conventional and real enmity (hostility).

> Whereas conventional hostility assumes the value and worth of the
> enemy, real hostility entails despise for the enemy; whereas conven-
> tional enmity assumes opponents of comparable strength, real hostil-
> ity is often associated with great inequalities between two opposing
> parties, and this in turn explains why terror, deceit and camouflage
> are the only way for the weaker side to attack the stronger. Moreover,
> while the unit of conventional enmity is the state and its forum is an
> inter-state war, real hostility is originally associated by Schmitt with
> civil and colonial wars and its fundamental unity is the partisan group.
> (Slomp 2009: 84)

We can now single out what Schmitt means by *absolute enmity* (*absoluter Feindschaft*) by focusing on the distinction he makes between two
types of partisan: the telluric partisan and the global revolutionary.
The telluric partisan is still a fighter who is rooted in a local time
and place – the partisan who acts to defend his country and territory.
Schmitt introduces four criteria to characterize this type of partisan:
"irregularity, increased mobility, intensity of political engagement,
and telluric character" (Schmitt 2007: 22). By contrast, the global
revolutionary is not bonded to any particular territory. His enemy is

not a specific enemy, but a universal enemy who becomes demonized. The bearers of absolute enmity perceive themselves as surrounded by Evil. Absolute enmity is unbridled and unlimited. Absolute enmity gained dominance in the second half of the twentieth century. Lenin became the exemplar of a new theory of war and the absolute enemy. "For Lenin, only revolutionary war is genuine war, because it arises from absolute enmity. Everything else is conventional play" (Schmitt 2007: 51–2).

> The war of absolute enmity knows no bracketing. The consistent fulfillment of absolute enmity provides its own meaning and justification. The question is only: Is there an absolute enemy, and if so who is he? For Lenin, the answer was obvious, and the fact that he made absolute enmity serious made him superior to all other socialists and Marxists. His concrete absolute enemy was the class enemy – the bourgeois, the essential capitalist was dominant. Cognizance of the enemy was the secret of Lenin's enormous effectiveness. His understanding of the partisan was based on the fact that the modern partisan had become the true irregular and, thereby, the strongest negation of the existing capitalist order; he was called to be the true executor of enmity. (Schmitt 2007: 52)

Schmitt does not restrict his understanding of absolute enmity to the revolutionary partisan. He blames a whole variety of phenomena for the growing dominance of absolute unlimited enmity, including the just war tradition and humanistic liberalism.[32] One of the deepest motivations for Schmitt's life-long polemic against all forms of liberal humanism is that (so he claims) it unleashes and "justifies" absolute enmity; it dehumanizes the enemy. In his 1963 Foreword to *The Concept of the Political*, Schmitt even extended his analysis of the absolute enemy to the Cold War:

> With the so-called Cold War, the whole conceptual framework that has so far supported the traditional system of defining and regulating war breaks down. The Cold War mocks all the classical distinctions between war, peace and neutrality, between politics and economics, between the military and the civilian, between combatant and non-combatant, and maintains only the distinctions between friend and enemy, on which it grounds its very origin and essence. (Schmitt 2002a: 18)

Strictly speaking, the absolute enemy is no longer human; he is not the brother (as Cain was the brother of Abel). *He is not even properly an enemy – but a foe.* Schmitt writes that it is no wonder that the old English word *foe*, which has been dormant for centuries, has been revived to characterize the absolute enemy. (*Kein Wunder, dass alte englishe Wort* foe *aus seinem vierhundertjährigen archaischen Schlummer erwacht und seit zwei Jahrzehnten wieder nebern* enemy *in Gebrauch gekommen ist* (Schmitt 2002a: 18–19).[33] "Foe" is the term for the "enemy" against whom one fights the last absolute war of humanity – the final "just war," the war to end all wars. The foe is the "enemy" that we want to destroy once and for all.[34]

Schmitt's discussion of the historical changes to the friend/enemy distinction from the time of the Westphalia Treaty up until the present offers penetrating insights into the changing nature of enmity and warfare. Even if we consider his historical typology of enemies to be somewhat "idealized," he was one of the first theorists to appreciate the significance of partisan guerilla warfare in the twentieth century – and how this changed the understanding and practice of war. In his analysis of the revolutionary actor, he anticipates the new forms of terrorist activity. His remarks made in 1963 are almost prophetic: "But what if the human type that until now has produced the partisan succeeds in adapting to the technical-industrial environment, avails himself of the new means, and becomes a new type of partisan? Can we then say that a technical-industrial partisan has developed? Is there any guarantee that the modern means of mass destruction always will fall into the right hands, and that an irregular struggle is inconceivable?" (Schmitt 2007: 78–9).[35] Frightening questions – but in light of 9/11, they take on an all too real urgency.[36]

My primary purpose in outlining Schmitt's typology of the different types of enemy and enmity is to bring into the open the normative-moral perspective that orients his analysis. We can see this clearly in the final section of, the *Theory of the Partisan* entitled "From Real Enemy to the Absolute Enemy." In this section, Schmitt's rhetoric and polemic reach a feverish pitch. "In the theory of war, it is always the distinction of enmity that gives war its meaning and character. Every attempt to bracket or limit war must have in view that, in relation to the concept of war, enmity is the primary concept, and that the distinction among different types of war presupposes a distinction among different types of enmity" (Schmitt 2007: 89). Once again he singles out the period of the *jus publicum europaeum* for praise and condemns what happens when war is no longer "bracketed." "[W]ith the bracketing of war, European humanity had achieved something extraordinary: renunciation of the criminalization of the opponent, i.e. the relativization of enmity, the negation of absolute enmity. *That really was extraordinary; even an incredibly human accomplishment, that men disclaimed a discrimination and denigration of the enemy*" (Schmitt 2007: 90, emphasis added). Schmitt is not merely describing a stage in the concrete historical development of war and enmity; nor is he simply elaborating a theory – an analytical tool – for understanding politics. He is expressing his deepest *moral* convictions; he is *praising* what he takes to be one of the great achievements of "European humanity," and he is *condemning* the absolute enmity that he takes to be so characteristic of our times.

Schmitt even suggests that with the eruption of absolute enemy (the foe), politics comes to an end. "The partisan was a real, but not an absolute enemy. That follows from his political character" (Schmitt 2007: 92). This is destroyed with the bursting forth of the "professional revolutionary." "But Lenin, as a professional revolutionary of global civil war . . . went still further and turned the real enemy into an absolute enemy" (Schmitt 2007: 93). This is still not the worst. Writing at the height of the Cold War, Schmitt declares: "Technical-industrial development has intensified the weapons of men to weapons of pure destruction. For this reason, an infuriating incongruity of protection and obedience has been created: half of mankind has become hostage to the rulers of the other half, who are equipped with atomic weapons of mass destruction. Such absolute weapons of mass destruction require an absolute enemy, and he need not be absolutely inhuman" (Schmitt 2007: 93).

Schmitt's Amoral Moralism

Returning to a theme that was so dominant in *The Concept of the Political*, Schmitt condemns the "moralism" whereby the absolute enemy is totally dehumanized.

> Thus, the ultimate danger exists not even in the present weapons of mass destruction and in a premeditated evil of men, but rather in the inescapability of a moral compulsion. Men who use these weapons against other men feel compelled morally to destroy these other men, i.e. as offerings and objects. They must declare their opponents to be

totally criminal and inhuman, to be a total non-value. Otherwise, they are nothing more than criminal and brutes. The logic of value and non-value reaches its full destructive consequence, and creates ever newer, ever deeper discriminations, criminalizations, and devaluations, until all non-valuable life has been destroyed.

In a world in which opponents mutually consign each other to the abyss of total devaluation before they can be destroyed physically, new types of absolute enmity must be created. *Enmity becomes so frightful that perhaps one no longer should speak of the enemy or enmity, and both should be outlawed and damned in all their forms before the work of destruction can begin.* (Schmitt 2007: 94, emphasis added)

After this impassioned condemnation of a world in which ever new forms of absolute enmity are being created, Schmitt dissembles and retreats to the position of the impartial theoretician. In the final sentences of the *Theory of the Partisan*, Schmitt the "theoretician" tells us: "The theoretician can do no more than verify concepts and call things by name. The theory of the partisan flows into the question of the concept of the political, into the question of the real enemy and of a new *nomos* of the earth" (*Der Theoretiker kann nicht mehr tun als die Begriffe wahren und die Dinge beim Namen nennen. Die Theorie des Partisanen mündet in den Begriff des Politischen ein, in die Frage nach dem wirklichen Feind und einem neuen Nomos der Erde*) (Schmitt 2007: 95). Bargu succinctly summarizes Schmitt's warning and severe moral judgment of our present situation.

Written as a supplement to *The Concept of the Political*, Schmitt's *Theory of the Partisan* warns against the transmutation of enmity, which is the concrete manifestation of the "friend-enemy distinction," into an abstract and absolute form. Symbolized by the standing that the figure of the partisan has gained since World War II, such enmity unravels the boundaries and rules of war sustained by the Eurocentric *nomos*. Because *jus publicum Europaeum* only permits states to claim *jus belli* and deploy regular armies, destruction can be contained and the enemy respected as an equal. According to Schmitt, warfare in the image of a *duel* between states is "humane-rational" and a remarkable achievement of European civilization. . . . With the *patriotic* partisan's ascent into prominence and the emergence of the *revolutionary* partisan, these distinctions collapse into one another.

Schmitt, of course, is critical of this development because he observes that the movement of the partisan to the center of warfare is a sign of global disintegration and disorder [*a-nomos*]. The radicalization of partisanship, Schmitt forewarns, unleashes a violence that turns the

whole social and political order into a battleground for absolute annihilation and the enemy into a criminal whose very humanity is denied.
(Bargu 2010: 3)[37]

Bargu is absolutely right in stressing Schmitt's warning about the
consequences of absolute enmity. It unleashes an unlimited violence
that thoroughly dehumanizes the enemy (and the friend). The enemy
is no longer an enemy but a foe – an "entity" to be annihilated. And
the way he expresses his criticism is revealing. This absolute violence
is no longer "human-rational." When we no longer respect our enemy
as a human being, a *brother*, we not only devalue and dehumanize our
enemy, we dehumanize *ourselves*.[38] Schmitt categorically states: "An
enemy is not someone who, for some reason or other, must be eliminated and destroyed because he has no value. The enemy is on the
same level as am I" (Schmitt 2007: 85).[39]

But although Schmitt clearly affirms this form of "equality"
between friend and enemy, he never unambiguously states that this
is the normative-moral perspective from which he is judging and
condemning unlimited violence. And, what is more important, he certainly never seeks to provide a justification for his normative-moral
stance. If he did, he would have to seriously engage in the type of
normative discourse that he ridicules, and which he claims has no
relevance for understanding "the political." Remember that when
Schmitt first introduced his definition of the political he told us that
he was not concerned with "normative ideals" and that the friend/
enemy concepts are "neither normative nor pure spiritual antitheses"
(*Sie sind keine normativen un keine "rein geistigen" Gegensätze*) (Schmitt
1996a: 28)

Earlier I referred to Schmitt's deceptive conflation of descriptive
and normative-moral concepts. We see this clearly in his discrimination of the three types of enemy: the conventional, the real, and
the absolute. In order to draw these distinctions, Schmitt implicitly
appeals to weighted value judgments. The distinguishing feature
of the *jus publicum europaeum* is *not* states confronting each other
as states, or even regular armies fighting wars with other regular
armies. Rather, it is the type of *equality* and *respect* that is manifested
in these friend/enemy encounters. "The enemy is on the same level
as am I." The enemy is not criminalized or demonized. The aim of
war is defeat, not annihilation. It is the way in which states conduct
their politics and fight their wars that defines conventional enmity.

But when he calls this a great "human-rational" achievement, he is clearly expressing his normative-moral judgment.

Schmitt voices his concern about the way in which the telluric partisan has moved from the margins of warfare to its center in the twentieth century, but he nevertheless expresses his qualified admiration for the way in which partisans bond with their fellow partisans and are willing to risk death to defend their country. The patriotism of the telluric partisan defines real enmity (as distinguished from absolute enmity). Why should this be admired? Here too, Schmitt's qualified praise of the telluric partisan expresses his normative-moral orientation.

Finally, Schmitt thoroughly condemns all those who unleash absolute enmity and unlimited violence. But what is *wrong* with Lenin's view that "only revolutionary war is genuine war because it arises from absolute enmity" (Schmitt 2007: 52)? What was *wrong* with the threat of mutual annihilation during the height of the Cold War? What is *wrong* with denying the humanity of one's foe? These may seem like shocking questions, but they are intended to bring into the open Schmitt's normative-moral stance in characterizing the various types of enmity. Schmitt may pretend that "the theoretician can do no more than verify concepts and call things by name," but if talk of "dehumanization" is not merely a rhetorical gesture, then some intellectual rigor is required in *justifying* the normative-moral claim that enmity *ought* to be limited.[40]

Let me turn the issue around. I think that Schmitt has been highly effective in demonstrating that ever since the Second World War there has been a disturbing growth and spread of absolute enmity. Wars have been conducted in a way that completely devalues human life and completely dehumanizes the "enemy." With ever new forms of sophisticated weapons, killing is achieved in impersonal ways. Frequently, wars and killing are conducted without any serious regard for the distinction between military personnel and civilians. This is equally true of both "terrorists" and nations that retaliate against "terrorism." We live in a world in which there is the real possibility of unleashing a violence that destroys the social and political order – annihilating even the friend/enemy distinction. No one knows whether this can be avoided. No one knows whether it is even possible to create a new *nomos* of the earth. But trying to prevent this catastrophe demands a forthright discussion of the relevant normative-moral issues concerning what we mean by dehumanization and how we *ought* to try to limit enmity. Unfortunately, Carl Schmitt is of little help in confronting these fundamental problems – problems that arise *immanently* from his own critique. Perhaps the most fundamental aporia in Carl Schmitt is that he leads us with clarity and brilliance to an appreciation of the normative-moral issues – and to the political issues – that must be confronted if we are to avoid absolute and unlimited violence; yet, at the same time, he dismisses – and undermines – the very possibility of seriously confronting them.

Chapter 2

Walter Benjamin: Divine Violence?

The Political Context

In 1921, the 28-year-old Walter Benjamin published an article entitled *"Zur Kritik der Gewalt"* (translated as "Critique of Violence") in the academic journal *Archiv für Sozialwissenschaft und Sozialpolitik*.[1] Benjamin had recently returned to Berlin from Switzerland, where he wrote his dissertation, *The Concept of Art Criticism in German Romanticism*. He had not yet begun writing his famous book *The Origin of German Tragic Drama*, which was submitted (and turned down) as a *Habilitation* at Frankfurt University. During the early 1920s Benjamin was intensely interested in politics and violence. His correspondence indicates that he was planning to write a book, *Politik*, that would deal with a critique of politics and violence. As with many of his projects, Benjamin did not complete it, but the fragments he wrote, "Leben und Gewalt" and "Abbau der Gewalt," like the essay he published, focus on violence.[2] Even though Benjamin had been living outside Germany between 1917 and 1919, there were immediate reasons why he should be so concerned with politics and violence. The turbulent events of the time – the collapse of Germany, the November revolution, the Spartacist uprising, the devastating consequences of the Treaty of Versailles, the shaky beginnings of the Weimar Republic, the violent protests and murders of political extremists (right and left) – thrust concrete issues about state, law, violence, militarism, pacifism, and parliament into the arena of public discussion. But when first published, "Critique of Violence," Benjamin's dense, elusive, and provocative article, scarcely evoked any notice or debate.[3] It lay virtually dormant and forgotten until the publication of a collection of his writings edited by Theodor W. Adorno and Gershom Scholem in 1955. Ten years later Herbert Marcuse edited a small selection of Benjamin essays in a popular Suhrkamp series entitled *Zur Kritik der Gewalt and andere Aufsätze: Mit einem Nachwort von Herbert Marcuse.*[4] And almost immediately "Critique of Violence" sparked an intense and controversial discussion.[5] A few passages from Marcuse's *Nachwort* (Afterword) vividly indicate how the essay was read during the stormy days of the radical student movement of the 1960s.

> The violence that is dealt with in Benjamin's analysis is not that which is criticized everywhere else; especially not when it is the violence employed (or attempted) by those below against those above. It is exactly this sort of violence that Benjamin, in some of the most extraordinary passages in his writing, considers to be a "pure" violence, that violence which might furnish a "mythical" [*sic*] remonstrance to the violence that has dominated history up to this point. The violence criticized by Benjamin is that of the Establishment, that which preserves its monopoly on legality, truth, and justice. Here the violence-laden character of the law is invisible, though it becomes ferociously evident during so-called "exceptional circumstances" (which are *de facto* nothing of the sort). These exceptional circumstances are simply the usual for the oppressed. (Marcuse 1965: 99)[6]

Marcuse emphatically declares that "in Benjamin's critique of violence, it becomes clear that messianism is a trope that expresses the historical truth: liberated humanity is only conceivable now as the radical (and not merely the determinate) negation of the given circumstance. . . . Benjamin's messianism has nothing to do with customary religiosity: guilt and restitution are for him *sociological* categories" (Marcuse 1965: 100). For Marcuse, it is perfectly clear that "Benjamin was unable to compromise on the concept of revolution. . . . His critique of social democracy is not primarily a criticism of that party which had become a prop of the status quo; it is rather a recollection of the truth and actuality (not as yet questioned) of the revolution as a *historical necessity*" (Marcuse 1965: 101, emphasis added). According to Marcuse, "Critique of Violence" is an uncompromising revolutionary tract. Later I will return to a more detailed examination of this interpretation of Benjamin's essay. But for now I simply want to indicate how "Critique of Violence" was read during the 1960s in Germany.

Since that time, Benjamin's essay has challenged thinkers through-out the world. The essay has virtually taken on a life (and an afterlife) of its own – and provoked radically diverse, conflicting interpretations and evaluations. There is scarcely a distinction, a claim, or allusion in the essay that has not been subject to the most intense scrutiny and debate. Thinkers as diverse as Theodor Adorno, Jacques Derrida, Jürgen Habermas, Giorgio Agamben, Gillian Rose, Dominick La Capra, Martin Jay, Axel Honneth, Judith Butler, Simon Critchley, Slavoj Žižek (and many others) have argued passionately about its meaning and consequences. And the fascination does not seem to be diminishing, but only increasing. In part, I think this is due to the apprehension that we are now no longer living through what Eric Hobsbawm labeled the "age of extremes" but through a new "age of violence." In seeking to make sense of violence and to distinguish types of violence (and nonviolence) there is an almost irresistible obsession to return to Benjamin's essay and to take one's stand in regard to it.

Law-Making and Law-Preserving Violence

In this chapter I want to focus on what is perhaps the most contro-versial distinction that Benjamin introduces, toward the very end of his essay – the distinction between mythic and divine violence. His remarks are extremely cryptic and have been subject to the most extreme interpretations. Yet they are crucial for determining how we read Benjamin's article and what we take to be its significance for the critique of violence. Let me cite the relevant passage in full, because we will keep returning to it.

> Far from inaugurating a purer sphere, the mythic manifestation of immediate violence shows itself fundamentally identical with all legal violence, and turns suspicion concerning the latter into certainty of the perniciousness of its historical function, the destruction of which thus becomes obligatory. This very task of destruction poses again, ulti-mately, the question of a pure immediate violence that might be able to call a halt to mythic violence. Just as in all spheres God opposes myth, mythic violence is confronted by the divine. And the latter constitutes its antithesis in all respects. If mythic violence is lawmaking, divine violence is law-destroying; if the former sets boundaries, the latter

boundlessly destroys them; if mythic violence brings at once guilt and retribution, divine power only expiates; if the former threatens, the latter strikes; if the former is bloody, the latter is lethal without spilling blood. The legend of Niobe may be contrasted with God's judgment on the company of the Korah, as an example of such violence. God's judgment strikes privileged Levites, strikes them without warning, without threat, and does not stop short of annihilation. But in annihilating it also expiates, and a profound connection between lack of bloodshed and the expiatory character of this violence is unmistakable. For blood is the symbol of mere life. The dissolution of legal violence stems (as cannot be shown in detail here) from the guilt of more natural life, which consigns the living, innocent and unhappy, to a retribution that "expiates" the guilt of mere life – and doubtless also purifies the guilty, not of guilt, however, but of law. For with mere life the rule of law over the living ceases. Mythic violence is bloody power over mere life for its own sake; divine violence is pure power over all life for the sake of the living. The first demands sacrifice, the second accepts it. (Benjamin 1996: 249–50)[7]

To begin to understand this passage, we have to work backwards, taking account of the shifting and unstable distinctions that Benjamin introduces earlier in his essay. In his opening sentences Benjamin tells us: "The task of a critique of violence can be summarized as that of expounding its relation to law and justice. For a cause, however effective, becomes violent, in the precise sense of the word, only when it enters into moral (*sittliche*) relations" (236). So from the very beginning Benjamin makes it clear that his critique is concerned with violence only insofar as it bears on moral issues, specifically the relation of violence to law and justice.[8] Initially, the two main traditions of law – natural law and positive law – presuppose what Benjamin calls a common "dogma" – the dogma that we can make a sharp distinction between just ends and justified means. "Natural law attempts, by the justness of the ends, to 'justify' the means, positive law to 'guarantee' the justness of ends through the justification of the means" (237). Both traditions presuppose that "justified means" and "just ends" are not irreconcilable. Restricting ourselves to this formulation doesn't get us very far unless we have "mutually independent criteria" (237) for determining just ends and justified means. Benjamin initially sets aside the question of the justness of ends and focuses his attention on the question of the means that constitute violence. It may seem promising to focus attention on the distinction between "so-called sanctioned violence and unsanctioned violence" or the meaning of the distinction between "legitimate and illegitimate violence" (238). But we will be moving around in circles unless we clarify what we mean by violence. Benjamin lays the groundwork for introducing his all-important distinction between law-making (*rechtsetzende*) and law-preserving (*rechtserhaltend*) violence thus: "All violence as a means is either lawmaking or law-preserving. If it lays claim to neither of these predicates, it forfeits all validity. It follows, however, that all violence as a means, even in the most favorable case, is implicated in the problematic nature of law itself" (243). Initially, the distinction between law-making violence and law-preserving violence seems straightforward. Law-making violence is the type of violence required to establish a law, whereas law-preserving violence is the type of violence required to enforce and preserve the law. But from the examples that Benjamin gives we realize that these two types of legal violence are mutually interdependent.[9] Perhaps the clearest example of this mutual interdependence would be those revolutionary situations that culminate in creating a constitution. The constitution created by the *pouvoir constituant* establishes constitutional law that is binding on subjects of the law. But this law would not be law unless it were enforced and preserved. It would not make sense to speak of law-making violence unless there were also law-preserving violence.[10] The distinction between these two types of violence is frequently blurred. Benjamin shows this in regard to the death penalty. "Its purpose is not to punish the infringement of law, but to establish new law. For in the exercise of violence over life and death, more than in any other legal act, the law reaffirms itself. But in this very violence something rotten in the law is revealed" (242). A clearer example of the blurring (or more precisely the suspension) of law-making and law-preserving violence is police violence. Police violence "is lawmaking, because its characteristic function is not the promulgation of laws but the assertion of legal claims for any decree, and law-preserving, because it is at the disposal of these ends" (243). Although we can make an *analytic* distinction between these two types of legal violence, they are really inseparable and oscillate. There is "a dialectical rising and falling in the lawmaking and law-preserving forms of violence. The law governing their oscillation (*Schwankungsgesetz*) rests on the circumstance that all law-preserving violence, in its duration, indirectly weakens the lawmaking violence it represents, by suppressing hostile counter-violence. . . . This lasts until either new forces or those earlier suppressed triumph over the hitherto lawmaking violence and thus found a new law, destined in its turn to decay" (251).

Before proceeding, I want to comment on the emphasis that Benjamin places on the intimate connection between law and violence. It may be objected that Benjamin's understanding of law is distorted because he fails to do justice to the positive functions of the "rule of law." Now, it is certainly true that his essay does not sketch a comprehensive understanding of law. But Benjamin is bringing out a feature of law that is frequently neglected, but is manifest in times of crisis – especially when the state takes itself to be seriously threatened. He emphasizes this when he initially considers the class struggle and the right to strike of organized labor. "[T]he right to strike conceded to labor is certainly a right not to exercise violence, but, rather, to escape from a violence indirectly exercised by the employer" (239). But from the point of view of labor, the right to strike is the right to use force (*Gewalt*) to attain certain ends. When confronted with a revolutionary general strike, the state considers this an "abuse," because such a strike was never intended when it granted labor the right to strike. "Labor will always appeal to its right to strike, and the state will call this appeal an abuse" (239). This conflict of interpretations between the state and labor reveals "an objective contradiction in the legal system" (239). "[T]he law meets the strikers, as perpetuators of violence with violence" (239). Benjamin notes that even if we focus on the idea of a contract, which has been at the heart of so much modern political and legal theory, we do not escape from the potential violence of the law.

> [A legal contract] however peacefully it may have been entered into by the parties leads finally to possible violence. It confers on each party the right to resort to violence in some form against the other, should he break the agreement. Not only that: like the outcome, the origin of every contract also points to violence. It need not be directly present in it as lawmaking violence, but is represented in it insofar as the power that guarantees a legal contract is, in turn, of violent origin even if violence is not introduced into the contract itself. (243–4)

So even with contract law, we can discern the mutual interdependence of law-making and law-preserving violence. The origin of every contract points toward violence, and as a contract it can be enforced, if necessary, by the use of violence.

In his essay "Violence and the Word," Robert Cover, the talented American law professor and jurisprudential thinker who died at a relatively young age (writing in a very different historical context), underscores the Benjaminian point about violence and the law.

> Legal interpretation takes place in a field of pain and death. This is true in several senses. Legal interpretative acts signal and occasion the imposition of violence upon others: A judge articulates her understanding of a text, and as a result, somebody loses his freedom, his property, his children, even his life. Interpretations in law also constitute justifications for violence which has already occurred or which is about to occur. When interpreters have finished their work, they frequently leave behind victims whose lives have been torn apart by these organized, social practices of violence. Neither legal interpretation nor the violence it occasions may be properly understood apart from one another. (Cover 1993: 203)

Although the violence involved in legal interpretation is what Benjamin calls law-preserving violence, Cover makes the same point about law-making violence and emphasizes their interdependence.[11]

In light of Benjamin's claim about the intrinsic connection between law and violence, the question arises as to whether any nonviolent resolution of conflict is possible. We will see that this question is relevant for interpreting divine violence; but even at this stage in his essay, Benjamin indicates that "nonviolent agreement is possible wherever a civilized outlook allows the unalloyed means of agreement" (244). The subjective preconditions for such nonviolent agreement include "courtesy, sympathy, peaceableness, [and] trust" (244). With a brief remark that he barely elaborates, he tells us "that there is a sphere of human agreement that is nonviolent to the extent that it is inaccessible to violence: the proper sphere of 'understanding,' language" (245). I underscore this because a proper appreciation of Benjamin's critique of violence is played out against the possibility of nonviolence as well as the idea of a type of violence that is radically different from legal violence.[12]

The Revolutionary Strike

Benjamin turns to Sorel – in particular Sorel's distinction between the political and the proletarian revolutionary general strike – to bring out the difference between a violent strike and a nonviolent strike. In what initially seems extremely paradoxical, Benjamin declares that the political strike is violent "since it causes only an external modification of labor conditions" (246). Political strikes strengthen the power and violence of the state. With a burst of moral outrage, he condemns a recent political strike by German doctors as "an unscrupulous use of violence which is positively depraved" (247). In contrast to such political strikes, the proletarian general strike "sets itself the sole task of destroying state power" (246). The first type of strike is violent, but the second – the proletarian general strike – "as pure means is nonviolent" (246). Why? Because "it takes place not in readiness to resume work following external concessions and this or that modification to working conditions, but in the determination to resume only a wholly transformed work, no longer enforced by the state, an upheaval that this kind of strike not so much causes as consummates" (246). Benjamin clearly reveals his sympathies when he declares that the second kind of strike, the proletarian general strike, is "anarchistic" (246). Properly understood, Sorel's notion of the revolutionary violence of the general strike turns out to be nonviolent. "Against this deep, moral, and genuinely revolutionary conception, no objection can stand that seeks, on grounds of its possibly catastrophic consequences, to brand such a general strike as violent" (246).[13] (I will return to this claim that the proletarian general strike as pure means is nonviolent when I discuss divine violence.)

Despite raising the issue of whether nonviolent resolution of conflict is possible and telling us that the relationships of private persons provide examples of this, Benjamin nevertheless affirms that "every conceivable solution to human problems . . . remains impossible if violence is totally excluded in principle" (247). This anticipates the dramatic turn that the essay will soon take – "the question necessarily arises as to what kinds of violence exist other than all those envisaged by legal theory" (247). Earlier, we recall, Benjamin questioned the dogma that just ends can be attained by justified means. He now expresses his doubt about whether justified means and just ends are reconcilable.

> How would it be, therefore, if all the violence imposed by fate, using justified means, were of itself in irreconcilable conflict with just ends, and if at the same time a different kind of violence came into view that certainly could be either justified or the unjustified means to those ends, but was not related to them as means at all but in some

different way? This would throw light on the curious and at first discouraging discovery of the ultimate insolubility of all legal problems. . . . *For it is never reason that decides on the justification of means and the justness of ends: fate-imposed violence decides on the former and God on the latter.* (247, emphasis added)

Manifestation

One of the reasons why Benjamin's essay is so frustrating and open to diverse interpretations is because he introduces key concepts without giving us much of a clue about what they even mean. Not only does he introduce the concept of fate without explaining what he means, the above passage contains the first mention of "God." This may come as a jolt, because up until now it appears that Benjamin's primary focus has been law-making and law-preserving violence. Our perplexity is increased when he speaks of "the nonmediate function of violence" as not "a means but a *manifestation*" (248, emphasis added). We gain a clue about what he means by "manifestation" from the example he uses from everyday experience. If a man is impelled by anger to visible outbursts of violence, this is a *manifestation* of violence, not a *means* to an end. The concept of manifestation (*Manifestation*) is a quasi-technical term for Benjamin. From his perspective the perplexities of natural law and positive law traditions stem from their restriction to the framework ("dogma") of means–end thinking. And as long as we stick with this framework, the violence of law will be problematic. The concept of manifestation is intended to provide an alternative mode of thinking – one that enables us to understand violence as pure means. In contrasting means–end "rationality" with manifestation, Benjamin is drawing upon the rich German Romantic expressivist tradition. When he initially introduces the concept of mythic violence, he tells us that its archetypical form is a "manifestation of the existence of the Greek gods" and "not a means to their ends" (248). Long before Benjamin had any association with the Frankfurt School, we detect the beginnings of his own critique of means–end rationality (*Zweckrationalität*).[14] But we will also see that the manifestation of the gods illustrated by mythic violence is not yet the pure violence – the pure manifestation – of divine violence. The manifestation of the existence of the gods is exemplified by the Greek myth of Niobe.[15] Niobe, the queen of Thebes, at a festival in honor of Leto (Latona) boasts that she is more fertile than the goddess. Niobe thereby challenges fate and, as a consequence, Artemis and Apollo are sent to kill Niobe's children. But Niobe's life is spared. She is turned into a pillar of stone and is destined to grieve and weep eternally. As Benjamin interprets this myth, the violence of Artemis and Apollo establishes a law; but it is not a punishment of Niobe for breaking a law that already exists. Their violence is a *manifestation* of the gods. "Niobe's arrogance calls down fate upon her not because her arrogance offends against the law but because it challenges fate – to a fight in which fate must triumph and can bring to light a law only in its triumph" (248). "Violence therefore bursts upon Niobe from the uncertain, ambiguous sphere of fate" (248). But although this violence brings about the cruel death of Niobe's children, it is not actually destructive, because "it stops short of claiming the life of their mother, whom it leaves behind, more guilty than before through the death of her children, both as an eternally mute bearer of guilt and a boundary stone on the frontier between men and gods" (248). Niobe's guilt results indirectly from her arrogance – her challenge to fate.

How is this mythical violence related to the previous distinction between law-making and law-preserving violence? Mythic violence is not only closely related to law-making violence, it is identical to it. Benjamin returns to his opening distinction between law and justice: "Lawmaking is powermaking, assumption of power (*Macht*), and to that extent an immediate manifestation of violence (*Gewalt*). Justice (*Gerechtigkeit*) is the principle of all divine endmaking, power (*Macht*) the principle of all mythic lawmaking" (248). Although Benjamin has explained how power is the principle of all mythic law-making, we still do not understand in what sense "justice is the principle of all divine endmaking."

Following Benjamin's thought trains, it is clear that the mythic manifestation of violence shows itself "fundamentally identical with all legal violence" (249), because there is no law-making violence without law-preserving violence. And it is also clear that when Benjamin speaks of mythic violence, he is not restricting himself to ancient Greek myths. Mythic violence is the violence of *present* law-making and law-preserving. It might appear that the introduction of mythic violence as *manifestation* might provide a way of escaping from the problematic character of legal violence; but actually it "turns suspicion concerning the latter [legal violence] into certainty of the perniciousness of its historical function, *the destruction of which thus becomes obligatory*" (249, emphasis added). Benjamin's critique thus far has focused on showing the intrinsic relation of law and violence, and also the problematic character of legal violence. But a critique demands a space for judging and discriminating what has been revealed. How is legal violence to be destroyed, and what might destroy it? Who (or what) assumes the obligation to destroy the mythic manifestation of immediate violence that is identical with legal violence? This is the place where Benjamin explicitly introduces divine violence. "Just as in all spheres God opposes myth, mythic violence is confronted with the divine. And the latter constitutes its antithesis in all respects" (249).[16]

We are reaching the culmination of the "Critique of Violence". The long passage contrasting mythic and divine violence, quoted at the beginning of this chapter, appears at this point in Benjamin's text. Any interpretation and evaluation of Benjamin's essay ultimately depends on how we interpret what he means by divine violence and on discerning what role it plays in his essay. Yet commentators on Benjamin's essay have interpreted divine violence in extremely diverse – even contradictory – ways. I want to turn to an examination of some of these readings – in order to bring out their strengths and weaknesses.

Marcuse's Interpretation of Divine Violence

Let's return to Marcuse's reading of Benjamin. Although his Afterword is extremely brief and ranges over five essays written by Benjamin during a turbulent twenty-year period, the essential thrust of Marcuse's interpretation is unambiguous. The violence that Benjamin is critiquing is the violence that has dominated history until the present, a violence that preserves the "monopoly on legality, truth, and justice" (Marcuse 1965: 99). According to Marcuse, the theological (or messianic) element in Benjamin's thinking has "nothing to do with customary religiosity: guilt and restitution are for him *sociological* categories" (Marcuse 1965: 99). Benjamin's "messianism is a trope that expresses the historical truth: liberated humanity is only conceivable now as the radical (and not merely the determinate) negation of the given circumstance. Consequently, Benjamin is emphatically a revolutionary thinker – a thinker "unable to compromise on the concept of revolution" (Marcuse 1965: 99). His critique of social democracy is not primarily a critique of the party that had become a prop of the status quo, but rather "a recollection of the truth and actuality . . . of the revolution as a historical necessity" (Marcuse 1965: 99). Real progress is not achieved by the amelioriza-tion of the labor process, but only by its supersession (*Abschaffung*) – by the type of emancipatory revolution that seeks to destroy the state. This Marcusian reading is "Sorelian" insofar as he highlights the radical revolution that is required to bring about emancipation from existing legal violence. Marcuse "demythologizes" the allusions to the divine and the messianic. "If the revolution is to be messianic, it can not remain oriented within the continuum. . . . For Benjamin the Messiah would be exclusively constituted by the will and the conduct of those who are suffering under the established order, the oppressed: in class struggle" (Marcuse 1965: 105). To support his interpretation, Marcuse might appeal to Benjamin's remarks in the concluding paragraph of his essay.

> On the breaking of this cycle maintained by mythic forms of law, on the suspension of law with all the forces on which it depends as they depend on it, finally therefore on the abolition of state power, a new historical epoch is founded. If the rule of myth is broken occasionally in the present age, the coming age is not so unimaginably remote that an attack on law is altogether futile. But if the existence of violence outside the law, as pure immediate violence, is assured, this furnishes proof that revolutionary violence, the highest manifestation of unal-loyed violence by man, is possible, and shows by what means. (251–2)

Since 1965, when Marcuse published his Afterword, there have always been those attracted to this revolutionary reading of Benjamin's essay. Benjamin critiques the oscillating cycle of legal and state violence. What is demanded is the destruction of this form of domination. And this can be achieved only by a revolutionary violence "constituted by the will and conduct of those who are suffering under the established order, the oppressed" (Marcuse 1965: 105). This is why the critique of violence is "the philosophy of its history" (299). Only when we understand the historical character of the oscillation between law-making and law-preserving violence is it possible to make the critical, discriminating, and decisive judgment that this cycle must be broken.

The difficulty with such a reading is that it fails to come to grips with the complexity of Benjamin's text; it doesn't really illuminate the contrasts that Benjamin draws between mythic and divine violence.[17] Marcuse tends to be dismissive of the "theological" dimension of Benjamin's thinking and reads references to the "divine" and the "messianic" as if these concepts could be adequately explained by non-theological sociological and political categories.

Butler and Critchley on Divine Violence

I want to turn to a very different interpretation of divine violence, one that pays close attention to Benjamin's text and argues that "divine violence" is properly understood as "nonviolent violence." This is a strikingly original interpretation developed by Judith Butler and supported by Simon Critchley.[18] Let us recall that although Benjamin's critique focuses on understanding violence, especially as it pertains to the law and the state, there is a larger horizon of this critique where he contrasts violence with nonviolence. We have already noted two instances of this. Benjamin claims that there can be a nonviolent resolution of conflicts, even though he initially limits this to "relationships of private persons." He makes the stronger claim (without elaborating it) that there is a sphere of human agreement that is wholly inaccessible to violence – the proper sphere of "'understanding,' language" (245).[19] We have also seen that Benjamin makes the seemingly paradoxical claim that the revolutionary general strike "as a pure means, is nonviolent" (246). The issue that Butler and Critchley seek to clarify is how "divine violence" is related to the theme of nonviolence.

Butler introduces a distinction between coercive violence and non-coercive violence. Coercive violence refers to the coercive force of law – the violence that is characteristic of law-making and law-preserving violence.[20] But divine violence is non-coercive and "bloodless"; it is "lethal without spilling blood." The aim of divine (nonviolent) violence is to destroy mythical violence. Consequently it annihilates, but it also *expiates*. In the Niobe myth, the killing of the children by Artemis and Apollo institutes the *guilt* that Niobe experiences after her children are murdered – a guilt that is only an indirect result of her actions. When she insulted Leto, she did not know that this would result in the murder of her children. Divine violence "purifies the guilty, not of guilt but of law." Still, one may ask, what justifies the claim that divine violence is nonviolent? Butler makes much of a passage where Benjamin counters the objection that – carried to its logical conclusion – divine violence appears to confer on human beings the lethal power to kill.

> For the question "May I kill?" meets its irreducible answer in the commandment "Thou shalt not kill." This commandment precedes the deed, just as God was "preventing" the deed. . . . No judgment of the deed can be derived from the commandment. And so neither the divine judgment nor the grounds for this judgment can be known in advance. Those who base a condemnation of all violent killing of one person by another on the commandment are therefore mistaken. It exists not as a criterion of judgment, but as a guideline for the actions of persons or communities who have to wrestle with it in solitude and, in exceptional cases, to take upon themselves the responsibility of ignoring it. Thus it was understood by Judaism, which expressly rejected the condemnation of killing in self-defense. (250)

Butler argues that God's commandment differs significantly from law as understood as mythic violence. It is an imperative "without the capacity to enforce in any way the imperative it communicates" – not the "vocalization of a furious and vengeful God" (Butler 2006: 204).[21] The commandment is to be understood as a *guideline* for action (*Richtschnur des Handelns*) – a guideline with which each of us must wrestle in solitude – and "in exceptional cases, to take on themselves the responsibility of ignoring it" (250).[22]

> As a form of ethical address, the commandment is that with which each individual must wrestle without the model of any other. One ethical response to the commandment is to refuse (*abzusehen*) it, but even then one must take responsibility for refusing it. Responsibility is something that one takes in relation to the commandment, but it is not dictated by the commandment. Indeed, it is clearly distinguished from duty, and indeed, obedience. If there is wrestling, then there is some semblance of freedom. (Butler 2006: 212–13)

Consequently, the commandment "Thou shalt not kill" places severe limits on us. It is not a mandate for pacifism, because under exceptional circumstances (like self-defense in Jewish law) killing is permitted. But it places a high ethical demand on each of us to struggle in solitude with those circumstances in which killing may be required. At the heart of divine violence is a demanding "ethical" (this is Butler's term, not Benjamin's) requirement.[23] Summarizing this "ethical" interpretation of divine violence, Butler declares that Benjamin is showing three interrelated points: "(1) that responsibility has to be understood as a solitary, if anarchistic, form of wrestling with an ethical demand; (2) that coerced obedience murders the soul and undermines the capacity of a person to come to terms with the ethical demand placed upon her; and (3) that the framework of legal accountability can neither address nor rectify the full conditions of human suffering" (Butler 2006: 215–16).

Critchley finds this "ethical" reading of divine violence attractive for independent reasons. He has developed an ethics of commitment, one that is infinitely demanding and is the basis for a politics of resistance. We see how close he is to Butler's reading of Benjamin's essay when he writes:

> What is in question here is the complex relationship between violence and nonviolence, in which a commitment to the latter might still require the performance of the former. Paradoxically, an ethics and politics of nonviolence cannot exclude the possibility of acts of violence. If we are to break the cycle of bloody, mythic violence, if we are to aspire to what Benjamin anarchistically calls in the final paragraph of the essay "the abolition of state power," if something like politics is to be conceivable outside of law and in relation to the sacredness of life, then what is required is the deployment of an economy of violence. Following Benjamin, the guideline for a true politics is nonviolence and its aim is anarchism, but this thumb-line cannot be a new categorical imperative of the Kantian kind. In the solitude of exceptional circumstances, the guideline of nonviolence might call for violence, for subjective violence against the objective violence of law, the police and the state. In the essay's closing lines, Benjamin provocatively writes, "Divine violence may manifest itself in a true war." (Critchley 2012: 219)

This is an attractive interpretation of divine violence.[24] Both Butler and Critchley are struggling with an issue that is in the very foreground of concrete ethical and political life today. Both are committed to an ethic of nonviolence, but with a keen awareness that this cannot be understood as a "new . . . imperative of the Kantian kind," because we cannot anticipate those exceptional circumstances in which some form of violence may be required. As a *guideline*, the imperative not to kill demands that each of us, in our "solitude," struggle with it in concrete situations that we face. There are not, and cannot be, any *principles* that are *sufficient* – that we can exclusively rely on – in deciding what is to be done. This is the locus of human freedom and responsibility. We may refuse the commandment; we may decide that the exceptional circumstances we face require violence on our part to fight the "objective violence" of the state. But if we do, we must take responsibility for this decision.[25] Critchley, drawing on his reading of Benjamin, makes this point vividly: "[T]here are contexts, multiple contexts, too depressingly many to mention, where nonviolent resistance is simply crushed by the forces of the state, the police, and the military. In such contexts, the line separating nonviolent warfare and violent action has to be crossed. Politics is always a question of local conditions, of local struggles and local victories. To judge the multiplicity of such struggles on the basis of an abstract conception of nonviolence is to risk dogmatic blindness" (Critchley 2012: 239). Thus, even when we take the guideline of the commandment with full seriousness, even when we are committed to nonviolence, we cannot exclude the possibility of bloody violence. "Benjamin's is a crucial point: in the political sphere, it makes little sense to assert and hold to some abstract, principled, *a priori* conception of non-violence" (Critchley 2012: 240).

Is this "ethical" interpretation of divine violence as a nonviolent violence really warranted by Benjamin's text? I have strong doubts. First, to mention the obvious, Benjamin never explicitly says anything like this. He never says that divine violence is nonviolent. Nor does he explicitly characterize divine violence as *ethical*.[26] He doesn't even relate his discussion of divine violence to his previous discussion of the nonviolent resolution of personal conflict. Even if – on independent grounds – we are sympathetic with the Butler/Critchley account of how "persons and communities" must wrestle with God's commandment in solitude, this is about how *humans* should react to the commandment, not about *divine* violence as such. And although Butler and Critchley stress the political significance of nonviolent violence, they both de-emphasize that Benjamin is speaking about *revolutionary violence*, "the highest manifestation of unalloyed violence by man." In this respect, Marcuse's "Sorelian" interpretation seems closer to the spirit of Benjamin. Butler and Critchley provide illuminating analyses of the Niobe myth for understanding mythic violence, but they barely discuss Benjamin's reference to the story of Korah in speaking of divine violence.

Although Korah is mentioned several times in the Bible, the story of his rebellion occurs in Numbers 16. Korah, along with others, rebels against the leadership of Moses and Aaron in the wilderness. Moses orders Korah and his company to appear at the Tabernacle with censers for incense on the following day, when the Lord will decide who are the rightful leaders of the people. Korah complies and appears with the congregation. The congregation is commanded to separate itself from Korah and his band. When this order is carried out, "the earth opened its mouth" and the conspirators "and all that appertained to them went down alive into the pit, and the earth closed upon them" while "a fire from the Lord consumed two hundred and fifty of their attendants" (Numbers 16: 18–35).

Benjamin introduces the story of Korah when he contrasts divine violence with mythic violence. Mythic violence is law-making, divine violence is law-destroying. "The legend of Niobe may be contrasted with God's judgment on the company of Korah, as an example of such violence. God's judgment strikes privileged Levites, strikes them without warning, without threat, and does not stop short of annihilation" (250). The death of Korah (and his band) is "bloodless" and "lethal without spilling blood," because Korah is buried alive without any warning. There is no basis for thinking that this "bloodless" violence is nonviolent. And we should not forget – although Benjamin doesn't mention it – that when the surviving people protest, when they murmur against Moses, the Lord – as the Hebrew Bible tells us – sends a plague that kills 14,700 of them. There is a further irony in the story of Korah when we realize what his offense was. It was an act of rebellion – a revolutionary act – against the authority of Moses and his law.

Immediately after introducing the story of Korah, Benjamin says that God's judgment annihilates but also expiates; there is a "deep connection between the lack of bloodshed and the expiatory character of this violence" (250). But there is no mention of expiation (*shüne*) in Numbers, and it is difficult to know what this expiation can mean for those who have been buried alive and burnt by fire – or for the survivors. On the contrary, God orders that the censers of those burned to death should be hammered into plating for an altar as a warning that "none should be like Korah."

Perhaps it will be argued that, despite some awkwardness in reconciling Benjamin's claims about the bloodless character of divine violence with the story of Korah, Benjamin affirms the identity of divine violence with revolutionary violence. And he does explicitly say that this revolutionary violence is nonviolent. But if we return to the context in which he makes this claim about the proletarian general strike, the contrast he draws – following Sorel – is between the type of political strike that enforces state violence and the violence of the general strike that aims to destroy the state. Like Sorel, Benjamin praises the "deep, moral, and genuine revolutionary" character of the general strike. And he does speak of "its possibly catastrophic consequences" (246). Even when he makes the point that a "rigorous conception of the general strike" is capable of diminishing the incidence of actual violence in revolutions," he, in effect, concedes that revolutions involve actual violence. The point of contrasting mythic and divine violence is to distinguish sharply two very different types of violence, but there is no *direct* basis in Benjamin's text for claiming that divine violence is nonviolent.

Žižek on Divine Violence

Critchley's interpretation of Benjamin's divine violence is developed in the context of his ongoing highly polemical debate with Slavoj Žižek.[27] I want to focus on Žižek's (mis)understanding of divine violence. It is always difficult to pin down what Žižek is saying because of the playful exuberance of his dialectical gamesmanship. In a series entitled "Big Idea/small books" Žižek has written a *tour de force* with the straightforward title *Violence*. The final chapter "Divine Violence" concludes with two sections: "Divine Violence: What It Is Not . . ." and ". . . And Finally, What It Is!" Žižek mocks Critchley's defense of a nonviolent violence and the anarchistic politics of resistance that Critchley defends – claiming that (like the political strike) it succeeds only in reinforcing the power of the state. And Critchley thinks that, when unmasked, Žižek champions a Leninist authoritarianism where "real politics cannot waste its time in resisting state power: it should 'grab' it and 'ruthlessly' exploit it" (Critchley 2012: 228). This is the antithesis of what Benjamin means when he calls for destroying the state. But this is not quite where Žižek ends up, because he also declares that "the threat today is not passivity, but pseudo-activity, the urge to 'be active,' to 'participate,' to mask the nothingness of what goes on" (Žižek 2008: 217). "Sometimes doing nothing is the most violent thing to do" is the last sentence of his book. So how, then, does he understand Benjamin's divine violence – what is it? "[D]ivine violence serves no means, not even that of punishing the culprits and thus re-establishing the equilibrium of justice. . . . It is a 'sign without meaning'" (Žižek 2008: 199–200). Despite Benjamin's explicit reference to God's actions annihilating Korah, Žižek's Lacanian reading is that "divine violence is *a sign of God's (the big Other's) own impotence*" (Žižek 2008: 201). Although divine violence is presumably a "sign without meaning," Žižek doesn't hesitate to tell us that it is "the domain within which killing is neither an expression of personal pathology (idiosyncratic, destructive drive), nor a crime (or its punishment), nor a sacred sacrifice. It is neither aesthetic, nor ethical, nor religious (a sacrifice to dark gods)" (Žižek 2008: 198). Despite his claim to tell us what divine violence really is, his description sounds more like a negative theology – telling us what it isn't. But he does say:

> Divine violence should thus be conceived as divine in the precise sense of the old Latin motto *vox populi, vox dei*: *not* in the perverse sense of "we are doing it as mere instruments of the People's Will," but as the heroic assumption of the solitude of sovereign decision. It is a decision (to kill, to risk one's own life) made in absolute solitude, with no cover of the big Other. If it is extra-moral, it is not "immoral," it does not give the agent license to kill with some kind of angelic innocence. When those outside the structured social field strike "blindly," demanding and enacting immediate justice/vengeance, this is divine violence. (Žižek 2008: 202)

When Žižek tells us that divine violence should be conceived of "as the heroic assumption of the solitude of sovereign decision," it sounds more as if he is describing Carl Schmitt rather than Walter Benjamin. To illustrate what he means by divine violence, Žižek recalls "the panic in Rio de Janeiro when crowds descended from the favelas into the rich part of the city and started looting and burning supermarkets. This was indeed divine violence. . . . They were like biblical locusts, the divine punishment of men's sinful ways" (Žižek 2008: 202). Frankly, this sounds more like the *manifestation* of anger that Benjamin cites when he introduces his concept of mythic violence (not divine violence). Such outbursts do not destroy state power and violence; they provoke the demand for more law and order – and are frequently quickly suppressed by state violence. Consequently they actually increase state power and violence.

It is difficult to resist the conclusion that Žižek is taking over Benjamin's term "divine violence" and giving it his own idiosyncratic contradictory "meaning(s)," which bear little resemblance to anything that Benjamin actually says. He ignores or downplays much of what Benjamin does say – especially about the significance of the commandment "Thou shalt not kill" – and he fails to deal forthrightly with Benjamin's central concern: how divine violence "might be able to call a halt to mythical violence." This is not going to happen by "doing nothing" unless Žižek believes – contrary to what Benjamin claims – in "miracles directly performed by God." At times, Žižek (and not just in his discussion of divine violence) seems to personify Hegel's skeptical self-consciousness: "a confused medley, the dizziness of a perpetually self-engendered disorder" (Hegel 1977: 125).

Derrida's Deconstruction of Benjamin's Essay

Despite the "confused medley" of Žižek's "allegro" movement,[28] he touches upon some perplexing issues in Benjamin's obscure passages. I believe that we can better understand these by turning to Jacques Derrida's deconstructive reading of Benjamin's essay. One of the primary reasons why there has been a constant, almost obsessive, return to the interpretation and reinterpretation of "Critique of Violence" is because of Derrida's now famous, detailed, risky, and extremely controversial deconstructive interpretation: "Force of Law: The Mystical Foundation of Authority." The context and circumstances for delivering his lecture (subsequently revised and published in the *Cardozo Law Review* in both French and an English translation) are crucial for understanding it. Derrida was invited to give the keynote address at a colloquium held at Cardozo in October 1989 entitled "Deconstruction and the Possibility of Justice." Although his essay consists of two parts (untitled), he read only the first part at Cardozo, and distributed a preliminary text of the second part. The first part deals with Derrida's own understanding of the relation of law (*droit*) and justice (*la justice*) – and is intended to be a preliminary for Part II, his deconstructive reading of "Critique of Violence." Subsequently, the second part was delivered at a colloquium organized by Saul Friedlander at the University of California, Los Angeles, on "Nazism and the 'Final Solution': Probing the Limits of Representation." When he delivered Part II, which deals directly with Benjamin's essay, he added an introduction, explaining why he thinks "it would perhaps not be entirely inappropriate to interrogate" Benjamin's text at such a conference. Derrida characterizes Benjamin's essay as "uneasy, enigmatic, terribly equivocal" and "as it were, haunted in advance (but can one say 'in advance' here?) by the theme of radical destruction, extermination, total annihilation, beginning with the annihilation of law and of right, if not of justice, and, among those rights, human rights, at least such as these are interpreted within a tradition of natural law of the Greek type or the *'Aufklärung'* type" (Derrida 1990: 973). At the end of his lecture, he includes a disturbing "Post-scriptum" that relates Benjamin's essay to Nazism and the Final Solution. Both parts of "Force of Law" are extremely rich – and they are illuminating not only about Benjamin but about Derrida's understanding of deconstruction and its relation to law and justice. In Part I Derrida categorically asserts: "Justice in itself, if such a thing exists, outside and beyond the law is not deconstructible" and "Deconstruction is justice" (Derrida 1990: 945).[29] I am primarily concerned with what he says (and doesn't say) about divine violence.

Although Derrida gives a line-by-line commentary and interpretation of the early parts of Benjamin's essay, his analysis of divine violence seems almost hurried – even though he introduces his discussion by saying that "here begins the last sequence, the most enigmatic, and the most profound in this text" (Derrida 1990: 1025). Initially, what is most striking – especially in light of the interpretations of Marcuse, Butler, and Critchley – is what he *doesn't* discuss. He mentions but passes rapidly over what is central for Butler and Critchley – the significance and interpretation of the commandment "Thou shalt not kill." He restricts himself to the straightforward comment: "That for Benjamin is the essence of Judaism which forbids all murder, except in the singular cases of legitimate self-defense, and which sacralizes life to the point that certain thinkers extend this sacralization beyond man, to include animal and vegetable" (Derrida 1990: 1029).[30] There is no discussion of Korah in Derrida's *main* text. He barely explores the relation of divine violence to revolutionary violence or to the general proletarian strike. He does emphasize how the Greek mythos kills with blood, whereas divine violence annihilates without bloodshed. And although he says that blood makes all the difference, he doesn't explicate what it means to annihilate without bloodshed. Blood is the symbol of mere life (*das blosse Leben*), which Derrida characterizes as biological life and associates with simple *Dasein*.[31] "In contrast, purely divine (Judaic) violence is exercised on all life but to the profit or in favor of the living (*über alles Leben um des Lebendigen willen*). . . . In other words, the mythological violence of *droit* is satisfied in itself by sacrificing the living, while divine violence sacrifices life to save the living, in favor of the living. In both cases there is sacrifice, but in the case where blood is exacted, the living is not respected" (Derrida 1990: 1027). Despite the ambiguity of concepts like life and *Dasein* (which Benjamin himself notes), Derrida thinks that "what makes for the worth of man, of his *Dasein* and his life, is that he contains the potential, the possibility of justice, the yet-to-come (*avenir*) of justice, the yet-to-come of his being-just, of his having-to-be just. What is sacred in his life is not his life but the justice of his life" (Derrida 1990: 1029). But Derrida doesn't explain precisely what this "not-yet-attained condition of the just man" means, or how it is related to divine violence.

Derrida concludes by returning to a theme that is central to deconstruction: *l'indécidabilité*, *Unentscheidbarkeit*, "All undecidability (*Unentscheidbarkeit*) is situated, blocked in, accumulated on the side of *droit*, of mythological violence, that is to say the violence that founds and conserves *droit*. But on the other hand all decidability stands on the side of divine violence that destroys *le droit*, we can even venture to say deconstructs it" (Derrida 1990: 1031). "To say that all decidability is found on the side of divine violence that destroys or deconstructs *le droit* is to say at least two things": "(1) That *history* is on the side of this divine violence, and history precisely in opposition to myth . . . (2) If all decidability is concentrated on the side of divine violence in the Judaic tradition, this would come to confirm and give meaning to the spectacle offered by the history of *droit* which deconstructs itself and is paralyzed in undecidability" (Derrida 1990: 1031). The undecidability of mythological violence is contrasted with the decidability that is concentrated on the side of divine violence. But Derrida questions this sharp contrast. Or, more accurately, he thinks that Benjamin's text both affirms this sharp distinction and undermines it. He emphasizes the *conditional* way in which Benjamin puts the issue when he writes: "But if the existence of violence outside the law, as pure immediate violence, is assured, this furnishes proof that revolutionary violence, the highest manifestation of unalloyed violence by man, is possible, and shows by what means" (252).

Derrida asks: "But why is this statement in the conditional? Is it only provisional and contingent? Not at all. For the *decision* (*Entscheidung*) on this subject, the determinant decision, the one that permits us to know or to recognize such a pure revolutionary violence *as such*, is a *decision not accessible to man*. Here we must deal with a whole other undecidability" (Derrida 1990: 1033).[32] Thus, according to Derrida, there are *two* competing violences, but *undecidability* stands at the core of both divine and mythic violence: "On one side the decision without decidable certainty, on the other the certainty of the undecidable but without decision. In any case, in one form or another, the undecidable is on each side, and is the violent condition of knowledge or action. But knowledge and action are always dissociated" (Derrida 1990: 1035). The reason why it is so important (and so central to Derrida and deconstruction) to show the undecidability of both mythical and divine violence is because "the undecidable is not merely the oscillation or the tension between two decisions, it is the experience of that which, though heterogeneous, foreign to the order of the calculable and the rule, is still obliged ... to give itself up to the impossible decision, while taking account of law and rules. *A decision that didn't go through the ordeal of the undecidable would not be a free decision*" (Derrida 1990: 963, emphasis added).

Derrida's "conclusion" about the different ways in which undecidability lies at the very heart of both forms of violence is "consistent" with his own deconstructive practice and is intended to show that the seemingly sharp and "antithetical" distinction that Benjamin draws between these two forms of violence is not as clear and distinct as Benjamin suggests. This is precisely what Derrida wants to show (or rather, claims to have shown) with all of the major distinctions that Benjamin introduces in his essay – including mythic and divine violence, law-making and law-preserving violence, the political strike and the proletarian general strike, and especially law and justice. This doesn't mean that we can't draw these distinctions. On the contrary, it is only by drawing them that the text deconstructs these rigorous distinctions. But it does mean that we *never* escape from undecidability.

Throughout "Force of Law" (and many of his other writings) Derrida makes much of the "signing" of a text – taking responsibility for it. And he tells us that each time we sign, we speak in an "evaluative, prescriptive, non-constative manner" (Derrida 1990: 1037). Where and how does Derrida sign *his* text, "Force of Law"?

I suggest we witness this in his "Post-scriptum." Let us recall that the deconstructive reading of Benjamin's text was presented at a conference dealing with Nazism and the Final Solution. Initially, this seems completely inappropriate, because Benjamin's text was written in 1921, long before the rise of the Nazis and the Final Solution. Derrida concedes this, but nevertheless thinks that, despite the enigmatic and overdetermined quality of Benjamin's text, it has a certain "coherence," a certain "logic." He therefore thinks that it is risky, but appropriate, to entertain some hypotheses about "the large aspects of the problematic and interpretative space in which his discourse on the final solution might have been inscribed" (Derrida 1990: 1041).[33] Derrida (in his typical "on the one hand but on the other hand manner") first considers how much in Benjamin's essay – especially his understanding of the logic of the state and the extreme extension of mythical violence – could be drawn upon to condemn the "logic" of Nazism. But, on the other hand, "No anthropology, no humanism, no discourse of man on man, even on human rights can be proportionate to either the rupture between the mythical and the divine, or to a limit experience such as the final solution" (Derrida 1990: 1043).

Derrida signs – "speaks in an evaluative, prescriptive, non-constative manner" – by telling us directly where he stands in the final paragraphs of his Post-scriptum. Because Derrida's "final conclusion" has provoked such strong – indeed violent – criticism, let me quote it at length.

> What I find, in conclusion, the most redoubtable, indeed (perhaps, almost) intolerable in this text, even beyond the affinities it maintains with the worst (the critique of *Aufklärung*, the theory of the fall and of original authenticity, the polarity between originary language and fallen language, the critique of representation and of parliamentary democracy, etc.), is a temptation that it would leave open, and leave open notably to the survivors or the victims of the final solution, to its past, present or potential victims. Which temptation? The temptation to think the holocaust as an uninterpretable manifestation of divine violence, insofar as this divine violence would be at the same time nihilating, expiatory and bloodless, says Benjamin, a divine violence that would destroy current law through a bloodless process that strikes and causes to expiate. . . . *When one thinks of the gas chambers and the cremation ovens, this allusion to an extermination that would be expiatory because bloodless must cause one to shudder. One is terrified at the idea of an interpretation that would make of the holocaust an expiation and indecipherable signature of the just and violent anger of God.*

It is at that point that this text, despite all its polysemic mobility and all its resources for reversal, seems to me finally to resemble too closely, to the point of specular fascination and vertigo, the very thing against which one must act and think, do and speak, that with which one must break (perhaps, perhaps). . . . I do not know whether from this nameless thing called the final solution one can draw something which still deserves the name of a lesson. But if there were a lesson to be drawn, a unique lesson among the always singular lessons of murder, from even a single murder, from all the collective exterminations of history (because each individual murder and each collective murder is singular, thus infinite and incommensurable), the lesson that we can draw today – and if we can do so we must – is that we must think, know, represent for ourselves, formalize, judge the possible *complicity* between all these discourses and the worst (here the final solution). In my view, this defines a task and a responsibility the theme of which (yes, the theme) I have not been able to read in either Benjaminian "destruction" or Heideggerian "*Destruktion.*" It is the thought of difference between these destructions on the one hand and a deconstructive affirmation on the other that has guided me tonight in this reading. It is this thought that the memory of the final solution seems to me to dictate. (Derrida 1990: 1045, emphasis added)

There is no doubt about Derrida's signature – and it has outraged many who claim that this is a perverse reading of Benjamin's text. But, given Derrida's deconstructive understanding of *undecidability*, this reading is not a contingent but a *necessary* consequence. Derrida is *not* saying that the temptation to adopt this interpretation follows from Benjamin's understanding of divine violence, but that because of the undecidability of Benjamin's text, we can't exclude such an interpretation – or at least the "temptation" to interpret divine violence in this way.

Rose's Response to Derrida

The reactions to Derrida's "final" words have been extremely strong. Gillian Rose is one of his severest critics.[34] She claims that Derrida misreads Benjamin, and that he actually *exposes* the "crisis of deconstruction." She accuses Derrida of projecting his own Heideggerian ontology on to Benjamin by developing "an eschatological and originary reading of Benjamin's essay" (Rose 1993: 85). "As a result of

Derrida's originary approach to law-founding and law-conserving violence, Benjamin's account of modernity can only appear reactionary: cast solely in political terms, the hidden yet overblown law-founding violence of the politics in modern democracies is beyond the control of parliaments" (Rose 1993: 85). What Derrida misses is that "Benjamin's political reflections presuppose a social theory of capitalist institutions, and amount to a search for a theory of revolutionary practice which will be neither reformist nor justify force as a means of right-making" (Rose 1993: 85). "The evocation of divine force, which can never be a *means*, is returned to the modern context so that the educative 'philosophy of history of violence' may demonstrate that as long as force is used 'mythically' as right-making *means* it will prevent the abolition of state power" (Rose 1993: 85–6). Benjamin, she claims, does not fit within deconstruction or within Heideggerian ontology. Actually – and Derrida misses this – Benjamin is much closer to Rosa Luxemburg, because he "is exploring the relation of theory and practice for a truly democratic revolution which will inaugurate radical democracy at every moment and not postpone it to a post-revolutionary future when force, the 'means', will have achieved its 'ends'" (Rose 1993: 86). Derrida's insistence that Benjaminian oppositions "deconstruct themselves," that they exhibit a *"différanti-elle* contamination," leaves open the possibility for "a false Messiah to proclaim a tyranny" (Rose 1993: 86).[35]

> They leave us with the dilemma of mysterious, primeval violence versus mythical, formal law, between incomprehensible end and bloody means. When what needs investigation is the *fate* of modern law – the diremption and discrepancy between its formal promises and the social actuality they presuppose and reproduce. Then violent acting out of nationalist or racist phantasies engendered by these discrepancies may be comprehended instead of being exalted to a pure originary violence or degraded to the violence of pure formal law as such. This would be to demystify law without compensatory myth and without hallowing history as *holocaust*. Only if we resist the temptation of the ontology of "originary contamination" can we begin to discern the complicities of our political history. To do that we need to be able to represent, to formalize, to think, to know, to judge – all the activities from which Messianic deconstruction would disqualify us. (Rose 1993: 86–7)

These are strong words – and in a way, they bring us back to the spirit (if not the letter) of Marcuse's interpretation of Benjamin.

More generally, these several interpreters are fighting for the soul of Benjamin. The issue is not exclusively whether one is to read Benjamin as a philosophical, political, theological, or political-theological thinker. Rather, what underlie the conflict of interpretations are the concrete consequences of Benjamin's thinking. Benjamin's sharp critique of means–end thinking in the law can be generalized to a critique of instrumental reason. Insofar as critique also means discrimination and cut (*krinein*), he makes a sharp cut between the institutionalization of the dogma of means–end analysis in the law and manifestation (*Manifestation*). He also draws a sharp distinction between the type of manifestation exhibited by mythic violence and the "pure means" of divine violence. But this still leaves open precisely how "pure means" is to be interpreted.

The Undecidability of Divine Violence

Is Benjamin primarily appealing to the idea of divine violence in order to enable us to understand that a political revolution is a "historical necessity"? Is he primarily directing us to probe "the relation of theory and practice for a truly democratic revolution which will inaugurate radical democracy at every moment"? Is he enabling us to think through the guideline (*Richtschnur*) of nonviolence which demands that we struggle with it in solitude; that we face up to our responsibility in those exceptional circumstances where a violent response may be required? What are we to make of the contrast that Benjamin draws between "spilling of blood" and a God who "strikes without bloodshed" when he associates the former with the legend of Niobe and the latter with the burying of Korah? Is divine violence "a sign without meaning"? Is Benjamin heightening the sense of undecidability and the aporias that we must *experience* in making decisions? Is Benjamin's discourse about divine violence undecidable, such that it opens us to "an interpretation that would make of the holocaust an expiation and indecipherable signature of the just and violent anger of God"? *Benjamin's remarks about divine violence are too condensed, opaque, and elliptical to interpret in any definitive manner.* I am not convinced that Derrida's understanding of *radical* undecidability is inherent in Benjamin's text, but there is a more modest undecidability that invites conflicting interpretations.

There are further reasons to be uneasy about Benjamin's enigmatic essay. There are many relevant issues that Benjamin leaves open – or, at the very least, fails to provide sufficient guidance for us to answer. Suppose we return to what he explicitly says about law – in particular, law-making and law-preserving violence. It isn't clear from his essay whether Benjamin is condemning *all* law and legal systems. Certainly the rhetoric of the essay suggests as much. Even if we concede that Benjamin focuses on a feature of law that has been neglected, basic distinctions and discriminations need to be made. Crudely speaking, there are "good" and "bad" forms of *Gewalt*. Violence – or the potential threat of violence – is frequently necessary to guarantee justice. The images that come to mind when Benjamin declares that "something rotten in law is revealed" may be laws like the fugitives law in the United States that were designed to return Blacks to their slaveholders, or the laws against miscegenation. But what about the laws that are designed to put an end to these injustices (like the civil rights legislation of the 1960s) and which also threaten violence to those who violate the law? Given the historical situation of Germany in the early 1920s, we can understand and even sympathize with Benjamin's stress on the violence of law. But ultimately it is too simplistic to fail to discriminate the multiple positive functions of law – the ways in which law (based on the threat of violence) can further justice. We can also ask: what would be the surrogate for law if the state were destroyed? Benjamin is silent about this. It is disingenuous to say that this falls back on means–end thinking. It is not adequate, and is potentially disastrous (as we know all too well from history), to say that this must be decided by those who come after the revolution. "The critique of violence is the philosophy of its history" – presumably *real history*, not some abstract idea of history.

One may admire, as both Benjamin and Sorel did, the "deep, moral, and genuinely revolutionary quality of the proletariat general strike." But it is too facile to suggest that whereas state power has "eyes for effects," the "catastrophic consequences" of such a revolution are not sufficient for branding such a strike as violent. Even if we agreed with this claim, how could we possibly act responsibly in a situation unless we took account of the possible catastrophic consequences of what we were doing? There is a danger in Benjamin's thinking of so emphasizing the purely *expressive* manifestation of revolutionary action that we ignore the purpose or the consequences of what we are doing.[36] If we are to struggle with the commandment not to kill, then we must struggle with the *possible consequences* of what we decide to do – otherwise we are not struggling but play acting. We can't just stop by abstractly contrasting the two alternatives: reinforcing the state violence or destroying the state power. If we are to act responsibly, we have to ask what concretely is involved in destroying the state.

Nervousness about Divine Violence

Consequently, there are good reasons why even sympathetic readers of "Critique of Violence" express "nervousness."[37] Dominick La Capra claims that "the notion of the state or mythical (fate-imposed) violence functions in a dubiously homogenizing fashion in Benjamin's argument. . . . It leads him to lump all states together independent of their constitutions or political and economic regimes. All are violent in a 'rotten' manner" (La Capra 1990: 1071). He also thinks that the manner in which Benjamin claims that divine "violence is bloodless remains perhaps intentionally opaque. . . . Benjamin here practices a most insistent silence. . . . And silence itself cuts both ways, for it does not guard against the most abusive interpretation of divine violence – interpretations that may even be encouraged by messianic-apocalyptic pathos" (La Capra 1990: 1072).[38] Martin Jay expresses a similar concern when he writes that the "apocalyptic embrace of divine violence" carries serious risks. "[Benjamin's] bold assertion of the liberating function of divine violence [is] an assertion that high-lights the tension between religion and morality rather than their full compatibility." Benjamin, Jay claims, comes remarkably close to suggesting the "cleansing role of divine violence" (Jay 2003: 182). He speaks of Benjamin's "nihilist streak evident in his antinomian evocation of divine violence" (Jay 2003: 21). Axel Honneth, who gives a very perceptive detailed analysis of "Critique of Violence," never-theless thinks that the "secret goal" of Benjamin's essay is "the idea of a sort of cultural revolution that would bring down the centuries-old system of legal relations altogether. . . . In the end, Benjamin is convinced, we can only be liberated from [the] spell of law by a revolution that, in a sacral way, immediately produces justice through the performance of violence" (Honneth 2009: 125). Habermas thinks that Benjamin's conception of fate "affirms a natural-historical con-tinuum of the perpetually same and rules out cumulative changes in the structures of domination. This is where a redemptive critique is set into motion" (Habermas 1979: 55). Benjamin, Habermas affirms, wants to ban "the instrumental character of action from the realm of political praxis in favor of a 'politics of pure means'." Benjamin Morgan claims that "Benjamin's critique doesn't arrive at a criterion for judging which violence is just and which is not; it arrives at an aporia where the possibility of human judgment is no longer secure" (Morgan 2007: 52). Agamben writes:

> The definition . . . of "divine violence" constitutes the central problem of every interpretation of the essay. Benjamin in fact offers no positive criterion for its identification and even denies the possibility of recognizing it in the concrete case. What is certain is only that it neither posits nor preserves law, but rather de-poses (*entsetzt*) it. Hence its capacity to lend itself to the most dangerous equivocations which is proven by the scrutiny with which Derrida, in his interpretation of the essay, guards against it, approximating it – with a peculiar misunderstanding – to the Nazi "Final Solution." (Agamben 1998: 63–4)

The Seductive Allure of Benjamin's Essay

Considering the acknowledgment by virtually all commentators of the opaque, enigmatic, elusive quality of Benjamin's essay and the "violent" disagreements about the meaning of divine violence, the question arises, why is there so much fascination with this essay? Why do thinkers struggling to understand violence feel compelled to return to it over and over again? A skeptical response might be that it is precisely because the essay is so enigmatic that – like a Rorschach test – it invites the most diverse interpretations. The conflicting interpretations frequently reveal a great deal more about the interpreters than about any fixed meaning of the text. Readers like Marcuse and Rose clearly want to emphasize how Benjamin's critique of law and the state opens the space for "revolutionary practice which will be neither reformist nor justify force as a *means* of right-making." Because Butler and Critchley are deeply concerned with an ethics and politics that is committed to nonviolence, but recognize that there are situations in which violence may be required to fight "objective" violence, they stress the role of Benjamin's interpretation of the commandment "Thou shalt not kill" as a guideline that allows for exceptions. Derrida, despite his serious reservations about divine violence, seems more concerned to show the close affinity between Benjamin and deconstruction – and specifically how a deconstructive reading sheds light on the ambiguities of the text.

Still, we want to know why so many thinkers are drawn to this short text. I suggest that the reason why Benjamin's text is so alluring is that he incisively raises the key *questions* that any critique of violence must confront. He compels us to see the extent to which law involves violence – even those aspects of the law that may initially seem to be innocent of violence. He is especially insightful in exposing how this violence becomes apparent and problematic in times of crisis – when states feel threatened. He shows just how difficult it can be to draw any hard and fast distinction between "good" and "bad" violence, between "sanctioned and unsanctioned violence", between "legitimate and illegitimate violence." His examples of military and police violence show how the distinction between law-making and law-preserving violence is suspended and/or blurred – a problem that is still very much with us. He raises deep questions about which forms of political activity actually have the effect of reinforcing state power. If anything, this question is even more intractable today, when states and their leaders seem to have an enormous capacity to crush, absorb, defuse, and co-opt protest movements. He warns against the dangers of a continuous cycle of violence and counter-violence. His appeal to the pure manifestation of divine violence can best be approached as gesturing to the possibility of alternative ways of *thinking* and *acting*. The value of Benjamin's essay is in the *questions* that it opens up and compels us to confront – questions that still haunt us – and not in any *answers* or solutions that he provides, because he doesn't provide answers.

I want to conclude by offering an interpretation of a passage from Benjamin's final paragraph:

> If the rule of myth is broken occasionally in the present age, the coming age is not so unimaginably remote that an attack on the law is altogether futile. But if the existence of violence outside the law, as pure immediate violence, is assured, this shows that revolutionary violence, the highest manifestation of unalloyed violence by man, is possible, and shows by what means. Less possible and also less urgent for humankind, however, is to decide when unalloyed violence has been realized in particular cases.[39]

I do *not* think that Benjamin is speaking about a *future* new age – a coming golden age – that will appear after the Revolution and bring an end to the state and the cycle of mythic forms of law. Rather, I think he is speaking about the *present* (his present and, more importantly, our present). And what he is telling us is that "the rule of myth" can be (occasionally) broken. When this happens, then we have a glimpse that an alternative "revolutionary violence" is possible. We see – or rather *experience* – that there is a genuine alternative to the cycle of law-making and law-preserving violence.[40] This opening shows (*erweisen*) that the critique of existing violence is not futile – that there are moments when we can feel, think, and experience a genuine revolutionary alternative.[41] When Benjamin adds: "Less possible and also less urgent for humankind, however, is to decide when unalloyed violence has been realized in particular cases (*Nicht gleich möglich noch auch gleich dringend ist aber für Menschen die Enscheidung, wann reine Gewalt in einem bestimnten Falle wirklich war*)," I interpret this as a warning that we can never be certain that our actions are genuinely revolutionary. We can't possibly know with certainty whether the consequences of our actions break the cycle of mythical violence or reinforce it. This risk and uncertainty is inescapable. All we can know is that we must honestly face up to our responsibility for our actions.

Chapter 3

Hannah Arendt: On Violence and Power

The Historical Setting

In 1970 Hannah Arendt published her controversial essay *On Violence*.[1] The essay grew out of her participation in a heated panel on "The Legitimacy of Violence" that took place three years earlier at the famous Theatre for Ideas – a meeting place for New York intellectuals. Chaired by Robert Silvers of the *New York Review of Books*, the other members of the panel were Noam Chomsky, Conor Cruise O'Brien, and Robert Lowell. And in the audience there were also active discussants, including Susan Sontag and Tom Hayden, a leader of the SDS.[2] Arendt had lived through the turbulent 1960s with mixed emotions. She was an enthusiastic supporter of the early civil rights movement, the anti-Vietnam War movement, and the nonviolent student sit-ins in universities. (She even joined her students who were occupying a building at the University of Chicago.) But she was alarmed by the growth of the Black Power movement and the increasingly shrill rhetoric of violence in the student movement throughout the world. Arendt never hesitated to express her opinions forcefully, even when they were unpopular. Many readers of *On Violence* were (and still are) offended. Her harsh remarks about Negroes and the Black Power movement were condemned as "racist" (even though she strongly condemned racism in the same essay).[3] And some of her comments – especially if taken out of context – are shockingly offensive. Speaking about the student movement in the United States, she says: "Serious violence entered the scene only with the appearance of the Black

Power movement on the campuses. Negro students, the majority of them admitted without academic qualification, regarded and organized themselves as an interest group, the representatives of the black community. Their interest was to lower academic standards" (Arendt 1970: 18). She adds fuel to the fire when she declares that a large minority of the Negro community stands "behind the verbal and actual violence of the black students." She is equally condemning of the "academic establishment" in its "curious tendency" to yield to "Negro demands, even if they are clearly silly and outrageous" (Arendt: 1970: 19). It is as if the rhetoric and instances of actual violence touched a deep, sensitive nerve in Arendt – perhaps a reminder of what she had experienced in Germany in the early 1930s. But, given her provocative rhetoric, it is not difficult to understand why so many were shocked by and dismissive of her essay. This is unfortunate, because Arendt, I want to argue, develops some of the most penetrating reflections on violence in the political realm. The truth is, as we shall see, that Arendt's concern with violence can be traced back to some of her earliest writings. Arendt insisted that thinking grows out of personal experiences. She begins her essay by reviewing the recent experiences that were the occasion for her reflections. *On Violence* is filled with references to contemporary events, newspaper articles, reports, and books, which are probably barely known or remembered today. In her brief review of the literature on violence, especially Sorel, Fanon, and Sartre, she makes some acute observations. She notes that Sorel, despite his thinking about the class struggle in military terms, "ended by proposing nothing more violent than the famous myth of the general strike, a form of action which we today would think of as belonging rather to the arsenal of nonviolent politics. Fifty years ago even this modest proposal earned him the reputation of being a fascist, notwithstanding his enthusiastic approval of Lenin and the Russian Revolution" (Arendt 1970: 12). She discusses Fanon's *The Wretched of the Earth*, which many radical students were hailing as the credo and justification for violence. But her main target for criticism is Jean-Paul Sartre, for his "irresponsible glorification of violence." She accuses Sartre of misunderstanding Marx in his "amalgamation of existentialism and Marxism" when in the preface to *The Wretched of the Earth* he writes: " 'To shoot down a European is to kill two birds with one stone . . . there remain a dead man and a free man,'. . . . This is a sentence Marx could never have written" (Arendt 1970: 13). Sartre doesn't realize his sharp disagreement with Marx when he declares that "'irrepressible violence . . . is man recreating himself,' and that it is through 'mad fury' that 'the wretched of the earth' can 'become men'" (Arendt 1970: 12).[4] She draws an unfavorable comparison between Sartre and Fanon: "Fanon himself, however, is much more doubtful about violence than his admirers. . . . Fanon knows of the 'unmixed and total brutality [which], if not immediately combated, invariably leads to the defeat of the movement within a few weeks'" (Arendt 1970: 14, n. 19).[5]

The Antithesis of Power and Violence

"It is against the background of these experiences that I propose to raise the question of violence in political terms."[6] This is the opening sentence of the second section of her essay. I want to explore how Arendt deals with violence in this essay, supplementing it with observations that she makes in her other writings. I also want to work back to some of her earliest reflections on violence in the 1940s, when she called for the formation of a Jewish army to fight Hitler.

Although Arendt tells us that there has been a reluctance to deal with violence as a phenomenon in its own right, there is nevertheless a consensus of theorists from the left to the right who think that "violence is nothing more than the most flagrant manifestation of power." She quotes C. Wright Mills, who starkly affirms: "All politics is a struggle for power; the ultimate kind of power is violence." This declaration echoes "Max Weber's definition of the state as 'the rule of men over men based on the means of legitimate, that is allegedly legitimate, violence'" (Arendt 1970: 35). This well-entrenched paradigm of power, which has a long history, claims that power is the rule of an individual, group, or state over others. Power is understood to be *power over*.[7] This concept of power, which she calls the "command–obedience relationship," has a deeply entrenched history and has been reinforced by the Hebrew-Christian "imperative conception of law" (Arendt 1972: 138). If this is the way we think of power, then it makes perfect sense to claim that the ultimate kind of power is violence. This is precisely the conception of power that Arendt challenges – and her point is not merely one of linguistic propriety. It goes to the very heart of her political thinking. Power and violence are not only distinguishable; they are antithetical. Where power reigns, there is persuasion, not violence. And when violence reigns, it destroys power. She is critical of the question that many political theorists and philosophers have taken to be "the most crucial political issue": "Who rules Whom?" (Arendt 1970: 43). Arendt insists that serious political thinking requires making careful distinctions. The failure to do so indicates not only "a certain deafness to linguistic meanings, which would be serious enough, but it has also resulted in a kind of blindness to the realities they correspond to" (Arendt 1970: 43). And she distinguishes "power," "strength," "force," "authority," and "violence." Each of these key terms refers to distinct and different phenomena. Although my focus will be on power and violence, let me briefly review her range of distinctions.

"*Power* corresponds to the human ability not just to act but to act in concert. Power is never the property of an individual; it belongs to a group and remains in existence only so long as the group keeps together. When we say of somebody that he is 'in power' we actually refer to his being empowered by a certain number of people to act in their name. The moment the group, from which the power originated to begin with (*potestas in populo*, without a people or group there is no power), disappears, 'his power' also vanishes" (Arendt 1970: 44).

"*Strength* unequivocally designates something in the singular, an individual entity: it is the property inherent in an object or person and belongs to its character, which may prove itself in relation to other things or persons, but is essentially independent of them" (Arendt 1970: 44). Virgil's graphic description of Aeneas's physical prowess in his battles against his enemies is an exemplar of strength.

"*Force*, which we often use in daily speech as a synonym for violence, especially if violence serves as a means of coercion, should be reserved, in terminological language, for the 'forces of nature' or the 'force of circumstances' (*la force des choses*), that is, to indicate the energy released by physical or social movements" (Arendt 1970: 44–5).

Authority, Arendt tells us, is the most elusive of these phenomena and the term is most frequently abused. "Its hallmark is unquestioning recognition by those who are asked to obey; neither coercion nor persuasion is needed" (Arendt 1970: 45). Examples of authority are the relation of parent and child, teacher and student. Authority can be vested in an office – for example, in the hierarchical offices of the Catholic Church. In each case, authority may be questioned, ridiculed, and undermined.

"*Violence*, finally . . . is distinguished by its instrumental character. Phenomenologically, it is close to strength, since the implements of violence, like all other tools, are designed and used for the purpose of multiplying natural strength until, in the last stage of their development, they can substitute for it" (Arendt 1970: 46).

At first glance these distinctions seem arbitrary – as if she were offering stipulative definitions – without justifying them. They certainly do not correspond to the ways in which we ordinarily use these terms, and, more significantly, they do not correspond to any standard uses of these terms by political theorists or philosophers. Furthermore, her characterizations are so condensed that they invite all sorts of questions. Arendt denies that they are arbitrary, although she admits that they "hardly ever correspond to watertight compartments in the real world" (Arendt 1970: 46). But if we are to be persuaded that they are not arbitrary, then we need a fuller account of their meaning and rationale – and this is the issue I want to pursue in regard to power and violence.[8]

Arendt's description of power is not an isolated attempt at redefinition. Rather, it links up with a whole network of concepts that she had been elaborating ever since *The Human Condition* (and even earlier): action, speech, plurality, natality, public space, isonomy, opinion, persuasion, and public freedom. Collectively, these concepts texture her vision of political life and constitute the background for her approach to power and violence. In the opening pages of *The Human Condition* – in her analysis of the three modes of activity of the *vita activa*, labor, work, and action – Arendt states: "Action, the only activity that goes on directly between men without the intermediary of things or matter, corresponds to the human condition of plurality, to the fact that men, not Man, live on earth and inhabit the world. While all aspects of the human condition are somehow related to politics, this plurality is specifically *the* condition – not only the *conditio sine qua non*, but the *conditio per quam* – of all political life" (Arendt 1958a: 7).

Plurality has a distinctive meaning for Arendt: it involves individuality, distinction, and equality. Every individual brings a distinctive perspective to a common world. Plurality is rooted in our natality, the capacity to begin, to initiate action spontaneously. "To act in its most general sense, means to take an initiative, to begin . . . to set something into motion" (Arendt 1958a: 177).[9] Action and speech are intimately related, because it is by our words and deeds that we reveal our unique distinctiveness in the company of others. Political equality, the equality that characterizes plurality, is what the Greeks called *isonomy*. In the polis "men meet one another as citizens and not as private persons. . . . The equality of the Greek *polis*, its isonomy, was an attribute of the *polis* and not of men, who received their equality by virtue of citizenship, not by virtue of birth" (Arendt 1977: 31).[10] We see more clearly why Arendt rejects the idea of political power as power of one individual or group *over* another – why she categorically rejects the idea that the crucial question of politics is "Who rules Whom?" Politics involves acting together; it is based upon human plurality and citizens encountering others as political equals. In the public space created by acting together, citizens debate and deliberate with each other; they seek to persuade each other about how to conduct their public affairs. Persuasion involves debate among political equals, where citizens mutually seek to clarify, test, and purify their opinions. Persuasion, not violence, is what "rules" in a polity. Speech and debate can be contentious and agonistic; they do not necessarily result in, or presuppose, consensus. But politics requires a commitment to persuasion, and when we fail to persuade, we must at least agree on fair procedures for making decisions.

We deepen our understanding of what Arendt means by politics and power by probing how she integrates tangible public freedom into this web of concepts. Referring to the *philosophes* of the French Enlightenment, she tells us that they had a shrewd insight into the *public* character of freedom. "Their public freedom was not an inner realm into which men might escape at will from the pressures of the world, nor was it the *liberum arbitrium* which makes the will choose between alternatives. Freedom for them could exist only in public: it was a tangible, worldly reality, something created by men to be enjoyed by men rather than a gift or a capacity, it was the man-made public space or marketplace which antiquity had known as the area where freedom appears and becomes visible to all" (Arendt 1977: 124). Public tangible freedom must be sharply distinguished from liberty. Liberty is always liberation *from* something or someone, whether it is liberation from poverty or oppressive rulers and tyrants. Liberty is a necessary condition for public freedom, but not a sufficient condition. Public freedom is a positive political achievement that arises when individuals act together and treat each other as political equals. I believe that the distinction between liberty and public freedom is one of Arendt's most important, enduring, and relevant political insights. Over and over again – especially after the fall of Communism in 1989 – we have had to learn the painful lesson that liberation from oppressive rulers is not *sufficient* to bring about public freedom. One of the greatest disasters of the political rhetoric that was used to "justify" the military invasion of Iraq by the United States and its allies was the false belief that liberation from the oppressive rule of Saddam Hussein would initiate public freedom in the Middle East. The idea that liberation "automatically" leads to democratic public freedom is a dangerous illusion.

We can now more fully appreciate Arendt's distinctive concept of power and why she sharply distinguishes it from strength, force, authority, and violence. Power, as we have indicated, is not to be understood in a vertical, hierarchical manner, where it is taken to mean control or domination over another individual or group. Power is a horizontal concept: it springs up and grows when individuals act together, seek to persuade each other, and treat each other as political equals.

> [P]ower comes into being only if and when men join themselves together for the purpose of action, and it will disappear when, for whatever reason, they disperse and desert one another. Hence, binding and promising, combining and covenanting are the means by which power is kept in existence; where and when men succeed in keeping intact the power which sprang up between them during the course of any particular act or deed, they are already in the process of foundation, of constituting a stable worldly structure to house, as it were, their combined power of action. (Arendt 1977: 175)

Power, then, along with tangible public freedom, stands at the center of Arendt's political vision. Consequently, violence is the *antithesis* of power. "Power and violence are opposites; where the one rules absolutely, the other is absent" (Arendt 1970: 56). Violence is anti-political. So, strictly speaking, the very idea of "political violence" is self-contradictory; and the idea of nonviolent power is redundant. Violence is distinguished by its instrumental character; it uses tools, weapons, and sophisticated technological devices designed to multiply strength. "Violence can always destroy power: out of the barrel of a gun grows the most effective command, resulting in the most instant and perfect obedience. What never can grow out of it is power" (Arendt 1970: 53). Violence always stands ready to destroy power and public freedom. Arendt is brutally realistic, for she knows all too well that "in a head-on clash between violence and power, the outcome is hardly in doubt" (Arendt 1970: 53). And when there is a loss of power, there is an enormous temptation to resort to violence. "Power is indeed of the essence of all government, but violence is not. Violence is by nature instrumental; like all means, it always stands in need of guidance and justification through the end it pursues" (Arendt 1970: 51). In the "real world" we rarely find power and violence in their "pure states": "*[N]othing . . . is more common than the combination of violence and power, nothing less frequent than to find them in their pure and therefore extreme form*" (Arendt 1970: 46–7, emphasis added).[11]

> Power springs up whenever people get together and act in concert, but it derives its legitimacy from the initial getting together rather than from any action that then may follow. Legitimacy, when challenged, bases itself on an appeal to the past, while justification relates to an end that lies in the future. Violence can be justifiable, but it never will be legitimate. Its justification loses in plausibility the farther its intended end recedes into the future. No one questions the use of violence in self-defense, because the danger is not only clear but also present, and the end justifying the means is immediate. (Arendt 1970: 52)

What is Arendt Doing?

Suppose we stand back and ask: What is Arendt doing in laying out these conceptual differences between power and violence? Is this only a theoretical exercise that displays her intellectual ingenuity? Or worse, is she guilty of doing what some of her critics claim – indulging in nostalgia for an idealized Greek polis that never actually existed? I think that both of these caricatures are off the mark. In her own terms, she is engaging in "an exercise of political thought as it arises out of the actuality of political incidents," the type of exercise that takes place in the gap between past and future, which she describes so eloquently in her preface to *Between Past and Future* (Arendt 2006: 3–15). Behind the immediate events of the 1960s, there is a much deeper stratum that provoked her thinking about politics, power, and violence. One of her earliest attempts to outline her vision of politics as based on plurality and the spontaneity of human action is to be found in the darkest chapter of *The Origins of Totalitarianism*, where she dwells on the horrors of the Nazi concentration and extermination camps. "Total domination, which strives to organize the infinite plurality and differentiation of human beings as if all of humanity were just one individual, is possible only if each and every person can be reduced to a never-changing identity of reactions, so that each of these bundles of reactions can be exchanged at random for any other" (Arendt 1958b: 438). The aim of totalitarian ideologies, she writes, "is not the transformation of the outside world or the revolutionizing transmutation of society, but the transformation of human nature itself" and "the concentration camps are the laboratories where changes in human nature are tested" (Arendt 1958b: 458). The aim of total domination is to destroy human plurality, individuality, and spontaneity – to make human beings as human beings superfluous. This is what Arendt called "radical evil."[12] It is as if "dwelling on horrors," dwelling on a new unprecedented radical evil, Arendt began her act of recovery of our humanity. Claude Lefort makes this point succinctly when he writes:

> Arendt's reading of totalitarianism, in both its Nazi and Stalinist variants, governs the subsequent elaboration of her theory of politics. She conceptualizes politics by inverting the image of totalitarianism, and this leads her to look, not for a model of politics – the use of the term "model" would be a betrayal of her intentions – but for a reference to politics in certain privileged moments when its features are most clearly discernible: the moment of the Greek City in Antiquity and, in modern times, the moments of the American and French Revolutions. The moment of the workers' councils in Russia in 1917, and that of the Hungarian workers' councils of 1956, might also be added to the list. (Lefort 1988: 50)[13]

Arendt witnessed another "privileged moment" of politics in the early civil rights movement and the anti–Vietnam War movement. The generations participating in these events display "sheer courage, an astounding will to action, and . . . a no less astounding confidence in the possibility of change"; she praises their nonviolent "participatory democracy" (Arendt 1970: 16, 19).

My central thesis is that in elaborating the difference between power and violence, Arendt is providing us with a *critical* perspective for thinking about our current political life. Although she departs from the tradition of thinking of power as "power over," she captures something quintessential about power – the way in which it can arise spontaneously when human beings act together, the way in which it can grow, the way in which it can become revolutionary. Given her scathing critique of any and all appeals to historical necessity and her own commitment to radical contingency, as well as the unpredictability of action, she reminds us that as long as natality and the human capacity to act together are not obliterated, the tangible public freedom that is the expression of power can spring forth.[14] As I have indicated, Arendt knows that in the "real world" power and violence are rarely separated; but this is no reason to confuse these antithetical concepts. By keeping them distinct, we sharpen our critical understanding of this "real world."

Lefort speaks about those "privileged moments" that exemplify the type of politics and power that she describes. Arendt called these moments the "revolutionary spirit" – a treasure that we are in danger of forgetting and losing.[15] "The history of revolutions – from the summer of 1776 in Philadelphia and the summer of 1789 in Paris to the autumn of 1956 in Budapest – *which politically spells out the innermost story of the modern age*, could be told in parable form as a tale of an age-old treasure which, under the most varied circumstances, appears abruptly, unexpectedly, and disappears again, under different mysterious conditions, as though it were a fata morgana" (Arendt 2006: 4, emphasis added). Arendt is frequently read as a severe critic of the modern age – and she certainly was, insofar as the modern age has seen the increasing spread of bureaucracy ("the rule of nobody") and the triumph of social and economic concerns that tend to obliterate action and politics. But, at the same time, she thought that it was only in the modern age that the revolutionary spirit appeared (as distinct from older rebellions).[16] The sudden emergence (and disappearance) of this revolutionary spirit spells out the innermost political story of the modern age. Her analysis of the revolutionary spirit refines our understanding of the relation of politics, power, and violence. Arendt begins *On Revolution* by declaring: "Wars and revolutions – as though events had only hurried up to fulfill Lenin's early prediction – have thus far determined the physiognomy of the twentieth century" (Arendt 1977: 11). The "aim of revolution was, and always has been, freedom," even though the word "freedom" frequently disappears from the revolutionary vocabulary (Arendt 1977: 11). Wars are much older than revolutions, and they have rarely ever been bound up with freedom. Historically, both wars and revolutions "are not even conceivable outside the domain of violence."

To be sure, not even wars, let alone revolutions, are ever completely determined by violence. Where violence rules absolutely, as for instance in the concentration camps of totalitarian regimes, not only the laws – *les lois se taisent*, as the French Revolution phrased it – but everything and everybody must fall silent. It is because of this silence that violence is a marginal phenomenon in the political realm; for man, to the extent that he is a political being, is endowed with speech. . . . The point here is that violence itself is incapable of speech, and not merely that speech is helpless when confronted with violence. (Arendt 1977: 18–19)

No one could accuse Arendt of being innocent or naive about the prevalence of violence in the "real world." But if we keep in mind how she has defined power and violence, we can appreciate why she separates politics from violence – why merging them is an obfuscating confusion. Violence, although it can be lethal, is mute; it is instrumental. But power requires speech and articulation. The *political* issue concerning violence is the "justification" of violence. "A theory of war or a theory of revolution, therefore, can only deal with the justification of violence because this justification constitutes its political limitation; if, instead, it arrives at a glorification or justification of violence as such, it is no longer political but antipolitical" (Arendt 1977: 19).

The Revolutionary Spirit

When we consider revolutions in the modern age, we need to discriminate between the elements of violence and the political significance of revolutions, which Arendt calls the "revolutionary spirit." Just as Arendt seeks to show that power must be distinguished from violence, so she also wants to argue that the revolutionary spirit must be distinguished from "revolutionary violence." Violence by itself can never bring about a revolution, even if it is necessary to achieve liberation.[17] The revolutionary spirit is the public tangible freedom that aims to create a new order (*novus ordo saeculorum*). Arendt argues that the American Revolution is the exemplar of the revolutionary spirit, not the French Revolution, which turned to terror and violence.[18] In speaking of the American Revolution she means the events that began in 1776 with the Declaration of Independence and culminated with the writing and ratification of the Constitution. It is the deliberation, the debates, the compromises, and the ultimate ratification of the Constitution – the creation of a *novus ordo saeculorum* – that epitomizes the revolutionary spirit. Although initially the men of the revolution did not think of themselves as creating a revolution, but rather as restoring basic human liberty, the Founding Fathers came to the realization that the "course of history suddenly begins anew, that an entirely new story never known or told before is about to unfold." This is the distinctive mark of the modern conception of revolution. "Crucial, then, to any understanding of revolutions in the modern age is that the idea of freedom and the experience of a new beginning should coincide" (Arendt 1977: 29). The network of concepts that Arendt elaborates in her political vision – plurality, natality, spontaneity, public space, participation in public affairs, testing and revising opinions with one's peers, debate, and persuasion – was concretely manifested in the founding of the Republic. The "success" of the American Revolution resulted, in part, from the long pre-Revolutionary tradition of political self-determination – a tradition of mutual covenants and agreements. The American Revolution is an exemplar of the revolutionary spirit because it stands "in flagrant opposition to the age-old and still current notions of the dictating violence, necessary for all foundations and hence supposedly unavoidable in all revolutions" (Arendt 1977: 213).

> In this respect, the course of the American Revolution tells an unforgettable story and is apt to teach a unique lesson; for this revolution did not break out but was made by men in common deliberation and on the strength of mutual pledges. The principle which came to light during those fateful years when the foundations were laid – not by the strength of one architect but by the combined power of the many – was the interconnected principle of mutual promise and common deliberation; and the event itself decided indeed, as Hamilton had insisted, that men 'are really capable . . . of establishing good government from reflection and choice', that they are not 'forever destined to depend for their political constitutions on accident and force'. (Arendt 1977: 213–14)[19]

This is not the end of the story of the American Revolution. Almost immediately, after the founding of the Republic, there was a failure to remember the revolutionary spirit, a failure that was preceded by the failure of the Revolution to provide this revolutionary spirit with a lasting political institution. Thomas Jefferson was one of the few who were deeply aware of this problem, and he called for dividing the country into "elementary republics," or wards – spaces in which the public freedom experienced by the founders of the Republic might be perpetuated. But nothing came of his plan. Not only the American Revolution, but all subsequent revolutions have been all too quickly suppressed – frequently by professional revolutionaries. The treasure of the revolutionary spirit is in danger of being lost and has been replaced by a distorted conception of revolutionary violence.[20]

Fabrication and Violence

Thus far, I have been discussing the question of violence in the political realm, as Arendt herself does in *On Violence*. But violence has an even broader significance in Arendt's thinking – although this broader conception of violence will eventually lead us back to power and politics. In the analysis of the *vita activa* in *The Human Condition*, Arendt distinguishes three fundamental activities: labor, work, and action. Labor corresponds to the biological process of the human body, and its human condition is life. "Work provides an 'artificial' world of things, distinctively different from all natural surroundings. Within its borders each individual life is housed, while this world itself is meant to outlast and transcend them all. The human condition of work is worldliness" (Arendt 1958a: 7). Action (which has been our primary concern thus far) corresponds to the human condition of plurality. *The Human Condition* is a complex work that may be read and interpreted from a variety of perspectives, but there are at least two dominant strands. The first consists of an explication, a phenomenological investigation of labor, work, and action – the three types of activities that constitute the *vita activa*. The second is a narrative, the story Arendt tells about the modern age. It is a story of a series of reversals. The major reversal is between the *vita contemplativa* and the *vita activa*. Whereas ancient philosophers and medieval theologians placed the highest value on the *vita contemplativa (bios theoretikos)* – the most divine-like form of human life – there has been an inversion in the modern age, actually a displacement by the *vita activa*. Furthermore, there has been a series of reversals within the *vita activa*. For the ancients, especially Aristotle, action (*praxis*) was the highest form of human activity – that in which human beings live ethical and political lives. Making (*poiesis*), the work of craftsmen or artists, has a lesser value than action (*praxis*). Labor, the activity necessary to sustain life, is the lowest form of activity. In the modern age there is a reversal of this hierarchy, whereby making and fabricating – the activities of *homo faber* – rise to the position that was formerly occupied by contemplation. This is followed by a second reversal, a glorification of labor, where *animal laborans* is victorious. Consequently, there is an inversion in the traditional hierarchy of action, work, and labor. Arendt claims that a "laboring mentality" has become so dominant and pervasive that we barely even recognize the independence of action and work.

When we examine her conception of work and fabrication, we discover what I have called her broader conception of violence. Fabrication consists in reification, in the making of things. Echoing the way in which Aristotle distinguishes between the natural world and the artificial world, Arendt stresses how *homo faber* is "the creator of the human artifice."

"Material is already a product of human hands which has removed it from its natural location, either killing a life process, as in the case of the tree which must be destroyed in order to provide wood, or interrupting nature's slower processes, as in the case of iron, stone, or marble torn out of the womb of the earth. *This element of violation and violence is present in all fabrication*, and *homo faber*, the creator of the human artifice, has always been a destroyer of nature" (Arendt 1958a: 139, emphasis added). We must interpret carefully what Arendt is saying. When considering the political significance of violence, Arendt has already stressed its instrumental character. When viewed from the perspective of power, "violence" has primarily a negative connotation; it is a threat to, and can destroy, power. (Power – especially when it involves large numbers of people – can isolate and destroy violence.) But if violence is present in all fabrication, then "violence" takes on a much more positive, or at least a more neutral, connotation. Work, fabrication, making things, is part of, and essential for, the human condition. It is through work that humans create a world – a world that is meant to outlast and transcend individual human lives. The category of means and ends governs making. We hear echoes of Aristotle's description of *poiesis* in his *Nicomachean Ethics* when Arendt writes: "The fabricated thing is an end product in the twofold sense that the production process comes to an end in it ... and that it is only a means to produce this end" (Arendt 1958a: 143). In her phenomenological investigation of labor, work, and action, Arendt delineates the hierarchical relations among these different activities, but she also stresses their interdependence. The most important task of creating the human artifice is the creation of a stable world within which action can take place. "The Permanence of the World and the Work of Art" is the final section of her chapter on work. Work, the making of things, is by no means restricted to manufacturing products for everyday life; it also involves creating works of art, "the most intensely worldly of all tangible things." "Thus, their durability is of a higher order than that which all things need in order to exist at all; it can attain permanence throughout the ages. . . . Nowhere else does the sheer durability of the world of things appear in such purity and clarity; nowhere else does this thing-world reveal itself so spectacularly as the non-mortal home for mortal beings" (Arendt 1958a: 167–8).

But if creating such a world – a world that is a home for human beings and a fit place for action and speech – involves violence, then it becomes clear that violence is not intrinsically negative. It has its proper function in creating a human world, which involves a transformation of nature. Yet there is a darker face to her Janus-like discussion of *homo faber*. *Homo faber* not only refers to human beings insofar as they are creators of an artificial world; it also names a *mentality* that can dominate and permeate *all* our thinking and acting. This mentality, which gained prominence in the seventeenth century, is exhibited by Hobbes – "the greatest representative" of "the political philosophy of the modern age" – when he speaks about *making* an artificial animal "called a Commonwealth, or State." "[T]he attempt to imitate under artificial conditions the process of 'making' by which a natural thing came into existence, serves as well or even better as the principle for doing in the realm of human affairs" (Arendt 1958a: 299). But for Arendt, this mentality, which has had such a powerful influence right up to the present, is blind to the contingency and unpredictability of action and events.[21] When this mentality becomes all-pervasive, it has disastrous consequences because it "legitimizes" violence – especially in the founding and forming of states.

> And, indeed, among the outstanding characteristics of the modern age from its beginning to our own time we find the typical attitudes of *homo faber*: his instrumentalization of the world, his confidence in tools and in the productivity of the maker of artificial objects; his trust in the all-comprehensive range of the means–end category, his conviction that

every issue can be solved and every human motivation reduced to the principle of utility; his sovereignty, which regards everything given as material and thinks of the whole of nature as of "an immense fabric from which we can cut out whatever we want to resew it however we like": his equation of intelligence with ingenuity, that is, the contempt for all thought which cannot be considered to be "the first step . . . for the fabrication of artificial objects, particularly of tools to make tools, and to vary their fabrication indefinitely"; finally, his matter-of-course identification of fabrication with action. (Arendt 1958a: 305–6)[22]

Violence as instrumental has a proper role in human life because it is involved in all fabrication. And fabrication is essential for producing things needed for everyday life and for creating works of art – creating a human world that will be a place fit for action and speech. But when the mentality of *homo faber* dominates our thinking and acting, it is dangerous for two basic reasons: it distorts reality (especially the unpredictability and contingency of human action), and it "legitimizes" violence in political life. Carried to its extreme, it entails, as C. Wright Mills declared, that violence is nothing more than the most flagrant manifestation of power.

Terror and Violence

I want to take up another strand in Arendt's thinking about violence that is mentioned in *On Violence*. She briefly discusses terror, telling us that "Terror is not the same as violence; it is, rather, the form of government that comes into being when violence, having destroyed all power, does not abdicate but, on the contrary, remains in full control. . . . Every kind of organized opposition must disappear before the full force of terror can be let loose." And in what might be taken as an implicit critique of Carl Schmitt's famous definition of "the political" she adds: "The decisive difference between totalitarian domination, based on terror, and tyrannies and dictatorships, established by violence, is that the former turns not only against its enemies but against its friends and supporters as well, being afraid of all power, even the power of its friends. The climax of terror is reached when the police state begins to devour its own children, when yesterday's executioner becomes today's victim. And this is also the moment when power disappears entirely" (Arendt 1970: 55).[23]

These remarks about terror and violence call to mind her discussion of terror and total domination in *The Origins of Totalitarianism*. Terror, as so many of her concepts, has a special meaning for Arendt. She is not referring to what – especially after 9/11 – we call "terrorists." Rather, as she indicates in the above passage, terror refers to a *form of government* – totalitarianism. Arendt argues that the totalitarianism of the twentieth century was unprecedented and must not be confused with or reduced to traditional conceptions of dictatorship and tyranny. Totalitarianism is a regime that is based on violence and seeks to destroy all power. In her discussion of total domination, she presents a graphic description of the concentration and extermination camps as "the most consequential institution of totalitarian rule" (Arendt 1958b: 441). They were "laboratories" of totalitarian regimes, where a systematic attempt was made to destroy the "juridical person" and "the moral person", finally "killing man's individuality." The aim of totalitarianism is to make human beings superfluous, to transform human beings into something that is not human. Transforming human nature itself, and making human beings superfluous, is what Arendt calls radical evil.[24] And she concludes her discussion of "Total Domination" with a dire warning: "Totalitarian solutions may well survive the fall of totalitarian regimes in the form of strong temptations which will come up whenever it seems impossible to alleviate political, social or economic misery in a manner worthy of man" (Arendt 1958b: 459).

In the final chapter of *The Origins*, Arendt raises the question of whether totalitarianism "has its own essence"; whether there is a "basic experience which finds its political expression in totalitarian domination" (Arendt 1958b: 461).[25] To grasp what is distinctive about totalitarianism as a form of government, we have to understand the distinctive role of ideology and terror. Ideologies, as used by totalitarian regimes, are "isms" which their adherents claim "can explain everything and every occurrence by deducing it from a single premise." From an external perspective ideologies are thoroughly irrational, but they carry their own internal logic and rationality to an extreme. "Ideological thinking orders facts into an absolutely logical procedure which starts from an axiomatically accepted premise, deducing everything else from it; that is, it proceeds with a consistency that exists nowhere in the realm of reality" (Arendt 1958b: 471). Terror is closely linked to ideology. Violence is certainly not unique to totalitarianism; tyranny and dictatorship also employ the

instruments of violence. But the terror that Arendt sees as characteristic of totalitarianism goes beyond more traditional uses of violence.
"[T]error in totalitarian government has ceased to be a mere form of
all opposition; it rules supreme when nobody any longer stands in its
way." "If lawfulness is the essence of non-tyrannical government and
lawlessness the essence of tyranny, then *terror is the essence of totalitarian
domination*" (Arendt 1958b: 464, emphasis added). "Under conditions
of total terror not even fear can any longer serve as an advisor of how
to behave, because terror chooses its victims without reference to
individual actions or thoughts, exclusively in accordance with objective necessity of the natural or historical process" (Arendt 1958b:
467). Returning to Arendt's remarks about terror in *On Violence*, we
see that although terror employs violence, it is "beyond" violence in
the sense that it is the total domination characteristic of totalitarian
regimes that arises when these regimes attempt to destroy all power
and all plurality.

The Justification of Violence

Although Arendt draws a sharp distinction between violence and
power, and claims that power is nonviolent, she was not a pacifist.
She certainly thought that there were times when violence is justified
for political purposes. One of the most dramatic instances of this was
her call for the formation of a Jewish army to fight Hitler. Shortly
after Arendt arrived in New York, she started to write articles for the
German-Jewish weekly *Aufbau*. Her first article, dated November 14,
1941, was entitled "Die jüdische Armee – der Beginn einer jüdische
Politik?" ("The Jewish Army – The Beginning of a Jewish Politics?").
Before the United States entered the Second World War, Arendt
called for a Jewish army drawn from volunteers all over the world to
fight Hitler, "in Jewish battle formations under a Jewish flag." She
argued that the formation of a Jewish army was essential for "the
struggle for the freedom of the Jewish people." Her justification for
a unique Jewish army is that "you can only defend yourself as the
person you are attacked as" (Arendt 2007: 137). This echoes her
famous remark when she escaped from Germany in 1933: "If one is
attacked as a Jew, one must defend oneself as a Jew. Not as a German,
not as a world-citizen, not as an upholder of the Rights of Man, or

whatever" (Arendt 1994: 12). Arendt's justification of the need for a Jewish army was that she thought it would be the beginning of a Jewish politics – the beginning of a demand by the Jewish people for a vital role in the fight for freedom. "We will never get that army if the Jewish people do not demand it and are not prepared by the hundreds of thousands with weapons in hand to fight for their freedom and the right to live as a people. Only the people themselves, young and old, poor and rich, men and women, can reshape public opinion, which today is against us. *For only the people themselves are strong enough for a true alliance*" (Arendt 2007: 138–9, emphasis original). Arendt wrote this (and many subsequent articles calling for a Jewish army) long before she had worked out her theoretical understanding of violence and power. But she clearly anticipated her later thinking insofar as she is calling for the Jewish people to act *politically* together to demand and volunteer for such an army. Although she doesn't explicitly mention "violence," it is perfectly clear that the aim of a Jewish army is to fight Hitler and the Nazis and to fight for the freedom of the Jewish people.[26] I have cited this early example of Arendt's call for the formation of a Jewish army to make clear that Arendt was fully aware of the complex relationship between power and violence. And there are times when violence can be politically justified in order to fight for freedom.

Arendt's Exaggerated Thinking

Throughout her intellectual career, from the time of her earliest writings about Jewish affairs and Zionism, Arendt was controversial. The most notorious controversy was provoked by *Eichmann in Jerusalem*, a controversy which continued until her death in 1975 and long after. Arendt thought of herself as an independent thinker (*Selbstdenker*), and she simply didn't "fit" any of the conventional academic or political labels. At a conference dedicated to her work, which she attended in 1972, Hans Morgenthau, the distinguished political scientist (and a personal friend), bluntly asked her, "What are you? Are you a conservative? Are you a liberal? Where is your position within contemporary possibilities?" Arendt forthrightly replied: "I don't know. I really don't know and I have never known. And I suppose I never had any position. You know the left think I am conservative, and the conservatives sometimes think I am left or I am a maverick or God knows what. And I must say I couldn't care less. *I don't think that the real questions of this century will get any kind of illumination by this kind of thing.*" (Hill 1979: 333, emphasis added).

She might have given the same reply if asked whether she was a philosopher, a political theorist, a cultural or literary critic.[27] Arendt simply didn't think in these terms, and she certainly did not "fit" any of the traditional academic professions; nor was she much concerned with dominant intellectual trends and fashions. She was not only an independent thinker, but an irritating thinker. When she deals with a problem or a thinker, she frequently writes as if there is one, and only one, correct view. And she had strong opinions concerning just about everything she discussed. When she had a fixed idea about something, she would rarely budge (or consider alternative interpretations). For example, she stubbornly insisted that both Hegel and Marx substituted a philosophy of history and a doctrine of historical inevitability for a genuine understanding of human freedom.[28] Her rhetoric is frequently essentialist. When she entitles essays "What *is* Freedom?" or "What *is* Authority?" she writes as if there is really one, and only one, correct answer to these questions. When she distinguishes "power," "strength," "force," "authority," and "violence," she doesn't say "I propose to introduce these distinctions for the following reasons"; rather, she presents these distinctions as if any clear-thinking person will see that these refer to "distinct phenomena" (Arendt 1970: 43). Sometimes these dogmatic pronouncements seem like sheer intellectual arrogance. She was frequently accused of exaggeration – even by sympathetic friends. In their extended correspondence, Karl Jaspers makes this accusation several times. In her letter to him dated January 22, 1952, she expressed her pique.

"Exaggeration" – of course. "Relationships between ideas," as you say, can hardly be presented any other way. And then they are not really exaggerations either. They are products of dissection. It's the nature of thought to exaggerate. When Montesquieu says that republican government is based on the principle of virtue, he is "exaggerating", too. Besides, reality has taken things to such great extremes in our century that we can say without exaggeration that reality is "exaggerated." Our thinking, which after all likes nothing better than rolling along its accustomed paths, is hardly capable of keeping up with it. My "exaggerated" kind of thinking, which is at least making an effort to say something adequate in a tone that is, if possible, itself adequate, will of course sound wildly radical if you measure it not against reality but against what other historians, going on the assumption that everything is in the best of order, have said on the same subject. (Arendt and Jaspers 1992: 175–6)

This passage is extremely revealing about Arendt's own thinking, and it has particular relevance for her reflections on violence. When Arendt introduces her categorical distinction between violence and power, she is clearly "exaggerating," and this might be taken as a reason for dismissing her work. After all, even *she* admits that nothing is "more common than the combination of violence and power, nothing less frequent than to find them in their pure and therefore extreme form" (Arendt 1970: 47).[29] If this is true, then what's the point of drawing such a strong distinction between them? I am inclined to reply: "That's precisely the point!" Arendt is not utopian. She doesn't think that in the "real world" power can prevail without any violence. But the point of her "exaggerated" claims is to get us to see, understand, and appreciate something that we are in danger of forgetting – that power and action are distorted when we fuse power and violence. Distinguishing power and violence enables us to discern those political "privileged moments" that have emerged almost spontaneously and which reveal the "innermost story of the modern age." What Arendt says about Walter Benjamin – in a beautiful and illuminating essay – is just as applicable to her.

> Like a pearl diver who descends to the bottom of the sea, not to excavate the bottom and bring it to light but to pry loose the rich and the strange, the pearls and the coral in the depths, and to carry them to the surface, this thinking delves into the depths of the past – but not in order to resuscitate it the way it was and to contribute to the renewal of extinct ages. What guides this thinking is the conviction that although the living is subject to the ruin of time, the process of decay is at the same time a process of crystallization, that in the depth of the sea, into which sinks and is dissolved what was once alive, some things "suffer a sea-change" and survive in new crystallized forms and shapes that remain immune to the elements, as though they waited only for the pearl diver who one day will come down to them and bring them up into the world of the living – as "thought fragments," as something "rich and strange," and perhaps even as everlasting *Urphänomene*. (Arendt 1968b: 205–6)

The purpose of this "excavation" is not simply to retrieve "pearls" from the *past*, but to serve as a reminder of what is in the *present* and is still real *future* possibility. As long as the human condition does not radically change, there is the possibility of actualizing nonviolent political power – or at least of maximizing this power by acting together, testing and clarifying our opinion in public spaces, and minimizing violence. Even if we fail in this endeavor, Arendt's "exaggerated" thinking provides critical standards for judging what we are doing and what is happening to us. Her distinctions are "products of dissection" that enable us to discriminate what we otherwise would not see if we assume that things are "rolling along" in their "accustomed paths." And this type of thinking is what is called forth precisely because "reality has taken things to such great extremes in our century [the twentieth century] that we can say without exaggeration that reality is 'exaggerated'."

There are many types of violence that Arendt does not discuss systematically, such as religious violence, rape, and suicide bombing. It isn't clear how she understands violent speech; presumably all violence is mute. And there are many questions about violence that she never asks, such as why violence is glorified, or how it is related to sacrifice. But what she does say about violence and power, as well as how the violence intrinsic to work becomes dangerous when the mentality of *homo faber* dominates thinking and acting, is fresh and illuminating and provides a much-needed perspective for understanding the extremes of the twentieth and twenty-first centuries.

The Relevance of Arendt

Still, one may wonder how relevant Arendt's reflection is to the political realities of our contemporary age. Even if one concedes that she illuminates "extraordinary politics" and "the revolutionary spirit," these "privileged moments" have been all too rare and brief by her reckoning. What does Arendt really have to tell us about everyday politics in this age of globalization? In her own reflections on freedom she hits upon a deep perplexity that she never quite resolved. In the concluding chapter of *On Revolution*, she argues that after the American Revolution – in post-revolutionary thought – there was not only a "failure to remember the revolutionary spirit" but, even more important, a failure to provide a lasting political institution for the public freedom that had been achieved in the founding of the Republic. "The perplexity was very simple, and stated in logical terms, it seemed unsolvable: if foundation was the aim and end of revolution then the revolutionary spirit was not merely the spirit of beginning something new but of starting something permanent and enduring; a lasting institution, embodying this spirit and encouraging it to new achievements, would be self-defeating" (Arendt 1977: 232). If the deliberation involved in writing and ratifying the Constitution exemplified a privileged political moment of political freedom, and the Constitution is supposed to "house" public freedom, then the perplexity is how to foster and encourage public freedom after the founding of the Republic.

In this context, Arendt sketches the idea of a council system that might serve as an alternative to the modern state.[30] But the problem that Arendt touches on raises profound issues that go beyond the American Revolution. Whether we use the Weberian language of extraordinary and ordinary politics, or the Kuhnian language of revolutionary and normal science, the problem is how is one to preserve something of the spirit of what is extraordinary and revolutionary in everyday normal politics. How are we to foster the growth of power and minimize violence? How are we to make public freedom tangible, not only in brief historical moments, but in enduring, long-lasting, political institutions? Arendt was acutely aware of these problems and perplexities, and she valiantly struggled with them. But I don't think she ever came up with a satisfactory "solution." In truth, I don't think that any thinker of the twentieth or twenty-first century has adequately resolved the issue of the processes of "normalization" that defeat the revolutionary spirit and undermine the "privileged moments" of "public freedom." But it would be a grave mistake to dismiss Arendt's reflections on violence and power because she failed to resolve a problem and perplexity that no one else has solved – and which may indeed be insoluble.

Whatever the deficiencies of Arendt's sharp and categorical distinction between power and violence, I have been arguing that they still provide us with a valuable critical perspective for coming to grips with power and violence in our world today. But I would like to focus on two criticisms, which I have already suggested, that show why her analyses need to be modified and supplemented. I want to return to what I have already claimed is an important distinction for her – between liberty and freedom. Liberty is always *liberty from*, whether liberty *from* hunger and poverty or liberty *from* oppressive rulers. Without liberty (at least for those who engage in politics) there *cannot* be public freedom. If we return to her description of the Greek polis, she makes the point that the isonomic politics – the public freedom – of the Greek polis took place among those citizens who were liberated from the necessity of labor. She tells us that totalitarianism is the form of government that seeks to eliminate all traces of public freedom. If Hitler and the Nazis were to be overthrown, it would happen only by violent means. This is a clear case where armed resistance – violence – is justified. But we do not need to appeal to such an extreme example. Consider her favorite example of a "successful" revolution – the American Revolution. She knows that the Revolution began with a war of *liberation*. She emphasizes that, at first, political leaders in the colonies demanded their rights as Englishmen. War broke out only when these demands were resisted. The idea of a genuine revolution emerged reluctantly – the revolutionary idea of creating a *novus ordo saeculorum*. In short, there would be no revolution unless there was a war of liberation. Although Arendt tells us that violence can be justified, she never really thematized the difficult issue of when, and under what circumstances, it can be justified – the violence that may be required to achieve liberty, which is itself the *necessary* condition for public freedom. Is violence, armed struggle, justified when, as Fanon suggests, it appears to be the *only* way to overthrow a repressive colonial regime – one that crushes any attempt by the colonized to achieve the type of power and public freedom that Arendt describes? Ironically – on Arendt's own grounds – the relation of violence and power is more closely connected than she indicates. If power is the mark of what is genuinely political, then the *justification* for the use of violence ought to be a *political* issue. This is precisely the sort of issue that ought to be open to debate, deliberation, and persuasion by those who contemplate employing violent means to achieve liberty from oppressive rulers.

There is an even more intimate connection between violence and power that she suggests but doesn't fully explore. Let's return to her early call for an international Jewish army to fight Hitler and the Nazis. Her early *Aufbau* article is entitled "The Jewish Army – The Beginning of a Jewish Politics?" Armies are meant to kill in wartime – to engage in violence. But Arendt is not simply arguing for the creation of a Jewish army; she sees this as the *beginning of a Jewish politics*. Arendt was sharply critical of the failure of the Jewish people in modern times to assume political responsibility. Her argument in her *Aufbau* article is that by organizing an international Jewish army the Jews will constitute themselves as a political people. A Jewish army is vital for the Jewish people "to fight for their freedom and the right to live as a people. . . . For only the people themselves are strong enough for a true alliance" (Arendt 2007: 138–9). If we take these words seriously, then it means that violence is not only justified to fight Hitler, but is also necessary to constitute the Jewish people as a political community. Of course, Arendt is addressing a very concrete issue at a specific time in history. It would be unwarranted to draw any general conclusions from this specific call for the formation of an international Jewish army fighting under the Jewish flag. Nevertheless, it raises an issue that Arendt never explored in any depth. Are there other situations in which violence can be justified to fight violent oppressors and to institute a politics of the people? Are there other examples where we can affirm: "For only the people themselves are strong enough for a true alliance?"[31] The criticisms that I am raising are not "external" criticisms; they are implicit in Arendt's analyses. They are *immanent* in the sense that they follow from her analysis of the relation of liberty and freedom, and from her description of what was required for the Jews in 1940 to become a political people.

Power, Violence, and the "Real World"

I would like to conclude by showing just how insightful Arendt has been for thinking and acting in the "real world." Shortly after the Hungarian uprising, she wrote one of her most enthusiastic essays. The twelve-day revolution, the formation of spontaneous councils, and the power that grew in the streets vindicated her belief in the emergence of the revolutionary spirit against overwhelming odds. The crushing of the uprising by Soviet tanks also showed how quickly and brutally violence can destroy power. But in this 1958 article, Arendt was almost prophetic about what might happen – and did happen in 1989. Although the uprising lasted only twelve days and was completely unexpected, it "contained more history than the twelve years since the Red Army had 'liberated' the country from Nazi domination" (Arendt 1958b: 480). "If there was ever such a thing as Rosa Luxemburg's 'spontaneous revolution' – this sudden uprising of an oppressed people for the sake of freedom and hardly anything else, without the demoralizing chaos of military defeat preceding it, without *coup d'état* techniques, without a closely knit apparatus of organizers and conspirators, without the undermining propaganda of a revolutionary party, something, that is, which everybody, conservatives and liberals, radicals and revolutionists, had discarded as a noble dream – then we had the privilege to witness it." (Arendt 1958b: 482). The creation of revolutionary councils was "the same organization which for more than a hundred years now has emerged whenever people have been permitted for a few days, or a few weeks or months, to follow their own political devices without a government (or a party program) imposed from above" (Arendt 1958b: 497). All sorts of councils – neighborhood councils, councils of writers and artists, student and youth councils – were spontaneously organized in Hungary, and in these councils public freedom became tangible. Arendt claims that under modern conditions, "the councils are the only democratic alternative to the party system." The rise of the councils "was the clear sign of a true upsurge of democracy against dictatorship, of freedom against tyranny" (Arendt 1958b: 501). Of course, the uprising was crushed almost as soon as it arose. But – especially considering the events of 1989 – Arendt's concluding remarks in "Reflections on the Hungarian Revolution" were insightful.

> Still, the danger signs [for the Soviet Union] of 1956 were real enough, and although today they are overshadowed by the successes of 1957 and the fact that the system was able to survive, it would not be wise to forget them. If they promise anything at all, it is much rather a sudden and dramatic collapse of the whole regime than a gradual normalization. Such a catastrophic development, as we learned from the Hungarian revolution, need not necessarily entail chaos – though it certainly would be rather unwise to expect from the Russian people, after forty years of tyranny and thirty years of totalitarianism, the same spirit and the same political productivity which the Hungarian people showed in their most glorious hour. (Arendt 1958b: 510)

Arendt did not live to witness the fall of Communism, but in light of her reflections on the Hungarian revolution, she would not have been surprised by its "sudden and dramatic collapse." And it is not surprising that her writings about totalitarianism, plurality, power, and politics were a source of inspiration for many of the dissident leaders who brought about the fall of Communism. When Adam

Michnik, one the leaders of the Polish Solidarity movement, was in prison during the early 1980s, he was reading the works of Hannah Arendt. He was not alone in being inspired by Arendt. The fall of Communism throughout Eastern Europe – certainly one of the most significant political events of the last decades of the twentieth century – is a dramatic instance of how the power of people can spontaneously arise, grow, and even defeat the potential violence of the state. I find it deeply ironical that Arendt, who is frequently accused of being "romantic," "nostalgic," "utopian," and "irrelevant," is one of the few political thinkers of our time who had a deep understanding of what might (and actually did) happen when nonviolent power grows and spreads – the power to bring about a dramatic collapse of what many had taken to be a "powerfully" entrenched and violent totalitarian regime.

If there is a constant theme that runs through all of Arendt's work, it is the need to think. In the prologue to *The Human Condition* she wrote: "What I propose, therefore, is very simple: it is nothing more than to think what we are doing." And although she doesn't thematize "thinking" in *The Human Condition*, she informs us that "the highest and perhaps purest activity of which men are capable [is] the activity of thinking" (Arendt 1958a: 5). In *Eichmann in Jerusalem*, when she sought to account for the banality of evil, she was struck by Eichmann's inability to think. He certainly was "intelligent" enough to calculate and plan, but this is not the same as thinking. As she tells us in *The Life of the Mind*, "It was this absence of thinking – which is so ordinary an experience in our everyday life, where we have hardly the time, let alone the inclination, to *stop* and think – that awakened my interest" (Arendt 1978: 4). In the preface to *Between Past and Future*, she described her essays as "exercises in political thinking."[32] She characterized the type of thinking that she practiced as "thinking without banisters" (*Denken ohne Geländer*). Thinking is an activity that must be carried out over and over again. Arendt certainly believed this about her own thinking. She insists that her reflections on power and violence should call forth further thinking; there can be no finality in the process of genuine thinking. And in her "exaggerated" thinking about violence, she has helped to illuminate the dark landscape of our times.

Chapter 4

Frantz Fanon's Critique of Violence

The Historical Context

In 1960 Frantz Fanon, who was born in the French colony of Martinique on July 25, 1925, was diagnosed with leukemia. In the last year of his life, fully aware that his disease was fatal, he dedicated himself to writing *Les Damnés de la Terre* (*The Wretched of the Earth*) – much of it dictated to his wife.[1] Published just after his death on December 6, 1961, with a preface by Jean-Paul Sartre, the book immediately took on a life of its own – but it was banned in France.

Fanon left Martinique in 1943 at the age of 18 to fight with the Free French Forces in the last days of the Second World War. After the war, he stayed in France to study medicine and psychiatry in Lyons. He also immersed himself in the intellectual milieu of France, which at the time was dominated by the existentialism and phenomenology of Jean-Paul Sartre and Merleau-Ponty, as well as by the revival of Hegel and Marx. In 1952 he published *Peau Noire, Masques Blancs* (*Black Skin, White Masks*), analyzing and critiquing what it was like to be Black in White Europe. A year later he accepted a position as *chef de service* (chief of staff) for the psychiatric ward of Bida-Jonville hospital in Algeria. On November 1, 1954, the Front de Libération Nationale (FLN) launched a series of attacks against military and civilian targets in what became known as Toussaint Sanglante (Bloody All-Saints' Day). This marked the dramatic beginning of the Algerian war of independence. Bida-Jonville was a French hospital, and in the early days of the war Fanon's patients included French soldiers who had tortured Algerians. Critical of French attempts to suppress the struggle for Algerian independence, Fanon resigned from the hospital in 1956. For the remainder of his life he dedicated himself to the cause of the FLN. De Gaulle (after the Évian agreements and referendums held in both Algeria and France that overwhelmingly favored independence) declared Algeria an independent country on July 3, 1962 – just seven months after Fanon's death. When Fanon died, he was already certain that the Algerian war had been won.

The Wretched of the Earth quickly became known as a polemical treatise that justified the use of violence in the struggle against colonialism. In part this was encouraged by Sartre's provocative preface where he declares:

> When the peasants lay hands on a gun, the old myths fade, and one by one the taboos are overturned; a fighter's weapon is his humanity. For in the first phase of the revolt killing is a necessity; killing a European is killing two birds with one stone, eliminating in one go oppressor and oppressed: leaving one man dead and the other man free, for the first time the survivor feels a *national* soil under his feet. In that moment the national does not forsake him: it is there wherever he goes and wherever he is – always by his side, it merges with his freedom. (p. lv)[2]

More than a million copies of *The Wretched of the Earth* have been published in English alone, and it has now been translated into more than twenty-five languages. It has been read as *the* guide-book for fighting oppression not just in Africa, but throughout the world, and for advocating the necessity of violence in fighting oppressors. There are certainly passages (frequently taken out of context) that seem to justify the cleansing and transformative power of violence – creating, as Sartre suggests, free men out of the colonized. And there is little doubt that when Fanon speaks of violence, he frequently means the deliberate murder of colonizers.

Given this well-entrenched reading of Fanon's book as a justification and even a glorification of violence, it may seem perverse to characterize Fanon as engaging in a critique of violence. But that is precisely the thesis that I want to defend. There are three aspects of the tradition of critique that I draw upon. The first is the sense in which critique requires a depth understanding of the phenomenon that is examined – penetrating what is on the surface in order to grasp its deep structural dynamics. The second consists in showing how such an analysis indicates the limits of the phenomenon. (These first two aspects of critique are canonized by Kant's famous use of *Kritik*.) The third aspect of critique, which becomes explicit in Marx's use of *Kritik*, is critique *as* revolutionary praxis. These three aspects of Fanon's critique of violence are interrelated, because it is only by a depth understanding that we can bring out the limits of violence and further revolutionary liberating praxis.

To clarify and justify my thesis about Fanon's critique of violence, it is necessary to examine the structure of *The Wretched of the Earth*. Too frequently only the first chapter is read, and read superficially. *Les Damnés* consists of five chapters and a brief conclusion: 1, "On Violence"; 2, "Grandeur and Weakness of Spontaneity"; 3, "The Trials and Tribulations of National Consciousness"; 4, "On National Culture"; 5, "Colonial War and Mental Disorders"; and finally, the "Conclusion." Before turning to the opening chapter, I want to examine the other chapters, because they will enable us to understand better the nuances of what Fanon says in his opening chapter, "On Violence."

In the three chapters that follow "On Violence," Fanon is basically concerned with obstacles that stand in the way of the genuine liberation of the colonized. He doesn't limit himself to the struggle to achieve national independence. He addresses the threats to liberation *after* independence. Fanon is worried about the *betrayal* of the struggle for liberation – what might happen after independence. The addressees of Fanon's text (unlike Sartre's preface) are not Europeans or colonists, but rather those engaged in the struggle for liberation – his comrades (*comarades*).[3]

Spontaneous Violence: Strengths and Weaknesses

In chapter 2, "Grandeur and Weakness of Spontaneity," Fanon is especially critical of the discrepancy between indigenous national parties and the rural masses. Colonized intellectuals in their metropolises have studied the mechanisms of political parties and have organized parties to put pressure on the colonial administration. The formation of these parties coincides with the "birth of an intellectual and business elite" (63). But this notion of a party in a colonized society is imported from the metropolis. "The great mistake, the inherent flaw of most political parties in the undeveloped regions has been

traditionally to address first and foremost the most politically conscious elements: the urban proletariat, the small tradesmen and the
civil servants, i.e., a tiny section of the population which represents
barely more than one percent" (64). But this "proletariat" is much
less prepared to take up "the unrelenting struggle for national liberation." It is "the kernel of the colonized people most pampered by the
colonial regime," and this embryonic urban proletariat is "relatively
privileged" (64). Unfortunately, "the large majority of the nationalist parties regard the rural masses with great mistrust and disdain.
These masses give them the impression of being mired in inertia and
sterility" (65). In order to understand the reasons for this distrust,
it is essential to realize that "colonialism has often strengthened or
established its domination by an organized petrification of the peasantry" (65). Consequently, the feudal agents who dominate the rural
masses "form a barrier between the young Westernized nationalists
and the masses" (65). "Every time the elite makes a gesture toward
the rural masses, the tribal chiefs, the religious rulers, and the traditional authorities issue repeated warnings, threats, and excom-
munications" (66). The distrust of the urban elite is matched by the
peasants' distrust of the town dweller. Yet, Fanon claims that in their
spontaneity the rural masses remain disciplined and altruistic. This
is not to be understood as a traditional opposition between town and
country. Rather, "it is the opposition between the colonized excluded
from the benefits of colonialism and their counterparts who manage
to turn the colonial system to their advantage" (67). This situation is
exacerbated by the colonists, who use this antagonism in their opposition to national parties by mobilizing the rural population against the
urban population. The national parties perceive the rural masses as a
threat. They make the mistake of attempting to disrupt "traditional
existence within the context of the colonial system. They imagine
they can jump-start the nation whereas the mesh of the colonial
system is still tightly interlocked. They make no effort to reach out to
the masses" (67–8). As long as such a situation prevails, not only do
the national parties fail to achieve liberation, but their actions reinforce the colonial system. Despite this mutual antagonism between
urban national parties and the rural population, the rural masses play
a key role in the struggle for liberation. There is social unrest among
the rural population and spontaneous insurrections. The reaction of
nationalist parties leaves sustained revolt up to the spontaneity of the
rural masses. But still they make no attempt to organize the rebellion.

They fail to politicize the masses, to enlighten their consciousness, and raise the struggle to a higher level. The threat to "genuine" liberation, a liberation that should include both the urban and the rural populations, remains even *after* an independent nation is established. There is a temptation toward dictatorship by nationalist parties in order to pacify the rural masses.

We see how far Fanon departs from any traditional Marxist account of the relation of the proletariat and the peasants when he declares that in undeveloped societies it is "the peasantry, who represent the only spontaneously revolutionary force in the country." But still, the national bourgeois and union leaders treat the peasants as a "makeshift force" (76). Fanon is critical of the role of the leaders of the national parties. He sees them as playing a double game. Officially they declare that their aim is to smash colonialism, but they want "to remain on good terms with colonial authorities" (76). Fanon is more optimistic about the cadres of the parties who have suffered from colonial persecution. Being activists in a national party is "the only way of casting off their animal status for a human one" (77). This disenfranchised group hounded by the police takes refuge in the interior of the country. Their "ears hear the true voice of the country, and their eyes see the great and infinite misery of the people"; they discover "that the rural masses have never ceased to pose the problem of their liberation in terms of violence, of taking back the land from the foreigners, in terms of *national struggle* and armed revolt" (79). If there is to be any real hope for a struggle of national liberation, then it can come only from the "explosive mixture of unexpected power" when "the men from the towns let themselves be guided by the people" (79).

Now, whatever one thinks of Fanon's analysis – especially his somewhat idealized description of the solidarity of the rural masses – it is clear that he thinks that they are the primary agents for armed struggle. Or, to put the point differently, to the extent that the urban local bourgeoisie or proletariat set themselves apart from the rural masses, there will only be compromises with colonialism, not genuine revolutionary liberation. Fanon characterizes this complex relation between national parties and rural masses as a *dialectic* that consists of several stages. Initially, when national parties restrict themselves to the towns and disdain the rural masses, they turn out to be ineffective in opposing colonialism. When insurrection occurs among the rural population, the urban parties become more and more irrelevant.

The dialectic of armed struggle is advanced when the leaders of the rural insurrection realize that they need to extend their insurrection to the towns. In opposition to a traditional Marxist analysis, Fanon argues that in the colonial situation insurrection starts in the rural peasant areas. It penetrates the urban centers when the lumpen-proletariat (who have been expropriated from the land) become the urban spearhead of the insurrection. "The lumpenproletariat, this cohort of starving men, divorced from tribe and clan, constitutes one of the most spontaneously and radically revolutionary forces of a colonized people" (81). At times, Fanon comes close to idealizing and romanticizing the rural population. "The villages witness a perma-nent display of spectacular generosity and disarming kindness, and an unquestioned determination to die for the 'cause.' All of this is reminiscent of a religious brotherhood, a church, or a mystical doc-trine" (84). Fanon is certainly not naïve. Once the uprising has begun, the colonial forces regroup and adapt their tactics. They concentrate large numbers of troops in precise locations. This counter-offensive "throws the euphoria and idyll of the first phase into question" (84). But the solidarity grows much stronger when the enemy offensive is launched. "Impetuous spontaneity" fails as a doctrine. A much more pragmatic realism replaces the earlier jubilation. The techniques of guerilla warfare are adopted. The leaders of the insurrection come to realize that spontaneous eruptions are not enough; the peasants need to be enlightened and instructed. The leaders "therefore, must transform the movement from a peasant revolt into a revolutionary army" (86). But just as the leaders of the revolt adapt and change their tactics, so do the military and police forces of the colonists. The enemy seeks to bribe natives to betray the revolution and even organ-izes mercenaries to fight against those struggling for independence.

In one of Fanon's most revealing and important passages he emphasizes that racism and hatred of Europeans are not sufficient to nurture a war of liberation.

> Antiracist racism and the determination to defend one's skin, which is characteristic of the colonized's response to colonial oppression, clearly represent sufficient reasons to join the struggle. But one does not sustain a war, one does not endure massive repression or witness the disappearance of one's entire family in order for hatred or racism to triumph. Racism, hatred, resentment, and "the legitimate desire for revenge" alone cannot nurture a war of liberation. . . . *Day by day, leaders will come to realize that hatred is not an agenda.* (89, emphasis added)[4]

Given his own socio-psychological insight, Fanon grasps how the colonists make sophisticated use of psychological warfare. They also try to defuse the insurrection by granting concessions. Fanon warns that certain compromises and concessions are in fact "shackles." They are intended to perpetuate a colonial system. Furthermore, the native population also grows more sophisticated. They come to realize that "primitive Manichaeanism" – Black versus White, Arab versus Infidel – is too simplistic. Some Blacks can be whiter than the Whites. "Some members of the colonist population prove to be closer, infinitely closer, to the nationalist struggle than certain native sons. The racial and racist dimension is transcended on both sides" (95).

Fanon insists that anti-racist racism, hatred, and resentment do not provide an agenda for a war of liberation. He also notes that there is a type of brutality that is counter-revolutionary. "There is a brutality and contempt for subtleties and individual cases which is typically revolutionary, but there is another type of brutality with surprising resemblances to the first one which is typically counterrevolutionary, adventurist, and anarchist. *If this pure, total brutality is not immediately contained it will, without fail, bring down the movement within a few weeks*" (95, emphasis added).

Fanon concludes his chapter on the "Grandeur and Weakness of Spontaneity" with a rhetorical flourish: "Violence alone, perpetrated by the people, violence organized and guided by the leadership, provides the key for the masses to decipher social reality. Without this struggle, without this praxis there is nothing but a carnival parade and a lot of hot air. All that is left is a slight readaptation, a few reforms at the top, a flag, and down at the bottom a shapeless, writhing mass, still mired in the Dark Ages" (96).

I have discussed this chapter in some detail for several reasons. If we stand back and ask what precisely Fanon is doing here, it is clear that he is certainly not offering a detailed empirical description of any specific revolutionary movement. He is, of course, drawing on his experience in Algeria, but his references to many other countries – for example, Kenya, Angola, and the Congo – indicate that his account is a generalized one. Furthermore, his narrative cannot be read as a dialectical account of the *necessary* stages from spontaneous insurrection to a revolutionary war of liberation. On the contrary, Fanon is acutely aware of all the things that can go wrong. If national parties think that they need to appeal only to the "proletariat" in the metropolitan centers, they will fail. If these parties seek to negotiate and compromise with the colonists, they may achieve superficial reforms but will only entrench the colonists. If no attempt is made to incorporate and educate the rural masses, then the agency of revolutionary praxis will be lost. Although the spontaneous local eruptions of rural populations may provide an initial impetus, spontaneity is not enough. A peasant revolt, even on a grand scale, needs guidance. And it must eventually be extended to the metropolis. There must be resistance to the socio-psychological warfare of the colonists, who – at the same time – try to mollify the colonized and also provoke internal divisions among them. Hatred, anti-racist racism, resentment, even "total brutality" if unchecked, can destroy the movement. Far from "glorifying" violence, Fanon argues that violence must be enlightened, controlled, and directed to achieve liberation. But what is most important is that the people – both the rural and the urban natives – must be enlisted in the "cause." The people become the agents of revolutionary praxis – the struggle for liberation.

The Failures of the National Bourgeoisie

Fanon's warnings about what can go wrong in the fight against colonialism become even sharper in his next two chapters. He is relentless in his critique of the "national bourgeoisie, which takes over power at the end of a colonial regime" (98). The national consciousness of the native bourgeoisie "is nothing but a crude, empty, fragile shell" (97). The great failure of this local bourgeoisie is its failure "to learn from the people, and make available to them the intellectual and technical capital it culled from its time in colonial universities" (99). "[T]he historical vocation of an authentic national bourgeoisie in an undeveloped country is to repudiate its status as bourgeois and an instrument of capital and to become entirely subservient to the revolutionary capital which the people represent" (98–9). The call for nationalization by this bourgeoisie "signifies very precisely the transfer into indigenous hands of the privileges inherited from the colonial period" (100). Fanon is extremely harsh in his critique of what he takes to be the "hedonistic mentality," hypocrisy, and cynicism of the national bourgeoisie. It mimics the Western bourgeoisie "in its negative and decadent aspects without having accomplished the initial phases of exploration and invention that are the assets of this Western bourgeoisie whatever the circumstances" (101). This post-colonial national bourgeoisie poses an even greater threat to the struggle for liberation than the colonizers. The enemies of true liberation are the national bourgeoisie, who encourage "the growth and development of racism that was typical of the colonial period" (108).

There is barely any explicit mention of violence in this chapter, but Fanon accuses this bourgeois caste of mimicking the viciousness of the original colonizers. After independence was achieved in the Ivory Coast, "outright race riots were directed against the Dahomeans and Upper Voltans who controlled much of the business sector" (103). "We have switched from nationalism to ultranationalism, chauvinism, and racism. There is a general call for these foreigners to leave, their shops are burned, their market booths torn down and some are lynched; consequently the Ivorian government orders them to leave, thereby satisfying the demands of the nationals" (103–4). After independence, the state "imposes itself in a spectacular manner, flaunts its authority, harasses, making it clear to its citizens they are in constant danger. The single party is the modern form of the bourgeois dictatorship – stripped of mask, makeup, and scruples, cynical in every aspect" (111).

Fanon not only damns the national bourgeoisie; he mocks it. It doesn't even have the advantages of a Western capitalist bourgeoisie – it is not geared to "production, invention, creation or work . . . Networking and scheming seem to be its underlying vocation" (98). One is reminded of Marx's famous remark from the Eighteenth Brumaire: "History repeats itself first as tragedy, second as farce." But for Fanon, the nationalist bourgeoisies are at once both a tragedy and a farce.

But what is the alternative? Fanon advocates the maximum active participation of the people. The people must be politically educated, and they must participate in all affairs of the government and the management of their own affairs. What is the role of the politician and the intellectual in this educative process?

> We, African politicians, must have very clear ideas about our peoples' situation. But this lucidity must remain deeply dialectical. The awakening of the people as a whole will not be achieved overnight; their rational commitment to the task of building the nation will be simple and straightforward; first of all, because the methods and channels of communication are still in the development stages; secondly, because the sense of time must no longer be that of the moment or the next

harvest but rather that of the rest of the world; and finally, because the demoralization buried deep within the mind by colonization is still very much alive. (135)

But when it comes to describing precisely what it means to educate the people, and how their self-determination is to be accomplished, Fanon is extremely vague. This is even reflected in his language. Fanon was always sensitive to the use of language – whether the language of hatred and violence or his own performative rhetoric, which is intended to arouse, provoke, and further revolutionary praxis. But although his critique of the national bourgeoisies – and all that they stand for – is concrete, specific, vivid, and harsh, when it comes to describing the alternative that he advocates, his language is abstract and almost clichéd. His text is filled with generalized talk of what "should" or "must" be done – not *how* to do it.[5]

National Culture

Fanon begins his fourth chapter, "On National Culture," with a sentence that is frequently quoted: "Each generation must discover its mission, fulfill it or betray it, in relative opacity. In underdeveloped countries preceding generations have simultaneously resisted the insidious agenda of colonialism and paved the way for the emergence of the current struggles" (145). This indicates Fanon's acute sense that the struggle for liberation depends on the *agency* of the people. If the national bourgeoisie remains in power, if *all* the people are not involved, then the revolution will be betrayed. Fanon is aware of the "relative opacity" of action. Both words are important. The opacity is "relative" but not *absolute*, because action can be based on a "rational" analysis of the concrete situation. But there is always some "opacity," because we never fully know the consequences of our actions. When Fanon characterizes his analysis as "dialectical," he is aware of this relative opacity. There is no historical *necessity* that liberation will be achieved. The most revealing feature of the above passage is that it shows how Fanon thinks about temporality. First, one must grasp the concrete political, economic, and socio-psychological effects of the long duration of colonization. Algeria, for example, was invaded by the French in 1830, became a French military colony in 1834, and was declared an integral part of French territory in 1848. Resistance to colonization did not begin on November 1, 1954. Long before 1954 Algerians "simultaneously resisted the insidious agenda of colonialism and paved the way for emergence of the current struggles." Second, the people must acquire a sense of temporality that extends beyond the next harvest. A liberation struggle does not happen all at once, but takes time – indeed, its temporality extends far beyond "formal" independence. Third – and this is perhaps the most central point – there is a change in outlooks and behavior that takes place as the struggle develops.[6] Sartre's suggestion that in killing a European the oppressed become "free" does violence to Fanon's much more nuanced phenomenological description of the temporality of liberation struggles – including both its setbacks and advances.[7]

The aim of colonization is "to convince the indigenous population it would save them from darkness" (149).

> The result was to hammer into the heads of the indigenous population that if the colonist were to leave they would regress into barbarism, degradation, and bestiality. At the level of the unconscious, therefore, colonialism was not seeking to be perceived by the indigenous population as a sweet, kind-hearted mother who protects her child from a hostile environment, but rather a mother who constantly prevents her basically perverse child from committing suicide or giving free rein to its malevolent instincts. The colonial mother is protecting the child from itself, from its ego, its physiology, its biology, and its ontological misfortune. (149)

Reacting to this systematic degradation, the colonized intellectual seeks to reclaim the past, to demonstrate that it was "not branded with shame but with dignity, glory and sobriety" (148). "The concept of negritude for example was the affective if not logical antithesis of that insult which the white man had leveled at the rest of humanity" (150). The reaction of Arab colonized intellectuals has been similar to that of Black Africans – celebrating the past glories of Islamic culture.[8] But this celebration of African and Arab culture, which downplays the significance of *national* culture, leads to a dead end. The tendency to speak in "universal" terms loses contact with national cultures. If colonized intellectuals strive for cultural authenticity, they "must recognize that national truth is first and foremost the national reality" (161). "When the colonized intellectual writing for his people uses the past he must do so with the intention of opening up the future, of spurring them into action and fostering hope" (167). If this hope is not to be hollow, then the colonized intellectual "must take part in the action and commit himself body and soul to the national struggle" (167). Returning to the theme of temporality, the colonial intellectual ought to focus on the future, not the past – or, to the extent that he appeals to the past, it must be for the sake of future liberation. Summing up his critique, Fanon declares: "We should not therefore be content to delve into the people's past to find concrete examples to counter colonialism's endeavors to distort and depreciate. We must work and struggle in step with the people so as to shape the future and prepare the ground where vigorous shoots are already sprouting. . . . National culture in the underdeveloped countries, therefore, must lie at the very heart of the liberation struggle these countries are waging" (168). In short, national culture is the collective thought process demanded for revolutionary praxis. Fanon frequently points out the "unacceptable contradictions" that arise because "the colonial situation has not been rigorously analyzed." Throughout he stresses this need for rigorous *rational* analysis. The awakening of national consciousness has its effects on all the arts, including pottery, ceramics, song, dance, and even rituals. The struggle for liberation releases a new energy in the cultural sphere; it is "the struggle for nationhood that unlocks culture and opens the doors of creation" (177). National consciousness is not to be identified with a narrow-minded nationalism. On the contrary, national consciousness "is alone capable of giving us an international dimension" (179). When the struggle for liberation is accomplished, there will be "not only the demise of colonialism, but also the demise of the colonized" (178). Liberation means the end of the colonial system – the end of the colonists and the colonized. It is then – and only then – that there arises a "new humanity, for itself and others (*pour soi et pour les autres*)" that "inevitably defines a new humanism" (178). Fanon's dialectical account of the colonial system is oriented to destroying it and creating a new humanism. It is striking that in this chapter, the word "violence" doesn't even appear – although, of course, Fanon's characterization of the emergence of a new national cultural consciousness is played out against the background of the oppressiveness of colonial violence. Fanon returns to the explicit discussion of violence in his fifth and final chapter, "Colonial War and Mental Disorders." He is sensitive to the terrible socio-psychological affects of colonial wars on *both* the colonists and the colonized.

The Socio-psychological Effects of Colonial Violence

In the three middle chapters of *The Wretched* Fanon barely mentions violence. But his entire discussion is set against the backdrop of the violence of the colonial system – specifically the violence of the colonists. The depth and complexity of this violence must be "rationally analyzed." The techniques of physical brutality of the police and military need to be carefully analyzed, as well as the "sophisticated" means employed to destroy the economic, political, and cultural life of the colonized. One must also analyze the attempt by the colonists to penetrate and distort the very psyche of the colonized. The colonist is committed to a "systematized negation of the other, a frenzied determination to deny the other any attribute of humanity" (182). He seeks to turn the colonized into animals that are less than human and who will revert back into savagery once the "civilizing" effect of colonization is abandoned. "When colonization remains unchallenged by armed resistance, when the sum of harmful stimulants exceeds a certain threshold, the colonized's defenses collapse, and many of them end up in psychiatric institutions" (182).

Fanon reports several different types of mental disorders that arose in the Algerian colonial war. They include the case of impotence in an Algerian following the rape of his wife, and the random homicidal impulses in a survivor of a massacre. He also analyzes the murder by two young teenage Algerians of their European playmate. But Fanon also includes the case of a European police inspector who tortures his wife and children, and a police officer who suffers from depression as a consequence of his torturing Algerians. In this last case, the police officer accidentally meets (and frightens) one of his former victims who is suffering from post-traumatic stress disorder. In all these instances, Fanon describes the terrible psychic pain of the violence of the colonial war on *both* the colonized and the colonists. Fanon also damns the pseudo-scientific literature that seeks to "demonstrate" that the North African is "hereditarily violent," dominated by a "predatory instinct," and who exhibits "unwieldy aggressiveness" (223). He cites the work of a Dr. Carothers, an expert from the World Health Organization, who put forth the idea that "the normal African is a *lobotomized European*" (227). Fanon categorically declares that criminality "is not the result of the Algerian's congenital nature nor the configuration of his nervous system" (230).

The criminality of the Algerian, his impulsiveness, the savagery of his murders are not, therefore, the consequence of how his nervous system is organized or specific character traits, but the direct result of the colonial situation. . . . Independence is not a magic ritual but an indispensable condition for men and women to exist in true liberation, in other words to master all the material resources necessary for a radical transformation of society. (233)

On Violence

I have deliberately begun by discussing and analyzing the four chapters of *The Wretched* that follow the chapter "On Violence" because I believe they provide the necessary context for understanding this opening chapter. Succinctly stated, Fanon's primary concern is the violence that is *constitutive* of the colonial system. Because this violence is so entrenched and vicious, he argues that compromise and negotiation cannot end colonialism – they reinforce the colonial system. True liberation requires that the colonial system be completely destroyed – the colonizer and the colonized. National independence alone doesn't achieve liberation. There is the danger that new leaders and the national bourgeoisies will mimic the worst aspects of the colonial system – and continue its violence. Furthermore, there is the danger of regression to tribal, ethnic, and religious violence. Fanon is fully aware of the limits of violence in the fight against colonialism. Hatred and gratuitous barbarity by themselves fail to achieve liberation; they actually undermine the struggle for liberation.[9]

"On Violence" begins with a dramatic declaration: "National liberation, national reawakening, restoration of the nation to the people or Commonwealth, whatever the name used, whatever the latest expression, decolonization is always a violent event" (1). Initially, decolonization is an "agenda for total disorder" because its aim is to disrupt and destroy the colonial system. Fanon does not mince his words: "In its bare reality, decolonization reeks of red-hot cannonballs and bloody knives. For the last can be first only after a murderous and decisive confrontation between the two protagonists" (3). The colonized can overthrow the colonial system only if they "are determined from the very start to smash every obstacle encountered" (3). "It is the colonist who *fabricated* and *continues to fabricate* the colonized subject. The colonist derives his validity, i.e., his wealth, from the colonial system" (2). The colonized are *not* to be identified with the indigenous people; the colonized are what the indigenous people *become* as a consequence of colonialization.[10] Fanon doesn't shy away from claiming that the colonized man looks upon the colonist with lust and envy. But even here Fanon stresses the violence of the colonist: "The violence which governed the ordering of the colonial world, which tirelessly punctuated the destruction of the indigenous social fabric, and demolished unchecked the systems of reference of the country's economy, lifestyles, and modes of dress, this same violence will be vindicated and appropriated when, taking history into their own hands, the colonized swarm into the forbidden cities" (5–6).

From the perspective of the colonists, the colonized are "absolute evil." Even the "zoological" language of the colonists reinforces the complete dehumanization of the colonized – they are inhuman savage beasts. Consequently, the colonized are deeply suspicious when they are asked to be "reasonable" – especially when the supremacy of White values is constantly reiterated with such violence. In a passage that recalls the moment in Hegel's dialectic of lordship and bondage when the slave realizes that he has "a mind of his own," Fanon declares that "the colonized subject thus discovers that his life, his breathing and his heartbeats are the same as the colonist's. He discovers that the skin of a colonist is not worth more than the native's" (10). Fanon points out that, at first, these intellectuals tend to accept the "enlightenment" values of the oppressors. During this period – before the liberation struggle of the people has begun – "the intellectual behaves objectively like a vulgar opportunist" (13). The colonized directs the "aggressiveness sedimented in his muscles against his own people" (15).[11] The emotional rage of the colonized is embodied in his muscles – in his lived body. Black turns on Black. Although the colonized is always presumed guilty, deep down he acknowledges no authority. He is dominated but not domesticated. Fanon doesn't romanticize the anger and hatred of the colonized. He is persecuted and is "forever dreaming of becoming the persecutor" (16). "The muscular tension of the colonized periodically erupts into bloody fighting between tribes, clans, and individuals" (17). The appeal to magic, to supernatural powers, the ecstasy of dance, and even ritual, tend to inhibit and contain the aggressiveness of the colonized. But the struggle for liberation takes shape only when the aggressiveness and violence that have been instilled in the colonized by the colonial system are realigned and change direction – when they are directed

toward the true enemy, the colonists. Fanon is critical of those colonized metropolitan intellectuals who are violent in their rhetoric but
reformist in their attitudes. Once again, contra Marx, Fanon declares
that it is only the peasantry that "has nothing to lose and everything
to gain." From his discussion of the grandeur and weakness of spontaneity, we have seen that although the spontaneous outbursts of the
peasantry provide the energy for revolutionary praxis, the peasants'
actions must be channeled and directed. This is the true educational
task of the revolutionary leaders. Because colonists engage in "naked
violence," they give in only "when confronted with greater violence"
(23). Throughout this chapter Fanon voices his disdain for those
native bourgeois leaders who are all too willing to seek compromise
and who are seduced by pleas for nonviolence. Unmasked, they are
really concerned to preserve their own privileged position. "They
are losers from the start" (25). Yet the rhetoric of nation building
by nationalist politicians does stir up subversive feelings among the
masses. "There is therefore a cunning of history which plays havoc
with the colonies (*Il y a donc une ruse de l'histoire, qui joue terriblement aux
colonies*)" (29). Gradually the struggle for liberation gains momentum.
It is aided by the awareness that other guerilla liberation movements
have succeeded (for example, the victory of the Vietnamese people at
Dien Bien Phu) and by the panic that begins to grip colonial governments. In Fanon's dialectical account, the panic of colonists leads to
"saber-rattling exercises." But this only strengthens the determination of the masses. "Far from breaking the momentum, repression
intensifies the progress made by the national consciousness" (32).
The colonized are determined to put their faith in violent methods.
After all, this is the lesson that has been beaten into them by the
colonists. "The existence of an armed struggle is indicative that the
people are determined to put their faith only in violent methods.
The very same people who had it constantly drummed into them that
the only language they understood was that of force, now decide to
express themselves with force" (42).

After almost seven years of torture and killings by the French,
"not a single Frenchman has been brought before a French court of
justice for the murder of an Algerian" (50). Fanon affirms that "at
the individual level, violence is a cleansing force. It rids the colonized
of their inferiority complex, of their passive and despairing attitude.
It emboldens them, and restores their self-confidence" (51). But he
immediately adds that the aim of this violence is to achieve tangible

national liberation – not simply to cause havoc. Eliminating colonialism is only a necessary condition for achieving true liberation. This is
why Fanon spends so much time discussing how the liberation struggle can be (and has too frequently been) betrayed. Fanon completed
his book before the French "granted" Algeria independence, but I
suspect that if he had lived, he might have argued that his worst fears
came true – the struggle for liberation was betrayed because of the
failure to actively include all the people (especially the peasants) in
the new nation.

At the height of the Cold War, Fanon was fully aware of how the
attitudes and policies toward underdeveloped countries of *both* sides
in this conflict were basically determined by their special interests
and advantages – not the interests of the colonized. Although it was
commonly thought that the Third World had to choose between the
capitalist system and the socialist system, Fanon warns that the Third
World must "refuse to get involved in such a rivalry" (55). And in a
way that sounds remarkably prophetic of our present reality, Fanon
is deeply critical of the way in which Western financiers demand of
the newly independent countries a type of "political stability and a
peaceful social climate which are impossible to achieve given the
appalling situation of the population as a whole in the aftermath of
independence. In their search, then, for a guarantee which the former
colony cannot vouch for, they demand that certain military bases be
kept on and the young nation enter into military and economic agreements" (60). One may be sympathetic with Fanon's call for an end to
the Cold War and the nuclear arms race, but deeply skeptical of his
inflated claim that the "young nations of the Third World" are powerful enough to explain to capitalist countries that "the underdeveloped regions must receive generous investments and technical aid"
(61). And in what sounds almost like pure fantasy, Fanon concludes
his chapter "On Violence" with a flourish. "This colossal task, which
consists of reintroducing man into the world, man in his totality, will
be achieved with the crucial help of the European masses who would
do well to confess that they have often rallied behind the position
of our common masters on colonial issues. In order to do this, the
European masses must first of all decide to wake up, put on their
thinking caps and stop playing the irresponsible game of Sleeping
Beauty" (62). The inflated rhetoric of this passage is matched by the
language of Fanon's polemical conclusion, where he directly addresses
his comrades – his brothers:

So comrades, let us not pay tribute to Europe by creating states, institutions, and societies that draw their inspiration from it.

Humanity expects other things from us than this grotesque and generally obscene emulation. . . .

For Europe, for ourselves and for humanity, comrades, we must make a new start, develop a new way of thinking, and endeavor to create a new man. (239)

Let us not forget that Fanon dictated these words of address to his comrades shortly before his death and before Algeria was declared independent. In writing *The Wretched of the Earth*, Fanon sought to provide an analysis of colonial violence and to further its defeat. When liberation is achieved, both colonizers and the colonized will be destroyed. There will be the opportunity for a new sense of human dignity.

The Critique of Violence

I want to return to my initial thesis that *The Wretched of the Earth* is a critique of violence. I called attention to three aspects of Fanon's critique: critique as a depth understanding of colonial violence; critique as indicating the limits of violence; and critique as the revolutionary praxis required for destroying colonial violence and for achieving genuine liberation. It should now be clear that the major theme of *The Wretched* – to which Fanon returns over and over again – is the analysis of *colonial violence*. He insists that one cannot properly understand and fight colonialism unless one develops a proper analysis of it. The colonizers violently construct this system; *it is the colonizers that fabricate the colonized subjects*. Colonial violence is not limited to physical brutality and torture. Far more vicious and insidious are the varieties of humiliation: dehumanizing the indigenous population, treating them as savage beasts, seeking to convince them that they will revert to dark savagery if the colonists leave. This systematic humiliation is embedded in the everyday language of the colonists. Drawing on his psychiatric training and his psychoanalytic knowledge, Fanon shows how the colonists shape the psyche of the colonized – even their unconscious fears. He is critical of the pseudo-scientific literature that "demonstrates" that African natives are inherently murderous, and that their aggressiveness is biologically rooted in their brains.

Fanon is fully aware of the local forms of tribal, ethnic, and religious violence. But this violence is not to be confused with or assimilated to the violence instituted by the colonial system. The colonists attempt to foster local tribal violence in order to undermine the struggle of liberation. They enlist native mercenaries to fight those fighting for independence.

Fanon wants us to understand why there is so much rage and aggressive behavior in the colonized – a rage inflamed by the excessive repressive measures of the colonists. He is realistic and unsentimental about this violence. Initially, the colonized seek revenge. "The gaze that the colonized subject casts at the colonist's sector is a look of lust, a look of envy. Dreams of possession. Every type of possession: of sitting at the colonist's table and sleeping in his bed, preferably with his wife" (5). The colonized dream of taking the place of the colonist.

What about the limits of violence – the second aspect of Fanon's critique of violence? Here we need to make some distinctions. There are *no* limits on the varieties and intensity of the violence directed *against* the colonized by the colonists. Torture, massacres, linguistic and psychological humiliation, are part of their standard repertoire. "The arrival of the colonist signified syncretically the death of indigenous society, cultural lethargy, and petrifaction of the individual" (50). The colonists destroy indigenous culture. The colonists do not engage in *total* genocide because it would be self-defeating, undermining the purpose of colonialism: to exploit the native population and the rich natural resources of the territory.

But what is far more important, and unfortunately frequently neglected in many discussions of Fanon, is his emphasis on the *limits* of the violence of the colonized. He certainly does think that the rage, hatred, anger, and aggressiveness that are instilled and provoked in the colonized by the colonists are the sources of energy for the liberation struggle. And he also thinks that "the violence of the colonized . . . unifies the people" (51). But he knows full well that this "spontaneous" aggressiveness is *not* sufficient to carry on the struggle. I want to quote more fully a key passage that I cited earlier.

> Racism, hatred, resentment, and "the legitimate desire for revenge" alone cannot nurture a war of liberation. These flashes of consciousness which fling the body into a zone of turbulence, which plunge it into a virtually pathological dreamlike state where the sight of the

other induces vertigo, where my blood calls for the blood of the other, where my death through mere inertia calls for the death of the other, *this passionate outburst in the opening phase, disintegrates if it is left to feed on itself.* Of course the countless abuses perpetuated by the colonialist forces reintroduce emotional factors into the struggle, give the militant further cause to hate and new reasons to set off in search of a "colonist to kill." But, day by day, leaders will come to realize that hatred is not an agenda. (89, emphasis added)

We can now better understand why Fanon entitles his second chapter "Grandeur and Weakness of Spontaneity" ("Grandeur et faiblesses de la spontanéité"). The grandeur refers to the spontaneous rebellion of the people – especially the rural population who are not cowed by the colonists. But the weakness of spontaneity is that it "does not sustain a war." The war is not a single battle, but a succession of directed local struggles. Because spontaneous violence is self-defeating, Fanon underscores the need to channel, direct, even *restrain* this spontaneous violence.[12] This is why proper leadership is so important – a leadership that is responsive to the people. Fanon knows full well just how difficult it is to achieve such leadership.

Throughout *The Wretched* Fanon shows all the things that can go wrong – everything from the colonists' attempts to co-opt the people by granting minor concessions, to getting natives to fight among themselves. But he is most damning of the failures of a "bourgeois caste" and national leadership that are more concerned with protecting their privileges than in the liberation of the people. Unrestrained violence does not achieve liberation and real freedom – it undermines it. By engaging in such unrestrained violence, the colonized become the savages that the colonizers take them to be. Fanon insists that the aim of liberation is to *destroy the cycle of violence and counter-violence.* Writing about Algeria in 1959, he declares: "There is no one . . . apart from those Frenchmen who have dragged their country into this horrible adventure, who does not yearn to see the end of this slaughter and the birth of the Algerian nation" (Fanon 1994: 27).

The third moment of critique – critique as revolutionary praxis – is implicit in the first two moments and needs only to be made explicit. Fanon is certainly not writing a neutral third-person account of the colonial system. He is passionately involved, and the book is at once analytical, polemical, and a call to his comrades to engage in a revolutionary praxis. *The Wretched* is addressed to his comrades, not only in Algeria or even in all of Africa, but to all who are fighting against colonial systems. The violence of the colonized is necessary because this is the only way to overthrow the *entrenched* violence of the colonizers; it is the only way to destroy the colonial system. But this violence must be transformed into a sustained armed struggle. "Reasonable" discussion and negotiation will not end colonialism – certainly not in Africa. For the colonizers, this "reasonableness" is simply a device to conserve the colonial system. A constant theme in *The Wretched* is that national independence is only a necessary, not a sufficient, condition for genuine liberation. After independence, a colonial mentality persists. There is an enormous temptation for national leaders to imitate some of the worst practices of the colonizers – even to employ violence against their own people. Fanon accuses the colonized bourgeoisie of cynically brandishing the notions of nationalization and Africanization of the managerial classes. "In fact, its actions become increasingly tinged with racism" (103). This is a disaster. Only if there is a serious attempt to listen to the people and to engage them in full participation will freedom concretely be realized. Only then is there the possibility of creating a "new humanity."

Fanon's Ambiguous Legacy

Looking back on *The Wretched of the Earth* from the perspective of fifty years later, one can understand why it has been a source of inspiration, not just in the fight against colonialism, but in the fight against all sorts of oppression throughout the world. Fanon's prose is still alive and provocative. But judging by what has subsequently happened in many African countries, Fanon's *fears* about the betrayal of the revolutionary struggle have unfortunately been vindicated. There is little evidence that in any formerly colonized country there has been a serious attempt to listen to, engage, and gain the participation of the wretched of the earth. One of the weakest features of Fanon's "dialectical" analysis is his portrayal of "the people" and his confidence in their potential participation in all the affairs that concern them. He has a romanticized vision of who the people are, and what they are capable of doing. Ironically, his descriptions of the role of a national bourgeoisie, the persistence of a colonial mentality, the temptation to use violence against one's own people, and the reversion to forms of internal tribal, ethnic, and racial violence are far more accurate as *predictions* of what has happened in many African post-colonial societies. His expectations for a "new humanism" now seem like fantasies.

A judicious evaluation of what has and has not been achieved in former colonial countries during the past fifty years is a complex issue – and beyond the scope of this chapter. We should not forget, however, that Fanon was writing at a time when the Algerian revolution was still being fought. His vision of how the Third World might lead the way is primarily intended to be *inspirational* rather than *analytical*. But even if this is granted, Fanon can be faulted for providing so little guidance about what is to be done once independence is achieved, in order to realize concretely the type of new society that he envisions.

I am not concerned with drawing up a balance sheet of Fanon's insights and blindnesses as to what happens once colonized countries gain their independence. I do want to stress the integrity with which he struggles with the problem of violence. He presents a damning analytical and phenomenological account of how colonialism works. Indigenous peoples only become *colonized* under the colonial system; and it is the inhuman abuses of the colonizers that spur the spontaneous violence of the colonized. This spontaneous violence has to be channeled and limited; it has to be directed into a disciplined armed struggle. Otherwise it leads to disintegration and self-defeat. This requires a leadership that listens to the people and is responsive to their needs. Armed struggled is required, Fanon argues, because colonial systems – especially in Africa – will use any means they can to preserve the colonial system. In such a situation, negotiation, discussion, and reasonableness become cynical devices to preserve colonialism. Fanon shows that if we really understand how the colonial system in Africa works – its violent structure and dynamics – then it becomes clear that nonviolent strategies cannot overthrow African colonial systems. On the contrary, nonviolence perpetuates colonialism. His own experience in Algeria confirmed his belief that the French were not open to any negotiation or compromise that would seriously challenge the colonial system they instituted.[13] We may raise serious critical doubts about Fanon's talk of transforming society, creating a new humanity, starting history afresh. But his critique of violence is intended to show that this "new society" would put an end to colonial violence. In his concluding remarks, he admonishes his comrades not to drag man "in the directions which mutilate him." "The notion of catching up [with Europe] must not be used as a pretext to brutalize man, to tear him from himself and his inner consciousness, to break him, to kill him" (238). He calls for starting "over a new history of man" – one that will overcome "the racial hatred, slavery, exploitation and above all, the bloodless genocide whereby one and a half billion men have been written off" (238). His critique of violence has the goal of ending, once and for all time, colonial violence – *the violence of the colonists and the colonized.*

Chapter 5

Jan Assmann: The Mosaic Distinction and Religious Violence

The Mosaic Distinction

In 1997, Jan Assmann, one of the world's leading Egyptologists, published a provocative and controversial book entitled *Moses the Egyptian: The Memory of Egypt in Western Monotheism*. He begins his book in a most dramatic fashion:

> Draw a distinction.
>
> Call it the first distinction.
>
> Call the space in which it is drawn the space severed or cloven by the distinction. It seems as if George Spencer Brown's "first Law of Construction" does not apply solely to the space of logical and mathematical construction. It also applies surprisingly well to the space of cultural constructions and distinctions and to the spaces that are severed or cloven by such distinctions.
>
> The distinction I am concerned with in this book is the distinction between true and false in religion that underlies more specific distinctions such as Jews and Gentiles, Christians and pagans, Muslims and unbelievers. Once the distinction is drawn, there is no end of reentries or subdistinctions. We start with Christians and pagans and end up with Catholics and Protestants, Calvinists and Lutherans, Socinians and Latitudinarians, and a thousand more similar denominations and subdenominations. Cultural or intellectual distinctions such as these construct a universe that is not only full of meaning, identity, and orientation, but also *full of conflict, intolerance, and violence*. Therefore, there have always been attempts to overcome the

conflict by reexamining the distinction, albeit at the risk of losing cultural meaning.

Let us call the distinction between true and false in religion the "Mosaic distinction" because tradition ascribes it to Moses. (Assmann 1997: 1, emphasis added)

Although this distinction is ascribed to Moses, he was not the first to draw it. His precursor was Akhenaten, who instituted a form of monotheistic religion in the fourteenth century BCE. We encounter a seeming paradox. We know that Akhenaten was a real historical person, a pharaoh who ruled briefly in the fourteenth century BCE, even though the memory of him was virtually obliterated until the rediscovery of Armana in the nineteenth century. Moses, however, is a figure of memory. There is no independent historical evidence that he ever existed apart from the testimony of the Hebrew Bible and a few legends about him. "Since memory is all that counts in the sphere of cultural distinctions and constructions, we are justified in speaking not of Akhenaten's distinction, but of the Mosaic distinction. The space severed or cloven by this distinction is the space of Western monotheism. It is this constructed mental or cultural space that has been inhabited by Europeans for nearly two millennia" (Assmann 1997: 2).

One might think from the title of his book that, as an Egyptologist, Assmann is concerned with the *historical* issue of whether Moses was "really" an Egyptian. There is a long tradition, dating back to at least Hecataeus and Manetho, which claims that Moses was not a Jew, but a rebellious Egyptian priest or nobleman. But the historical question of Moses' origin and identity is not Assmann's primary concern. Rather, he seeks to trace the twists and turns of how Moses and Egypt have been remembered in the course of Western history, right up to the twentieth century. He characterizes his inquiry as a contribution to "mnemohistory." "Unlike history proper, mnemohistory is concerned not with the past as such, but only with the past as it is remembered. . . . Mnemohistory is not the opposite of history, but rather is one of its branches or subdisciplines. . . . It concentrates exclusively on those aspects of significance and relevance which are the product of memory – that is, of recourse to a past – and which appear only in the light of later readings. . . . The past is not simply 'received' by the present. The present is 'haunted' by the past and the past is modeled, invented, reinvented, and reconstructed by the present" (Assmann

1997: 9).[1] The aim of mnemohistory is to study traditions as phenomena of cultural memory. Assmann, of course, knows that "memories may be false, distorted, invented, or implanted." Consequently, there is a subtle and complex relationship between history proper and mnemohistory. We would not be able to claim that a memory is distorted or false unless we had independent historical procedures for ascertaining what actually happened. Memory cannot be validated as a historical source without being checked against "objective" evidence. But although mnemohistory must itself satisfy the canons of historical accuracy, the key issue for a historian of memory is not whether the memory is historically accurate. "[F]or a historian of memory, the 'truth' of a given memory lies not so much in its 'factuality' as in its 'actuality'" (Assmann 1997: 9).

Returning to the Mosaic distinction, what is really distinctive about it? After all, isn't it true that all religions draw a distinction between "us" and "them"? Doesn't every construction of identity generate alterity – insiders and outsiders? In a very general sense, this is true, but it misses the vital point that Assmann stresses. Cultures and religions not only generate otherness by constructing identity, but also develop techniques of translation. Indeed, ancient polytheism developed a variety of techniques of translation. In the polytheistic religions of the ancient world, different peoples worshipped different gods, but "nobody contested the reality of foreign gods" (Assmann 1997: 3).[2] In Mesopotamia, for example, the practice of translating divine names goes back to the third millennium BCE. But the Mosaic distinction simply did *not* exist in the world of polytheistic religions. The Mosaic distinction introduces a new type of religion – a "'counter-religion' because it rejects and repudiates everything that went before and what is outside itself as 'paganism'. . . . Whereas polytheism, or rather 'cosmotheism,' rendered different cultures mutually transparent and compatible, the new counter-religion blocked intercultural translatability. False gods cannot be translated" (Assmann 1997: 3).

The "grand narrative" of Exodus is the classic source of the Mosaic distinction. Israel is sharply contrasted with Egypt. The story of the Exodus is more than an account of the events of Israel escaping from Egypt. Exodus is a symbolic story, and Moses is a symbolic figure. Israel and Egypt symbolize many oppositions, but the fundamental one is the gaping abyss that separates the one and only *true* religion from all other false, idolatrous, polytheistic, pagan religions. The first two biblical commandments make this clear.

Thou shalt have no other gods before me.
Thou shalt not make unto thee any graven image.

In short, there is one and only one *true* God – all other gods and all other religions are *false*. The repudiation of idolatry grew stronger in the course of Jewish history. Idolatry is an abomination. The hatred between the Israelites and "idolators" was mutual: "Whereas the Jews depicted idolatry as a kind of mental aberration, of madness, the Egyptians associated iconoclasm with the idea of a highly contagious and bodily disfiguring epidemic. The language of illness continues to typify the debate on the Mosaic distinction to the days of Sigmund Freud" (Assmann 1997: 5). The monotheistic religion based on the Mosaic distinction is *revolutionary*.

> Monotheistic religions structure the relationship between the old and the new in terms not of evolution but of revolution, and reject all older and other religions as "paganism" or "idolatry." Monotheism always appears as a counter-religion. There is no natural or evolutionary way leading from the error of idolatry to the truth of monotheism. This truth can come only from outside, by way of revelation. The narrative of the Exodus emphasizes the temporal meaning of the religious antagonism between monotheism and idolatry. "Egypt" stands not only for "idolatry" but also for a past that is rejected. . . . Egypt represents the old while Israel represents the new. The geographical border between the two countries assumes a temporal meaning and comes to symbolize two epochs in the history of humankind. (Assmann 1997: 7)

We begin to see why Assmann characterizes the Mosaic distinction – the foundation of Western monotheism – as "the murderous distinction" (Assmann 1997: 6). The violent smashing of idols becomes symbolic of the total rejection of false religions.

To fully grasp the background of Assmann's inquiry, we need to introduce a further refinement in his understanding of cultural memory. Assmann distinguishes between the "memory of conversion" and "deconstructive memory." "Remembering Egypt could fulfill two radically different functions. First, it could support the distinction between true religion and idolatry. We may call this function of memory 'the memory of conversion'" (Assmann 1997: 7). In their ritual memory, Jews are obligated to recall their liberation from Egypt. Remembering is an act of constant disavowing of idolatry and supports the conversion to the true religion of one and only one true

God. The many admonitions in the Hebrew Bible and Jewish rituals to remember (*zakhor*) reinforce the Mosaic distinction.

But there is an inverse function of memory. Remembering Egypt can also serve the purpose of calling into question the Mosaic distinction. This is what Assmann calls "deconstructive memory." It is a counter-memory to the memory of conversion. "If the space of religious truth is constructed by the distinction between 'Israel in truth' and 'Egypt in error,' any discoveries of Egyptian truths will necessarily invalidate the Mosaic distinction and deconstruct the space separated by this distinction" (Assmann 1997: 8). When Assmann speaks about deconstructive memory, he means something straightforward. Deconstructive memory is the type of memory that questions, challenges, and, ultimately, undermines traditional dichotomies. This distinction between the "memory of conversion" and "deconstructive memory" helps to clarify why he entitles his book *Moses the Egyptian*.

As a figure of memory, Moses the Egyptian is radically different from Moses the Hebrew or the Biblical Moses. Whereas Moses the Hebrew is the personification of confrontation and antagonism – between Israel = truth and Egypt = falsehood – Moses the Egyptian bridges this opposition. In some respects he embodies the inversion or at least the revision of the Exodus myth. Moses the Hebrew is the Deliverer from Egypt and therefore the symbol of Egyptophobia. The Hebrew Moses of the Bible has kept an image of Egypt alive in Western tradition that was thoroughly antithetic to Western ideas, the image of Egypt as the land of despotism, hubris, sorcery, brute-worship, and idolatry. While the Biblical Moses personifies the Mosaic distinction, Moses the Egyptian embodies its mediation. He personifies the positive importance of Egypt in the history of humankind. (Assmann 1997: 11)

The story of *Moses the Egyptian* is the deconstruction – the undermining – of the Mosaic distinction. Assmann explores the suppressed history and repressed memory of the trauma that resulted from Akhenaten's revolutionary counter-religion and traces the legend about Moses the Egyptian back to Manetho, an Egyptian priest who wrote a history of Egypt in the first half of the third century BCE. Several other ancient "historians" (Egyptian and non-Egyptian) elaborated different versions of this legend, but it was Strabo who came closest to a reconstruction of the Egyptian Moses' religion as a monotheistic counter-religion.[3] Strabo's "portrait of Moses was to be recognized in the eighteenth century as that of 'a pantheist or, to speak according to more recent usage, Spinozist'" (Assmann 1997: 38).[4] Strabo also comes closest to the reconstruction of Moses' origin and identity in Freud's *Moses and Monotheism*.

> According to Strabo, an Egyptian priest named Moses, who felt dissatisfied with Egyptian religion, decided to found a new religion and emigrated with his followers into Palestine. He rejected the Egyptian tradition of representing the gods in zoomorphic images. His religion consisted of the recognition of only one divine being whom no image can represent: "which encompasses us all, including earth and sea, that which we call the heavens, the world and the essence of things – this one thing only is God." The only way to approach this god is to live in virtue and in justice. (Assmann 1997: 38)

In sum, Strabo, who bluntly states that Moses was an Egyptian priest, characterizes monotheism as a counter-religion that was a radical break with idolatry. There is no independent historical evidence that any of these accounts of Moses the Egyptian are factually true (just as there is no independent evidence about the existence of Moses the Hebrew – except the biblical account). But in mnemohistory, the central issue is not the factual truth of what is reported, but *how* and *why* persons and events are remembered in distinctive ways.[5]

Assmann's depiction of this ancient "historical" account of Moses the Egyptian serves as the background for his main inquiry: the Moses/Egypt discourse that has its beginnings in the seventeenth century and culminates in Freud's *Moses and Monotheism* – the deconstructing and abolishing of the Mosaic distinction.[6]

The Deconstruction of the Mosaic Distinction

I will give a brief summary of this rich narrative of the Moses/Egypt discourse that begins with Spencer, because my central concern is how the Mosaic distinction is related to religious violence.[7] This history begins with John Spencer (1630–93), an English Hebraist who sought to demonstrate the Egyptian origins of the ritual laws of the Hebrews.[8] According to Spencer, Moses was not an Egyptian but rather an "Egyptianized" Hebrew. Like many other participants in the discourse of Moses the Egyptian, a key text for him is a single verse in the New Testament (Acts 7: 22) declaring that Moses was well versed in all the wisdom of Egypt. To support his reasoning, Spencer adopted the principle of "normative inversion" that can already be found in Maimonides. This is a principle that "consists in inverting the abominations of the other culture into obligations and vice versa" (Assmann 1997: 31).[9] But unlike Maimonides, who "constructs" a pagan people (the "Sabians") and contrasts them with Moses' legislation, Spencer actually engaged in historical research into the ritual laws of the Egyptians. His intention was not to vindicate Egyptian ritual practices and laws; on the contrary, his image of Egypt is characterized by an extreme Egyptophobia. But Spencer helped to make Egyptian practices visible. His work was groundbreaking for two reasons. First, he inquired into the historical reasons for each particular law and institution. In doing so he, in effect, was challenging an orthodoxy that clings to the notion of revelation and rejects any suggestion of historical origins. "Second, his work proved ground-breaking in that it revealed Egypt as the origin of most of the legal institutions of Moses" (Assmann 1997: 75). Spencer's contribution was complemented by that of his contemporary Ralph Cudworth, who focused on theological issues. He sought to substantiate the idea of a primitive monotheism common to all religions and philosophies, including polytheism and even atheism. The reception (not the subjective intentions) of Spencer's picture of Egyptian rituals and Cudworth's picture of Egyptian theology initiated a comprehensive view of Egyptian religion.

Pursuing the "logic" of his mnemohistory, whereby the investigations of earlier thinkers become significant because of the ways in which they are received, appropriated, and interpreted by subsequent thinkers, Assmann next takes up the contributions of John Toland and William Warburton.[10] Spencer, in effect, had shown that civilization, religion, and worship began "long before Moses' time" in Egypt. And Sir John Marsham (in 1672) confirmed Spencer's chronological argument. A few years after the publications of Spencer and Marsham, John Toland and Matthew Tindal, working in what has been called "the radical enlightenment," explained the consequences of the new chronological revolution.

> Whereas Spencer, Cudworth, and Warburton tried to change the orthodox distinctions from within, Toland and Tindal worked from without, trying to "ruin the sacred truths" in a revolutionary and sometimes aggressive way. Basing their work on the ideas of the French and

English Deists as well as on those of the Hermeticists and Spinozists, they sought a concept of natural religion common to all nations, above and beyond its historical forms in different cultures. In Spencer, they found the historical proof that Egypt was the homeland and origin of this religion. They combined Spencer's reconstruction of the Egyptian origins of the Mosaic Law with the Hermetic tradition and its reconstruction of Egyptian theology, the doctrine of the One being the All and the All being the One. Marsham had shown that Egyptian religion came first and predated Moses by eight or nine centuries. On the basis of the undoubted principle that "truth comes first, and what comes later is corruption," Egypt had to be regarded as the homeland of truth. (Assmann 1997: 91–2)

Once again we witness the disparity between subjective intentions and reception (appropriation) in this mnemological discursive history. Warburton, who traced the God of Moses back to the God of the Egyptian Eleusinian mysteries, resisted identifying the God of the mysteries with the God of the philosophers. Nevertheless, this is the way he was read. "The Deists and the Spinozists of the eighteenth century looked to Egypt as the origin and homeland of their concept of God and they drew their evidence from Warburton" (Assmann 1997: 100).

The next two main figures in this discourse history of the deconstruction of the Mosaic distinction are Karl Leonhard Reinhold and Friedrich Schiller. Reinhold is best known as a philosopher who was an adherent (and critic) of Kant, but he was also a Freemason. And, as a Mason, he published an important treatise, *The Hebrew Mysteries, or the Oldest Religious Freemasonry*, under a pseudonym.[11] Reinhold held the same thesis as Spencer in postulating the Egyptian origin of the Mosaic Law, and he follows Toland in making Moses a Spinozist *avant la lettre*, relying mostly on Strabo's account. "But unlike Strabo and Toland, Reinhold shows this religion to be not a counter-religion but a secret religion. The element of negation which made Strabo's Moses turn his back on Egypt and found a new religion in another country is replaced by concealment" (Assmann 1997: 117). And so a new element enters the Moses/Egypt discourse – the element of secrecy. "But Reinhold's and Warburton's concept of a mystery cult retains the characteristics of a counter-religion, in that the secret teachings consist not only in the belief in the One, but also in the refutation of polytheism" (Assmann 1997: 117).

Friedrich Schiller, almost by happenstance, discovered Reinhold's book (intended only for his fellow Masons) and realized its enormous significance. This discovery inspired his own famous essay *Die Sendung Moses* (*The Legation of Moses*). Schiller's essay closely paraphrases Reinhold's arguments. Like the Moses of Reinhold, Warburton, and Spencer, Schiller's Moses is ethnically Hebrew and culturally Egyptian, initiated into all the mysteries of the Egyptians. "For Schiller, the decisive discovery was the identification of the god of the philosophers, that is, the god of reason and enlightenment, with the deepest and most sublime secret of the Egyptian mysteries and the demonstration that it was this sublime and abstract God that Moses had come to accept in the course of his Egyptian initiation and that he dared – at least partly – to reveal this God to his people" (Assmann 1997: 126). This description of a sublime God, who is anticipated by the secrets of the Egyptian mysteries, shows the influence of Kant's reflections on the sublime (and, more generally, the eighteenth-century fascination with the sublime). According to Schiller, Moses had to transform the "sublime deity of the mysteries: abstract, anonymous, impersonal, invisible, and almost beyond the reach of human reason – in Kant's words 'the sublimest thought ever expressed'" (Assmann 1997: 126), into the object of a public religion.

For all the differences among the participants in this Moses/Egypt discourse history, there is something that they share in common. They base their arguments and speculations on the same body of evidence – the same collection of classical, theological, and rabbinic quotations. Assmann likens this to "a kaleidoscope to which every new scholar, living in a new age, belonging to a new generation, and confronting new controversies gives a different turn, so that the hundreds and thousands of pieces fall into a new pattern. This kind of intertextuality can be interpreted as a form of cultural memory that kept a certain body of knowledge accessible for more than two thousand years" (Assmann 1997: 144). The Moses/Egypt discourse, which spanned the seventeenth and eighteenth centuries, seriously challenges the symbolic formula Israel = truth, Egypt = falsity. But we still have not yet come to the culminating figure in this Moses/Egypt discourse: Sigmund Freud.

Despite the importance of Freud in Assmann's own narrative of the Moses/Egypt discourse and for understanding how cultural memory "works," Assmann expresses some reservations about including Freud in his history of the Moses/Egypt discourse. But he makes a striking claim: "The most outspoken destroyer of the Mosaic distinction was a Jew: Sigmund Freud" (Assmann 1997: 5). Yet, when he begins his discussion of Freud, Assmann acknowledges that Freud "was operating outside the paradigm of memory" (Assmann 1997: 145). Freud was familiar with the Greek and Latin sources that described Moses as an Egyptian, but he didn't cite any of these sources in *Moses and Monotheism*; nor did he mention any of the thinkers discussed in Assmann's discourse history from Spencer to Schiller.[12] Freud is operating in a "totally new paradigm: psychoanalysis," and not the paradigm of cultural memory. "The old paradigm sought and accounted for similarities between cultures such as Israel and Egypt on the basis of diffusionism. The only problem was to determine the source of diffusion: was Israel or Egypt the origin? Psychoanalysis provided a new model, which is basically universalist" (Assmann 1997: 145–6). Freud differs from the earlier participants in the "old paradigm" because he had access to historical information that was not available to them – the archeological discoveries of Armana and the iconoclastic monotheistic reign of Akhenaten.

Nevertheless, Assmann justifies his inclusion of Freud because he is struck by the strong continuity with Spencer, Warburton, Reinhold, and Schiller – especially in the first two parts of *Moses and Monotheism*. He puts aside his doubts about including Freud as a "final chapter" of the Moses/Egypt discourse when he declares:

> The agenda of the Moses/Egypt discourse was to deconstruct "counter-religion" and its implications of intolerance by blurring the basic distinctions as they were symbolized by the antagonistic constellation of Israel and Egypt. "Revelation" had to be (re)turned into "translation." Freud became involved not simply because he shared this agenda, but also because he felt he could contribute *the final and decisive proof* by availing himself of the discoveries of archaeology and history that had been inaccessible to his predecessors, from Manetho to Schiller. (Assmann 1997: 147, emphasis added)[13]

By summarizing Freud's narrative plot, we can see why Assmann claims that "the Moses/Egypt discourse seemed to come to a conclusion" (Assmann 1997: 148). I quote Yosef Yerushalmi's lucid summary.

> Monotheism is not of Jewish origin but an Egyptian discovery. The pharaoh Amenhotep IV [Akhenaten] established it as his state religion in the form of an exclusive worship of sun-power, or Aton, thereafter calling himself Ikhnaton [Akhenaton]. The Aton religion, according to Freud, was characterized by exclusive belief in one God, the rejection of anthropomorphism, magic, and sorcery, and the absolute denial of

an afterlife. Upon Ikhnaton's [Akhenaton's] death, however, his great heresy was rapidly undone, and the Egyptians reverted to their old gods. Moses was not a Hebrew but an Egyptian priest or noble, and a fervent monotheist. In order to save the Aton religion from extinction he placed himself at the head of an oppressed Semitic tribe then living in Egypt, brought them forth from bondage, and created a new nation. He gave them an even more spiritualized, imageless form of monotheistic religion and, in order to set them apart, introduced the Egyptian custom of circumcision. But the crude mass of former slaves could not bear the severe demands of the new faith. In a mob revolt Moses was killed and the memory of the murder repressed. The Israelites went on to forge an alliance of compromise with kindred Semitic tribes in Midian whose fierce volcanic deity, named Yahweh, now became their national god. As a result, the god of Moses was fused with Yahweh and the deeds of Moses ascribed to a Midianite priest also called Moses. However, over a period of centuries the submerged tradition of the true faith and its founder gathered sufficient force to reassert itself and emerge victorious. Yahweh was henceforth endowed with the universal and spiritual qualities of Moses' god, though the memory of Moses' murder remained repressed among the Jews, reemerging only in a very disguised form with the rise of Christianity. (Yerushalmi 1991: 3–4)

With the exceptions of the murder of Moses by the Semitic tribe and the Israelites' fusion of Yahweh with Moses' God, Assmann shows that we find anticipations of virtually every detail of Freud's narrative in the older Moses/Egypt discourse. As Freud states: "The Egyptian Moses had given to one portion of the people a more highly spiritualized notion of god, the idea of a single deity embracing the whole world, who was not less all-loving than all-powerful, who was adverse to all ceremonial and magic and who set before men as their highest aim a life in truth and justice" (Freud 1964: 50).

But there is a serious problem in seeing Freud as the culminating chapter of the Moses/Egypt discourse. Assmann acknowledges this when he says, "The only problem with Freud's God was that he did not believe in him. This god was not a theological or philosophical truth, but an archaeological discovery. Had Freud still believed in this 'one single all-encompassing' God or nature as Toland, Reinhold, and Schiller did, his book would perhaps have ended here" (Assmann 1997: 158). But I do not think that Freud's agenda in *Moses and Monotheism* is the same as that of the Moses/Egypt discourse. Freud's project is not to deconstruct the Moses/Egypt discourse. On the contrary, Freud "the godless Jew" wants to reveal what he takes to be the deeper hidden legacy of sublime imageless monotheism – a legacy epitomized by the phrase *der Fortschritt in der Geistigkeit* (the progress of spirituality, the advance in intellectuality).[14]

As I hope to show, Assmann's appropriation of Freudian themes is absolutely crucial for his understanding of cultural memory, the fate of the Mosaic distinction, and religious violence. We get a hint of this in his concluding remarks in *Moses the Egyptian*, where he briefly discusses two Freudian concepts: latency and the return of the repressed. After distinguishing two earlier models of antagonism he writes:

> Latency as a third model of religious antagonism and tension is the discovery of Sigmund Freud and constitutes his most important contribution to the discourse on Moses and Egypt. Freud's great discovery and lasting contribution to this discourse is the role which he attributed to the dynamics of memory and the return of the repressed. . . . But I think that . . . one should acknowledge that the concepts of latency and the return of the repressed are indispensable for any adequate theory of cultural memory. They need, however, to be redefined in cultural terms. Freud reminded us of the fact that there is such a thing as "cultural forgetting" or even "cultural repression." Since Freud, no theory of culture can afford not to take these concepts into consideration. The old concept of tradition has proved insufficient. (Assmann 1997: 215)

Assmann barely elaborates the meaning of these pregnant remarks. In what sense is latency a third model of antagonism? Why are the concepts of latency and the return of the repressed indispensable for any adequate account of cultural memory? What precisely is meant by cultural latency and a cultural return of the repressed? Why is "the old concept of tradition" insufficient? Answering these questions will have direct bearing on understanding the potential threat of religious violence.

The Storm of Protest and Assmann's Response

Almost as soon as *Moses the Egyptian* was published, the book provoked intense and vehement criticisms.[15] Assmann has been accused of misunderstanding monotheism, misreading the Bible – even of being anti-Semitic. His critics have rebuked him for attributing to *all* monotheistic religions (especially Jewish, Christian, and Muslim) an exclusionary tendency that is foreign to them. He presumably fails to do justice to the universal character of monotheism, which includes all of humanity. Others have leveled the opposite criticism, claiming that he wants to do away with a distinction that is *constitutive* of monotheism and return us to polytheism or cosmotheism. Theologians, historians of religion, biblical scholars, and many others have entered into the fray. It is rare that a scholarly book dealing with an esoteric subject has come in for such intense (and at times, vicious) criticism. One critic even ascribes to Assmann "the fundamental claim" that "[t]his Mosaic distinction has brought so much suffering and violence into the world that it ought finally to be done away with. The price that human history has had to pay for it to date is simply too high" (Assmann 2010: 6).[16] I don't think it surprising that his book has caused so much passionate debate. After all, Assmann says that the Mosaic distinction stands at the heart of revolutionary monotheism, and he does refer to it as a "murderous distinction."

In *The Price of Monotheism*, Assmann succinctly states his intention in writing *Moses the Egyptian*: "I wanted to retrace this newly discovered chapter in the history of the memory of Egypt in the West, from its ancient origins right down to its present-day consequences; and it may well be that, carried away by the exhilaration of discovery, I overstated my case. In essence, however, I wanted to attempt a historical or 'mnemohistorical' reconstruction, not to embroil myself in theological controversy" (Assmann 2010: 5). But regardless of Assmann's "subjectively intended meaning," he did embroil himself in theological, biblical, and historical controversies. In his mnemological discourse history Assmann emphasized "the semantic potentials" that a text releases and fosters in its readers, rather than the subjective intentions of an author. Instead of simply defending his original views, Assmann – in *The Price of Monotheism* – contributes to the discussion of the issues raised by his critics. On a number of key issues, Assmann clarifies, supplements, and revises his earlier views. Yet, on the basic issue of the centrality of the Mosaic distinction, he actually strengthens his original arguments. And he directly confronts the issue of religious intolerance and violence, which caused the greatest unease in his critics. So let's consider some of his key emendations to the concept of the Mosaic distinction.

In *Moses the Egyptian*, Assmann stressed the revolutionary significance of monotheism, which he traced back to Akhenaten. He now concedes that we need a more nuanced understanding of two kinds of monotheism: evolutionary and revolutionary. There are two different paths to monotheism, and two quite different forms of monotheism:

> One, the evolutionary path, leads to an inclusive monotheism, a mono-theism that is nothing other than a mature stage of polytheism. The other, the revolutionary path, leads to exclusive monotheism, a mono-theism that cannot be arrived at through any developmental process but only through a revolutionary break with all that went before it. The distinction between true and false religion pertains solely to this exclusive monotheism. (Assmann 2010: 36)

Although this complicates the story of monotheism, Assmann still emphasizes the distinctiveness of *revolutionary* monotheism – the mon-otheism of the Mosaic distinction. But then we may ask, When did this revolution take place?[17] In *Moses the Egyptian*, Assmann certainly suggests that it is a datable event – that it occurred in the reign of Akhenaten. But now he adds greater nuance to his original views. Rather than suggesting that there is a single datable event when the revolutionary Mosaic distinction was introduced, he now speaks about "monotheistic moments" – moments that occur in "fits and starts."

> Rather than speaking of a single "monotheistic shift," with an unam-biguous "before" and "after," one could therefore refer with equal justice to "monotheistic moments" in which the Mosaic distinction is struck with all severity – the first and second commandments, the story of the Golden Calf, the forced termination of mixed marriage under Nehemiah, the destruction of pagan temples in Christian late antiq-uity – before being watered down or almost forgotten in the unavoid-able compromises that determine the everyday practice of religious life. (Assmann 2010: 2–3)

But, although speaking about "monotheistic moments," rather than a single datable event, adds greater nuance to Assmann's account, it doesn't alter the significance of the Mosaic distinction. "[T]he Mosaic distinction is struck with all severity" over and over again. But what about the Bible itself? Is it accurate to describe the monotheism of the Hebrew Bible as revolutionary monotheism? Assmann now tells us that there is evidence of both evolutionary and revolutionary monotheism in the Hebrew Bible. How many religions stand behind the Old Testament? Assmann's direct answer is *two*!

Not one religion but two stand behind the books of the Old Testament. One scarcely differs from the primary religions that coexisted with it at the time in its adoration of a supreme god who dominates and far excels the other gods, without, however, excluding them in any way, a god, who, as creator of the world and everything in it, cares for his creatures, increases the fertility of the flocks and fields, tames the elements, and directs the destiny of his people. The books and textual layers ascribed to the "priestly" traditional and redactional line are particularly shaped by this religion. The other religion, by contrast, sharply distinguishes itself from the religions of its environment by demanding that its One God be worshipped to the exclusion of all others, by banning the production of images, and by making divine favor depend less on sacrificial offerings and rites than on the righteous conduct of the individual and the observance of god-given, scripturally fixed laws. This religion is on display in the prophetic books, as well as in the texts and textual layers of the "Deuteronomic" line of tradition. (Assmann 2010: 8)[18]

Consider how Assmann qualifies his original claims. He acknowledges that there are different paths to, and forms of, monotheism. We find evidence of both of these in the Hebrew Bible. Furthermore, the monotheistic shift is not a single datable event; rather, it designates "moments" that can occur and reoccur throughout history. But even with these qualifications, Assmann still firmly holds that there is a distinctive type of revolutionary monotheism based on the Mosaic distinction.

Assmann confronts another line of criticism. Some of his critics have objected that he distorts the meaning of monotheism by putting a mistaken emphasis on exclusion – rather than the unity and universality of God. Furthermore, the distinction of the "true" and "false" is really a Hellenic philosophical distinction that isn't applicable to religion. The story of the Exodus is not one of the contest of the "true" and "false" religion, but rather the story of the liberation of the Hebrews – the escape from slavery to freedom.

Assmann doesn't deny the significance of the traditional interpretation of Exodus as the liberation of the Hebrews from slavery. This is how the story is retold every year at the Passover Seder when Jews all over the world fulfill their obligation to remember how they were liberated from Egypt, and follow the injunction to pass this story on to their children and their children's children. But this doesn't diminish the significance of the symbolic contrast between the true God and the false idolatrous gods of the "pagans." There is a distinctive sense of "truth" when speaking about the Mosaic distinction (which is not to be confused with the critical concept of "truth" that was introduced by the Greeks). The Greeks revolutionized the world by introducing a new critical concept of truth, but the Jews revolutionized the world by introducing a revolutionary monotheism in which there is *one and only one true God*. "The Mosaic distinction introduces a new kind of truth: absolute, revealed, metaphysical, or fideistic truth" (Assmann 2010: 15).[19] Assmann replies vigorously to the persistent charge that his thesis about the Mosaic distinction is anti-Semitic:

> In many discussions in which I have taken part, this thesis has been branded "anti-Semitic." The charge would perhaps be justified had I interpreted this transformation of the world as a turn for the worse rather than for the better, and had I wanted to castigate the Jews for putting an end to a Golden Age of primary religion by introducing the Mosaic distinction. But this strikes me as absurd – no less absurd, in fact, than had I wanted to reproach the Greeks for disenchanting the world and delivering it over to rational calculation through their invention of scientific thought. It is in my view self-evident that in both cases, in scientific thought no less than in monotheism, we are dealing with civilizational achievements of the highest order, and it has never occurred to me to demand that they be abandoned. I am advocating a return neither to myth nor to primary religion. Indeed, I am not advocating anything; my aim is rather to describe and understand. (Assmann 2010: 13)[20]

But however eloquent we may find this *apologia*, we still want to know how the Mosaic distinction is related to religious violence. I suspect that Assmann regrets the phrase he used in *Moses the Egyptian* when he wrote: "In making Moses an Egyptian and in tracing monotheism back to ancient Egypt, Freud attempted to deconstruct the *murderous distinction*" (Assmann 1997: 6, emphasis added). In fairness to Assmann, we should note that in *Moses the Egyptian*, he never explicitly discusses the sense in which the Mosaic distinction is "murderous." But a fundamental issue needs to be brought out into the open. If the Mosaic distinction is as rigorous and as absolute as Assmann indicates, and if it introduces a new kind of religious truth – "absolute, revealed, metaphysical, or fideistic truth" – that is radically opposed to all false religions, then it would seem that the Mosaic distinction is *intrinsically* violent. This is a disturbing conclusion, because there are many passages (up to 600) in the Bible that mention internecine violence – some of which are "the typical scenes of violence that orchestrate the institution of monotheism" (Assmann 2008: 111). Even though the accusation of anti-Semitism may be grossly unfair (and I think it is completely unwarranted), Assmann says that the Mosaic distinction introduces not only a new kind of truth, but also a new kind of violence: *religious violence*. What, then, is this religious violence?

The Mosaic Distinction and Religious Violence

The relation between religion, especially monotheism, and violence has troubled thinkers since the Enlightenment (and long before). Voltaire wrote about the striking scenes of violence in the Hebrew Bible, and David Hume postulated an intrinsic relation between monotheism and violence. The issue has become especially acute in our time because of "the wave of religiously motivated violence that is presently descending on the world" (Assmann 2008: 109). Assmann raises the key questions that demand answers.

> Why do the biblical texts use the language and imagery of violence in their narrative representations of the foundation and success of monotheism? Does the idea of monotheism, the exclusive worship of one god instead of a divine world, or the distinction between true and false in religion, in which there is one true god and the rest are false gods, imply or entail violence? Are violence and intolerance, rigor and zealotry the price that exclusive monotheism has had to pay for sticking to the notion of a very personal and passionate God while stressing the idea of Oneness? (Assmann 2008: 109)

His answers to these questions are complex and subtle. Given their importance, not only for his project but for everyone today, I want to follow his reasoning as carefully as I can. I argue that his answers are seriously deficient. To paraphrase Hegel, there is a disparity – a conflict between his *intentions* and what he actually *says*. This is the type of tension that Assmann finds over and over again in the Moses/ Egypt discourse – and it is just as applicable to his own discourse. But I also want to show that Assmann opens a new way of thinking about the so-called "post-secular" age and the ever-present danger of religious violence.

Assmann realizes that there is a danger in the way he has formulated the above questions, for they seem to imply a misleading essentialism. He frequently speaks as if there is an essence or core of *all* monotheisms – at least, of all revolutionary monotheisms. This would, of course, include all the Abrahamic religions – Jewish, Christian, and Islamic. To avoid the pitfall of essentialism, he introduces two qualifications. "The first consists in speaking not of 'consequences' but rather of 'propensities'. Consequences are a matter of necessity and inevitability; they will sooner or later become real in one form or another. Propensities, conversely, are a matter of potentiality and probability; they leave us free with respect to how to deal with them" (Assmann 2008: 109). Assmann categorically states that he does not think that monotheism is "inherently or structurally violent and intolerant." But under certain historical conditions these propensities can and do lead to violence and intolerance. To anticipate, Assmann's thesis is that revolutionary monotheism is potentially violent; this *propensity* is built into the Mosaic distinction. But actual violence is not necessarily and inevitably a *consequence* of monotheism.

Assmann's second qualification is that when he speaks of "monotheism," he "means simply the principle that there be 'no god but God' or, in the form of the first commandment, '[Thou shalt have] no other gods', regardless of any further distinctions between monotheism, henotheism, monolatry and the like" (Assmann 2008: 110). But even with this qualification, "monotheism" refers to all the Abrahamic religions *insofar* as they affirm the principle "no god but God."

In order to distinguish himself sharply from those anti-Semites and polemicists who cite the language of violence in the Hebrew Bible for the purpose of fabricating a case against the Jews – or, more generally, against monotheism, he writes: "[I]t is important to stress the fact that among the three Abrahamic religions, Judaism is the only one that has never turned the implications of violence and intolerance into historical reality precisely because it has relegated the final universalizing of truth to eschatology and not to history" (Assmann 2008: 111). The specific question that he wants to answer is: "Why does biblical monotheism see itself as violent?" Assmann gives a close reading of a number of passages in which the language of violence is especially striking – for example, the story of the Golden Calf, especially the passage in Exodus 32: 26–8 where Moses tells "each man to kill his brother, and each man his fellow, and each man his kin" and a similar passage in Deuteronomy 13: 7–10 where God declares that you should kill anyone who incites you to worship other gods – whether it is "your brother, your mother's son, or your son, or your daughter or the wife of your bosom or your companion who is like your own self." There are also many instances of "zeal: killing and dying for God" (Assmann 2008: 115). The famous story of the Maccabees – a classic instance of Hebrew heroism – reveals that the Maccabees not only defended themselves against Antiochus IV. "They are recorded as having extinguished the life of entire Jewish towns and cities that had adopted the Hellenistic way of life according to the treatment that Deuteronomy prescribed for Canaanite and Israelite towns that had relapsed by adopting pagan rites" (Assmann 2008: 119).[21]

How are we to interpret this constantly iterated language of violence? The last passage gives the essential clue. Assmann claims that the biblical language of violence is to be properly interpreted as a feat of *memory*, not of history. Most of these violent passages are internally directed against those who slip back into idolatry and paganism. The language of violence and intolerance "belongs to the ways in which biblical monotheism represents and remembers its installation and not to the ways it has actually been installed" (Assmann 2008: 128). The "anti-Canaanism of Deuteronomy and its language of violence" express "the pathos of conversion: the passion of a life-changing commitment, the fear of relapse, and the resolve to exterminate the pagan within" (Assmann 2008: 124). Furthermore, Assmann stresses that what is initially more important is the *enduring* of violence rather than the *inflicting* of violence: "Once it is realized that the intolerance inherent to monotheism, which flows directly from the Mosaic distinction, initially appears in a passive or martyrological guise – that is, as a refusal to accept a form of religion known to be false, and a concomitant willingness to die rather than yield an inch on this point – then the problem of 'monotheisms and violence' can be seen to have as much to do with enduring violence as with perpetrating it" (Assmann 2010: 21). Once again we see the importance of the distinction between mnemohistory and history proper. The language of violence is a vehicle for memory – a way of reminding Israelites of the dangers and temptation of slipping back into paganism, an emphatic reminder that there is one and only one true God who demands absolute commitment and loyalty. The language of violence is "symbolic" of the resolve not to fall back into idolatry, not to be seduced by the "fleshpots of Egypt." When Assmann reflects on the significance of the legacy of the Mosaic distinction for us today, he declares:

If the violent potential of its semantic implications remains the price of monotheism, it is also important to remember for what this price has been paid. Monotheism means exodus, that is, enlightenment. It means the liberation of mankind from the constraints of the powers of this world, of the given. It means the discovery of an alternative realm of human commitment and investment beyond the traditional realms of state, society, and nature. It means the discovery of the inner man and new dimensions of subjectivity. As a final consequence, the distinction between true and false means the distinction between God and world. If this distinction enables man to go beyond the given powers of cosmos and politics in his search for God, it pushes us to go beyond even sacred texts and truths of traditional religion. (Assmann 2008: 125)

This is the closest that Assmann comes to stating his own credo – his own belief about the "price of monotheism" and the positive meaning for civilization of revolutionary monotheism. This passage also shows why he so strongly identifies with Freud's claim that the legacy of Moses' revolutionary monotheism is a primary source for "progress in intellectuality." But there are still disturbing questions. What kind of violence is this, and what is its relation to other types of violence? Assmann takes up the definition of religious violence in his conclusion to *Of God and Gods*. Before examining what he says, I want to make an excursus that will bring us back to Freud and his relevance for Assmann's conception of the dynamics of cultural memory.

Latency and the Return of the Repressed

In both his chapter on Freud in *Moses the Egyptian*, "Sigmund Freud: The Return of the Repressed," and his essay "Sigmund Freud and the Progress in Intellectuality," Assmann reports Freud's shocking claim that the Jews murdered Moses. He voices his skepticism about this alleged murder and about the way in which Freud connects Moses' murder with the "original" patricide of the primal father. "The trauma of monotheism, if there is such a thing, rests in my opinion not on a twofold parricide, whose victims were first the primal father and then Moses, but on a twofold deicide, whose victims were first the 'pagan' gods and then the god of monotheism himself" (Assmann 2010: 96–7).[22] Freud tells us that after Moses' murder, there was a backsliding of the Jews from the strict and demanding iconoclastic monotheism to a form of idolatry.[23] The "mob" that revolted formed an alliance with other Semitic tribes in Midian and adopted a new, fierce volcanic deity, Yahweh. The god of the Egyptian Moses was fused with Yahweh, and the deeds of the Egyptian Moses were fused with those of a Midianite priest who was also called Moses. Now, however incredible this story of the fusion of two religions and the two figures named "Moses" may seem if taken as a serious *historical* hypothesis, it nevertheless plays a crucial role in Freud's account of the legacy of monotheism. After a long period of latency (centuries), there is a return of the repressed – a return to the true doctrines of monotheism. In the section of *Moses and Monotheism* entitled "The Latency Period and Tradition," Freud writes: "We confess the belief, therefore, that the idea of a single god, as well as the rejection of magically effective ceremonial and the stress upon the ethical demands made in his name, were in fact Mosaic doctrines, to which no attention was paid to begin with, but which, after a long interval had elapsed, came into operation and eventually became permanently established" (Freud 1964: 66). Freud accounts for this "delayed effect" by employing two fundamental concepts of psychoanalysis: latency and the return of the repressed. Even though these concepts were originally elaborated to explain individual neurosis, Freud claims that they can also be applied to cultural memory.[24]

> The Jewish people had abandoned the Aton religion brought to them by Moses and had returned to the worship of another god who differed little from the Baalim of neighbouring peoples. All the tendentious efforts of later times failed to disguise this shameful act. But the Mosaic religion had not vanished without leaving a trace; some sort of memory of it had been kept alive – a possibly obscured and distorted tradition. And it was this tradition of a great past which continued to operate (from the background, as it were), which gradually acquired more and more power over people's minds and which in the end succeeded in changing the god Yahweh into the Mosaic god and in re-awakening into life the religion of Moses that had been introduced and then abandoned long centuries before. That a tradition thus sunk in oblivion should exercise such a powerful effect on the mental life of a people is an unfamiliar idea to us. (Freud 1964: 69–70)

But no matter how unfamiliar this idea may be, Freud argues that the Mosaic religion of strict monotheism – originally repressed – returned after a long period of latency. When Freud explained this central thesis in a letter to Lou Andreas-Salomé in 1935 (four years before the publication of *Moses and Monotheism*), she beautifully expressed his main idea in her own distinctive way.

> Hitherto we have usually understood the term "return of the repressed" in the context of neurotic processes: all kinds of material which had been wrongly repressed afflicted the neurotic mysteriously with phantoms of the past, because in them he sensed something primevally familiar, which he felt bound to ward off. But in this case we are presented with examples of the survival of the most triumphantly vital elements of the past as the truest possession in the present, despite all destructive elements and counter-forces they have endured. And as in the case of the original religion of Moses, such positive aspects of the process may have been at work also in other religions, and so there too the repressed was not confined to pathological survivals. (Quoted in Bernstein 1998: 119–20)[25]

We can now better understand Assmann's remark at the conclusion of *Moses the Egyptian*: "the concepts of latency and the return of the repressed are indispensable for any adequate theory of cultural memory" (Assmann 1997: 215). These concepts stand at the core of Assmann's mnemohistory. Specifically, he shows how the biblical account of Moses the Hebrew represses the cultural memory of Egypt. But there is a counter-memory that breaks forth after a long period of latency. This is the way he sees the battle between Moses the Hebrew and Moses the Egyptian. The former is the dominant "memory of conversion," and the latter the "deconstructive counter-memory." This is also why Assmann says that "the old concept of tradition has proved insufficient" (Assmann 1997: 215). A concept of tradition that focuses exclusively on what is *consciously* handed down throughout history and does not acknowledge cultural latency and the return of the repressed fails to grasp the dynamics of cultural memory.[26]

To complete Freud's narrative, we must consider what he takes to be the legacy of this true, strict Mosaic monotheism. Assmann calls this the second deicide – the killing off of Moses' God. The legacy of the monotheism is *der Fortschritt in der Geistigkeit* (the progress in spirituality, the advance in intellectuality).[27] Assmann gives a succinct summary of Freud's thesis: "I now think Freud was trying . . . to present the Mosaic distinction (in the form of the ban on graven images) as a seminal, immensely valuable, and profoundly Jewish achievement, which ought on no account to be relinquished, and that his own psychoanalysis could credit itself precisely with taking this specifically Jewish type of progress a step further" (Assmann 2010: 86).

Religious Violence: The Fifth Form of Violence

Assmann concludes *Of God and Gods* with a section entitled "Toward a Critique of Religious Violence." He tells us that, unlike Walter Benjamin, he thinks that we should distinguish not *two* but *five* forms of violence. The first type he calls raw or "affective" violence.[28] Raw violence arises from anger, greed, and fear. Violence motivated by anger typically manifests itself in revenge; violence out of fear expresses itself in self-defense or pre-emptive action; "and violence motivated by greed is usually masked as 'might is right'" (Assmann 2008: 142).

"The second form of violence, legal violence, is pitted against raw violence. This is the foundation of states and legal institutions that Benjamin calls 'mythical violence.' Legal violence is counter-violence. Unlike raw violence, legal violence distinguishes between just and unjust. The aim of legal justice is the creation of a sphere of law and justice in which raw violence is excluded" (Assmann 2008: 143).

A third form of violence is political violence. Assmann draws on Carl Schmitt to explain his meaning: in a state of emergency, political violence turns against institutionalized law and suspends a greater or lesser part of civil rights. Political violence aims at preserving power and depends upon stirring up a love for the state and a hatred of its internal and external enemies.

There are two remaining forms of violence, and "it is only through them that one enters the realm of religion" (Assmann 2008: 143). The fourth type of violence is "ritual violence."[29] "We have lost sight of this form because it has almost vanished from the domain of modern world religions. In early or 'pagan' religions all violence that is exerted in the name of religion is ritual violence" (Assmann 2008: 143). This is the type of violence that is so central in the work of René Girard.[30]

Finally, we come to the fifth and final form of violence: religious violence. This is violence with reference to the will of God. Assmann's thesis is *"that this form of violence occurs only in monotheistic religions"* (Assmann 2008: 144, emphasis added).

> What, then, is religious violence? By this term I mean a kind of violence that stems from the distinction of friend and foe in a religious sense. The religious meaning of this distinction rests on the distinction of true and false.... Religious violence ... is directed against pagans, unbelievers, and heretics, who either would not convert to the truth or have defected from it and are therefore regarded as enemies of God.
>
> In wondering about the origins of religious violence, my purpose was to deconstruct, by means of genealogical reconstruction, the connection between religion and violence. (Assmann 2008: 144)

Assmann's description of religious violence is extremely perplexing. It is almost as if Assmann is drawing back and turning away from what he has so brilliantly demonstrated.

> Religious violence is nothing original, nothing necessarily implied in the idea of monotheism. Monotheism originally meant the liberation of man from the omnipotence of political power. This was at first conceivable only as counterviolence, religious violence against political violence. Essentially this is a question not of violence against violence but of power against power. The basic idea behind biblical monotheism is to erect a counterpower against the all-encompassing power of the political. Religion can exert its counterpower against the political only if it has recourse to totally different means and values. The truth of this lesson, which is implied in many of Jesus' words and actions, and has been demonstrated in modern times by Mahatma Gandhi, who based his nonviolent but extremely powerful actions on the religious idea of "truth." It has now become imperative to dissociate religion from violence. Violence belongs to the sphere of the political, and a religion that uses violence fails in its proper mission in this world and remains entangled in the sphere of the political. The power of religion rests on nonviolence. Only through a complete rejection of violence is monotheism able to fulfill its liberating mission of forming an alternative counterpower to the totalizing claims of the political. (Assmann 2008: 145)

1.   Even if we accepted this classification of the forms of violence, it is problematic why Assmann says that it is only with the last two forms of violence – ritual and religious violence – "that one enters the realm of religion." Assmann has shown over and over again that the Bible is replete with examples of the first three forms of violence. Can

we possibly understand the Five Books of Moses without reference to God's anger and the fear that it provokes? Throughout the Bible, there are examples of "anger, greed, and fear." On Assmann's own account, Deuteronomy and Leviticus are basically all about "legal violence." It seems completely artificial to separate "religious violence" from "political violence" in the Bible. When the first-born of the Egyptians are murdered and the Egyptians are destroyed in the Red Sea, this is certainly a religious-political act – just as the conquest of Canaan exemplifies political violence. In short, Assmann's first three "forms of violence" are integral to the representation of religious violence in the Bible. We cannot simply "abstract" some idealized notion of religious violence. Of course, raw, legal, and political violence occur in contexts that have nothing to do with religion or monotheism, but they are integral to the Bible.

   2.   When Assmann introduces his "critique of religious violence," he tells us that we must carefully distinguish between "power, violence, and constraint" (although he gives only the barest sketch of their differences). When he distinguishes violence from power and constraint, he categorically states that "Violence is *physical violence*" (Assmann 2008: 142, emphasis added). Yet, when he comes to characterize religious violence, he tells us that "the power of religion rests on nonviolence." This certainly looks like a flat contradiction. How can violence be physical violence, yet religious violence be nonviolent?

   3.   Assmann writes that "the basic idea behind biblical monotheism is to erect a counterpower against the all-encompassing power of the political" (Assmann 2008: 145). But it is hard to square this claim with God's overtly *political* aim in founding a new nation, a new people, and a new kingdom with a land of its own. "Israel" and "Egypt" may be symbolic of the true and false religions, but the biblical account of the escape from Egypt, the killing of the Egyptians in the Red Sea, and the battles fought to triumph over the Canaanites are told as *political* happenings. Assmann appears to be doing precisely what he criticizes so many others for doing – substituting a "purified theological" version of biblical monotheism for what is actually written in the Bible.

   4.   There is something deeply confusing about the way in which Assmann draws a sharp distinction between political and religious violence. He appropriates Carl Schmitt's concept of the political, which rests on the distinction of friend and enemy, but adds the qualification that this distinction does not define the sphere of the

political but rather defines the sphere of political violence. But this distinction between "the political" and "political violence" doesn't make sense on Schmittian grounds. "The friend, enemy, and combat concepts receive their real meaning precisely because they refer to the real possibility of physical killing. War follows from enmity. War is the existential negation of the enemy" (Schmitt 1996a: 33).

5. Furthermore, when Assmann defines religious violence, he employs this very same Schmittian language of friend and enemy. Religious violence "stems from the distinction of friend and foe in a religious sense" (Assmann 2008: 144).[31] What is the difference between the "political" and the "religious" sense of friend and foe? Assmann writes that "the religious meaning of this distinction rests on the distinction between the true and false." But it is hard to see how this reference to the religious sense of "the true and the false" explains what is distinctive about religious *violence*. On the contrary, it seems to be just another way of describing the Mosaic distinction where Israel = true and Egypt = false.

6. Assmann's sharp distinction between "propensities" and "consequences" is a bit too simple and neat. He tells us that *propensities* are "a matter of potentiality and probability," whereas *consequences* "are a matter of necessity and inevitability" (Assmann 2008: 109). Although the Mosaic distinction is potentially violent, it is not actually violent, because violence is not a necessary and inevitable consequence of this distinction. "Precisely because one is dealing with propensities and not with consequences, a reflection upon their origin and structure is important in order to avoid turning from potentialities into realities of various kinds that have haunted the world and continue to do so" (Assmann 2008: 110). But this sharp distinction between propensities and consequences is dubious. Ordinarily (and in philosophic discourse) we do not assume that *all* consequences are "necessary and inevitable"; they may be likely or probable. There is an ancient philosophical tradition of drawing a distinction between the potential and the actual; potentialities may not be actualized. But a good deal of the history and memory of Christianity and Islam has occurred in those historical circumstances when the potential violence of the Mosaic distinction has turned into actual violence. It seems more than quixotic to say that this is the result of a "mistaken" political appropriation of the religious violence of monotheism and that "only through a complete rejection of violence is monotheism able to fulfill its liberating mission of forming an alternative counterpower to the

totalizing claims of the political" (Assmann 2008: 145). Assmann here seems to be speaking as a defensive "theologian" who wants to reassure us about the "true" mission of monotheism, rather than as a historian of cultural memory. Such an antiseptic view of monotheism fails to underscore how over and over again the Mosaic distinction has been used *to justify and legitimize* physical violence. Once we zealously commit ourselves to *our* god as the one and only true god, we have the *strongest* possible justification to destroy infidels. Assmann's "critique of religious violence" simply *doesn't* follow from what he has taught us about the Mosaic distinction and revolutionary monotheism. How are we to account for this gaping disparity?

Assmann passionately defends himself against the charge that the Mosaic distinction is a disaster and ought to be abandoned. Like Freud, he claims that monotheism plays a major role in bringing about " 'the progress of intellectuality' which ought not to be relinquished, no matter how dearly it may have been purchased." His intention is "to sublimate the Mosaic distinction, not revoke it" (Assmann 2010: 120). This means that we ought to make the Mosaic distinction an incessant object of reflection and redefinition. We must not give up the Mosaic distinction, but we must constantly challenge it. We need both to *affirm* it and *deconstruct* it. This is the moral of Assmann's mnemohistorical tale. But there is a darker story to be told about the Mosaic distinction – and at times Assmann indicates his awareness of this.

The Dark Side of Monotheism

In my excursus on Freud, I indicated how Assmann appropriates and uses the Freudian concepts of latency and the return of the repressed. "Freud reminded us of the fact that there is such a thing as 'cultural forgetting' or even 'cultural repression.' Since Freud, no theory of culture can afford not to take these concepts into consideration" (Assmann 1997: 215). We have seen how Assmann uses these Freudian concepts in his account of "monotheistic moments," which have returned with renewed severity after long periods of latency. Even if the Mosaic distinction is suppressed, repressed, or deconstructed, we can *never* rule out the possibility of a violent return of the repressed. There is *always* the danger of a bursting forth of the Mosaic distinction and the eruption of new violence. The present (and the future) is "haunted" by the past. Even if we grant Assmann's claim that the Mosaic distinction need not necessarily lead to violent consequences, the propensity for violence *is* inherent in the Mosaic distinction. And this means that under varied historical and political conditions, it may result in real physical violence. Assmann shows his awareness of this danger when he writes:

> What I believe to have discovered in Egypt is the repressed and for-gotten side of monotheism, the dark side of monotheism, so to speak, which has remained present in the cultural memory of the West as an object of negation and denial at best. *That we are dealing here with a case of "repression" in the classical (that is, Freudian) sense can be deduced from the eruptive forcefulness with which this repressed dark side has continually returned to haunt the West.* (Assmann 2010: 119–20, emphasis added)

If we pursue the "logic" of Assmann's argument – if we pursue the "semantic potentials" of what Assmann has shown – then they have the utmost significance for theories of modernity and secularization. Monotheistic religions are not disappearing from the contemporary world, and there is little reason to believe that they will disappear in the future. Assmann's reflections on cultural memory and the endur-ance of the Mosaic distinction provide a deep reason to be skeptical of theories of modernity *insofar* as they neglect the power of cultural latency and the cultural return of the repressed. There is always the danger that the Mosaic distinction will "return" and become a "mur-derous distinction." Assmann is certainly aware of this. "The atroci-ties of the twentieth century – including the horrors of September 11, 2001 – have lent a tremendous resonance to the sacred texts of our monotheistic tradition. It is impossible to speak of religion, especially with a focus on violence, without thinking of and referring to the Holocaust and/or to the events of 9/11. . . . The times are over when religion could be viewed as the 'opium of the people'. Nowadays, in the hands and minds of certain movements, religion appears as the 'dynamite of the people'" (Assmann 2008: 5).

I want to draw out some consequences of Assmann's line of thinking that he does not explicitly develop. Certainly beginning with the eighteenth-century Enlightenment (especially the French Enlightenment) there has been a strong tradition that reason will (and ought to) triumph over religion and superstition – including any form of monotheism that claims to be based on revelation. (Some historians argue that the Radical Enlightenment really begins with Spinoza.) There is the more moderate approach of Kant, who acknowledges a proper domain of religion – but a religion within the bounds of reason. From this Enlightenment perspective there is the belief (or, more frequently, *the hope*) that with the triumph of reason there will also be the end of religious violence. There is no doubt that Freud himself, especially as his views are expressed in *The Future of an Illusion*, is squarely in this Enlightenment tradition – although he is more skeptical about the possibility of eliminating violent wars. From this Enlightenment orientation, the development from religious superstition to rational justification is what we mean by progress. Now although this grand narrative of progress has been criticized from a great variety of perspectives, we should not underestimate its survival power and the way in which it has shaped many areas of inquiry – including theories of modernization, development, and secularization. Until just a few decades ago secularization theories dominated the sociology of religion. These theories sometimes took a descriptive, predictive, or prescriptive form. Religions (including monotheistic religions) were presumably in the process of disappearing; will eventually disappear, or ought to disappear. But today secularization theories are in complete disarray. Religions – especially the world monotheistic religions – are not disappearing, although they are undergoing transformations. There is scarcely any serious thinker who now believes that they will disappear – although they are becoming much less significant in certain parts of the world. There is only a relatively small group of people who believe that religion *ought to* disappear from everyday life. Does it make any sense to speak about the mission of monotheistic religion today? Assmann clearly thinks so. I have already quoted him: "Only through a complete rejection of violence is monotheism able to fulfill its liberating mission of forming an alternative counterpower to the totalizing claims of the political" (Assmann 2008: 145). But here Assmann is *not* speaking as a historian of religions or a historian of the memory of revolutionary monotheism. His mnemohistory provides a very different view of history and modernity. Given his understanding of cultural latency, forgetting, and the return of the repressed, we must take seriously how the present (and the future) are haunted by the past. The belief that we will ever be completely over and done with those "monotheistic moments" wherein the severity of the Mosaic distinction erupts with renewed force is itself an illusion. And when these eruptions happen, then there is the all too real possibility that the potential violence of the Mosaic distinction turns into murderous physical violence. Assmann is certainly not predicting that this will happen; he is insisting only that it is a dangerous illusion to think that the day will come when a "rational society" will no longer have to be concerned with the eruption of monotheistic moments. Assmann's warning is that such violent eruptions are *always* possible. Consequently, we must be on our guard against their potentially devastating consequences.

Assmann rarely speaks about Islam because this is not his area of expertise, but he is certainly conscious of the rise of Islamic fundamentalism and some of the violent forms that it has taken. The Mosaic distinction "has stamped the Jewish as well as the Christian and Islamic soul with its psychohistorical consequences." All three monotheisms draw a sharp borderline.

> The sole difference lies in the fact that Judaism draws it to exclude itself, whereas other monotheisms draw it to exclude others. By worshiping the one true god, the Jews isolate themselves from the peoples, who are of no other further interest to them. Through their strict adherence to the laws, they cultivate a life-form in which this voluntary isolation finds symbolic expression. Christianity made it its mission to put an end to this self-imposed isolation and open itself to all peoples. Now everything and everyone is excluded that refuses to take up this invitation. Monotheism thereby became invasive, at the very least, and occasionally aggressive as well. The same holds true for Islam, which redefines the borderline in political terms and distinguishes, not just true and false, but likewise between subjugation and warfare (the dar al-Islam and dar al-Harb) in religion. In each case, monotheism defines itself with reference to an opposite that it excludes as paganism. (Assmann 2010: 119)

The point of this passage is not to make invidious comparisons among Judaism, Christianity, and Islam. On the contrary, Assmann draws our attention to what these three monotheisms share – defining themselves "with reference to an opposite that it excludes." With the revolutionary monotheism (dating back to Akhenaten) there emerges the real danger that religious violence turns into physical violence. Akhenaten initiates his new religion with an act of destruction – not just "symbolic" destruction, but the physical destruction of the traces of Egyptian polytheism. No god but God! This gesture is repeated over and over again in ever recurring "monotheistic moments." We can never, with complete confidence, rule out the cultural return of the repressed after long periods of latency. Any theory of modernity, secularization, or progressive enlightenment that forgets this is radically deficient.

I believe that it is because Assmann deeply understands this "dark side" of monotheism that he so strongly endorses Freud's thesis that *der Fortschritt in der Geistigkeit* is itself a central legacy of the Egyptian Moses' monotheism – a monotheism dedicated to truth and justice. This "progress" is certainly not inevitable; it is always under threat; it demands passionate commitment for its furtherance. Instead of opposing monotheism to Enlightenment, Assmann (like Freud) sees the two movements in close proximity. We might call this Assmann's "ambivalence thesis." I am using "ambivalence" in Freud's sense wherein affirmation and negation are *simultaneous and inseparable.*[32] On the one hand, religious violence is constitutive of the Mosaic distinction and can readily turn into physical violence. On the other hand, the legacy of the Mosaic distinction is also the progress in intellectuality/spirituality. In practical terms, this means that there is a constant task (what Kant called an *Aufgabe*) to oppose the actualization of this potential violence, to subject the Mosaic distinction to "incessant reflection and redefinition . . . if it is to remain, for us, the indispensable basis of an advance in humanity" (Assmann 2010: 120).

Assmann has taught us a profound lesson about religious violence, but not the one he explicitly affirms. Religious violence is, and will remain, a real propensity; it can all too easily turn into murder, rape, torture, and killing. This is why we must always be alert to this danger and oppose it. We must *affirm* and *deconstruct* the Mosaic distinction – a never-ending *Aufgabe*.

Chapter 6

Reflections on Nonviolence and Violence

I began this study with an analysis of Carl Schmitt's concept of the political. We should remember that two of his most famous and influential books that deal primarily with political issues were written long before he had any association with the Nazis. *Political Theology* was originally published in 1922, and *The Concept of the Political* was first published as an essay in 1927. Despite Schmitt's active complicity with the Nazis and his vulgar anti-Semitism, he certainly has been one of the most provocative and controversial political and legal thinkers of the twentieth century. Even if one sharply disagrees with him, he raises difficult issues concerning jurisprudence, constitutional theory, and the status of the law. One of the dominant reasons why many political thinkers from the right and the left have been attracted to Schmitt is because of his relentless criticism of liberalism. Crudely speaking, if one is convinced that everything that is wrong with the contemporary world can be traced back to the "pernicious" influence of liberalism (and neo-liberalism), then one may be tempted to champion Schmitt. Few thinkers can match Schmitt in his multi-dimensional attack on all varieties of liberalism, including political, legal, and economic liberalism. Furthermore, if one is convinced that a "realistic" approach to politics in the contemporary world must bracket or avoid any form of normative discourse, then Schmitt will be one's "hero."

The question that orients my discussion of Schmitt is what we learn from him about violence. Schmitt does not "glorify" violence, although he does "glorify" decisiveness. His famous friend/enemy distinction, which defines "the political," does not *by itself* sanction physical killing, but the concepts of friend and enemy "refer to the real possibility of physical killing"(Schmitt 1996a: 33). I have pursued the aporias in Schmitt's thinking about violence. Despite his explicit claims about the sharp distinction between "the moral" and "the political," and despite his disparagement of the appeal to norms, a substantive normative-moral orientation pervades his work. More strongly, his *condemnation* of liberal humanitarianism and the "dehumanization" of absolute enmity only makes sense from this normative-moral orientation – one that he never seeks fully to articulate or justify. What is worse is that although his "critique" presupposes this normative-moral orientation, he mocks and scorns the very idea of appealing to normative considerations in understanding "the political." One of the pernicious consequences of Schmitt's view of decision in politics – a consequence that is still so prevalent today in many thinkers – is his almost exclusive emphasis on the "event" of decision – decision that presumably springs out of nothingness. By so emphasizing (exaggerating) the *happening* of decision, Schmitt obscures the considerations that are relevant for making key political decisions. He fails to elaborate the complex issues involved in justifying practical political judgments that *inform* decision and action. Over and over again, Schmitt (and Schmittians) point out the gap between an appeal to norms and concrete decisions. But the *truth* that there is a gap between norm and decision, that there is always an element of risk in making a decision, and that concrete decisions cannot be "deduced" from norms and principles, is distorted into the *false* claim that norms and principles are basically irrelevant to making political decisions. For all its seductive attractiveness, this is ultimately a dangerous doctrine – whether advocated by right or left thinkers. Schmitt is insightful about how "limited enmity" has turned into "absolute enmity" in the twentieth century, and how limited war becomes total war. He shows how twentieth-century warfare (including guerilla warfare) has blurred the distinction between killing soldiers and killing innocent civilians. The goal of total war is no longer to *defeat an enemy* but to *annihilate* a *foe*. But Schmitt never analyzes how the Nazi regime – more than any other twentieth-century regime – *systematically* intensified the killing of innocent civilians and the elimination of its foes. In the final analysis, Schmitt does not provide us with the conceptual resources for condemning absolute enmity.

Even if we accept his analytical distinction between conventional, real, and absolute enmity, there is no basis in Schmitt for condemning any form of violence. Schmitt's talk about "dehumanization" turns out to be empty rhetoric. If we take his political theology with full seriousness, as Heinrich Meier does, and argue that this is the real basis of his judgments, it is still unclear what precisely the ground is for condemning absolute enmity and violence. When Schmitt claims that "the theoretician can do no more than verify concepts and call things by name" (Schmitt 2007: 95), this is really just a dodge to obscure and hide his normative-moral stance.

When we turn to Benjamin's very early essay "Critique of Violence," we are initially struck with both the similarities and the differences between Benjamin and Schmitt. Benjamin and Schmitt were approximate contemporaries – Schmitt was born in 1888, and Benjamin in 1892 – but their backgrounds could not have been more different. Schmitt was brought up in a conservative German Catholic environment in the provincial city of Plettenberg, Westphalia. He was trained as a lawyer and enlisted in the German army during the First World War. He was a leading jurisprudential thinker during the Weimar Republic. Benjamin came from a wealthy, assimilated cosmopolitan Jewish Berlin family and was sent to a progressive boarding school where he was influenced by the liberal educational reformer Gustav Wyneken. He broke with Wyneken in 1914 in response to a public lecture in which Wyneken praised the ethical experience that the outbreak of the war provided for the youth. Benjamin managed to stay out of the army. In the turmoil of Germany after its defeat, Schmitt and Benjamin shared a concern with the fragile state of the Weimar Republic, its unstable parliamentary government, and the constant eruption of violent events. "Critique of Violence" appeared *before* Schmitt's *Political Theology* (1922) and *The Concept of the Political* (1927). There was a brief correspondence between Benjamin and Schmitt. Schmitt read Benjamin's essay, and Benjamin was a close reader of Schmitt's early work. When Benjamin wrote his *Trauerspiel*, he discussed sovereign violence in the seventeenth century in relation to Schmitt's theory of sovereignty. One must be extremely wary of an anachronistic interpretation of the Schmitt–Benjamin connection. Both Benjamin and Schmitt had their doubts about parliamentary government. Schmitt might well have agreed with Benjamin when he wrote: "When the consciousness of the latent presence of violence in a legal institution disappears, the institution falls into decay. In our time, parliaments provide an example of this. They offer the familiar, woeful spectacle because they have not remained conscious of the revolutionary forces to which they owe their existence" (Benjamin 1996: 244). But the key text that inspired Benjamin's essay is Sorel's *Reflections on Violence*, and throughout his discussion of mythic violence and divine violence Benjamin seeks to illuminate revolutionary violence. Following Sorel, Benjamin claims that the aim of revolutionary violence is to overthrow state violence – what Sorel calls *la force*. Distinguishing the political general strike from the revolutionary proletarian strike, Benjamin declares that the first is violent, "the second, as a pure means, is nonviolent" (Benjamin 1996: 246). Why? Because the political strike reinforces state power, whereas the proletarian general strike seeks to abolish the state. I have argued that Benjamin's remarks about divine violence are so condensed and cryptic that they are open to the most extreme interpretations. These interpretations range from Marcuse's reading of Benjamin's essay as a revolutionary tract that shows the "historical necessity" of revolution, to those interpretations that claim that Benjamin's apocalyptic language licenses unrestrained violence. In the course of his essay, Benjamin speaks of different types of violence (*Gewalt*), although he doesn't offer a systematic classification. But he draws the major distinction between mythic and divine violence. "[T]he mythical manifestation of immediate violence shows itself fundamentally identical with all legal violence" (Benjamin 1996: 249). The destruction of mythical violence "becomes obligatory," and only divine violence can destroy this mythical violence. Divine violence is "in all respects" the antithesis of mythical violence. But what is divine violence? The readers of Benjamin's essay answer this question in diverse – and frequently contradictory – ways.

Although I have expressed doubts about whether Benjamin's text warrants the interpretations of Butler and Critchley, I want to consider some of their key claims, because they shed light on a more general question of the relation between nonviolence and violence. They both stress that Benjamin's critique of violence must be seen in the context of his remarks about nonviolence. And they both emphasize a passage that immediately follows Benjamin's introduction of the concept of divine violence. Benjamin raises the question whether pure or divine power "confers on men even lethal power against one another." He tells us that this cannot be conceded. "For the question 'May I kill?' meets its irreducible answer in the commandment 'Thou shalt not kill'" (Benjamin 1996: 250). We cannot deduce from this commandment a "condemnation of all violent killing of one person by another." The commandment exists "not as a criterion of judgment but rather as a guideline for the actions of persons or communities who have to wrestle with it in solitude and, in exceptional cases, to take on themselves the responsibility of ignoring it. Thus it was understood by Judaism, which expressively rejected the condemnation of killing in self-defense" (Benjamin 1996: 250). The commandment "Thou shalt not kill" is *not* to be understood as a *law* in the sense of either law-making or law-preserving violence. Drawing on Franz Rosenzweig's interpretation of the Jewish commandments, Butler suggests that "the commandment is emphatically not an instance of legal violence or coercion. . . . Rather, the commandment establishes a point of view on law that leads to the destruction of law as coercively binding. . . . The commandment 'Thou shalt not kill' cannot be a law on the order of laws that are destroyed. It must be a kind of violence that opposes violence" (Butler 2006: 209–11). But if the commandment is *not* a law in the same sense of law-making or law-preserving violence, then how are we to understand it? For Butler and Critchley the commandment is *not* to be assimilated to a type of categorical imperative that allows of no exceptions. It is a guideline (*Richtschnur*) for action – one that ought to be followed, but such that there can be exceptions.[1] Although there is a powerful mandate not to kill, there may be exceptional circumstances in which killing is permissible. The classic example in Judaism is the permissibility to kill in self-defense.[2] There can be no general law or universal principle that enables us to decide in advance what really counts as an exceptional case. Persons and communities have to wrestle with this issue in solitude. If they *ignore* the commandment, if they decide that they are confronting an exceptional case in which killing may be necessary, then they must "take on themselves the responsibility of ignoring it." According to the Butler/Critchley interpretation, divine violence turns out to be a type of nonviolence because the divine imperative is not to kill, even though it doesn't rule out physical violence in "exceptional circumstances."

Regardless of whether or not the Butler/Critchley position is an accurate interpretation of what Benjamin means by "divine violence," they are both committed to nonviolence as an overriding *ethical* demand – what Critchley calls an infinite ethical demand. This demand is compatible with the claim that there are exceptions such that violence is not only permissible but can be *justi-fied*. A basic ethical commitment to nonviolence that recognizes that there can be exceptions is an attractive position. There have been historical circumstances when armed struggle is justified. A para-digmatic example was fighting Hitler and the Nazis in the Second World War. And Fanon's *The Wretched of the Earth* can be read as a justification of armed struggle to destroy the rigidity and entrench-ment of the colonial system in Africa. But, of course, such a view of the interplay of nonviolence and violence raises many difficult issues. For example, returning to Benjamin, how is one to understand the authority of the commandment "Thou shalt not kill," especially if one does not believe that the commandments were handed down by God to Moses. And even if one grants that there is no universal rule or law to decide what counts as an "exceptional circumstance," what kinds of considerations are relevant for deciding that we are confronting an exceptional case that justifies violent killing? Even if it is granted that one must struggle with this decision in "solitude," how is this to be done? Are there any guidelines for evaluating the pros and cons for when violence is justified? Benjamin's "Critique of Violence" leaves too many issues open – even in light of the Butler/Critchley interpretation of divine violence as a form of nonviolence.

Hannah Arendt takes up issues that are unresolved in Benjamin's text. After considering Arendt's distinctions between power and vio-lence, I want to explore how Fanon complements Arendt's analysis. Arendt and Benjamin were very close personal friends during the years they spent in Paris after fleeing Germany in 1933. Benjamin encouraged Arendt to complete her unfinished book on Rahel Varnhagen, which she had begun in Germany. When Arendt finally escaped from Hitler's Europe and sailed to New York in 1941, she was carrying a copy of Benjamin's now famous "Theses on the Philosophy of History." To escape from Europe to America, Arendt and her husband left France illegally and crossed into Spain in the same vicinity where Benjamin had been turned back by French officials – and where he subsequently committed suicide. Arendt was respon-sible for introducing the writings of Benjamin to an American public when she published *Illuminations* in 1968 – a collection of some of his most famous essays. Her introduction to this collection – a por-trait of Benjamin as a person and as a writer – is one of the most beautiful and loving essays that she wrote. She did not, however, include Benjamin's "Critique of Violence" in *Illuminations*. The essay appeared in a second collection of Benjamin essays, *Reflections*, published after Arendt's death. Arendt never discusses or even mentions Benjamin's "Critique of Violence" in any of her published writings. To the best of my knowledge, she never even refers to it in any of her unpublished manuscripts or private correspondence. When she reviews the discussions of violence in her essay *On Violence*, she refers to Sorel, Sartre, Pareto, and Fanon (among others), but there is no mention of Benjamin. Nor does she ever explicitly discuss "mythical violence" or "divine violence." Furthermore, her views on law are far more varied and nuanced than anything suggested in Benjamin's essay.[3] What are we to make of this complete silence? I suspect that she considered Benjamin's early essay something of an intellectual embarrassment, not a true measure of Benjamin's literary genius.[4]

If we return to the theme of the relation of nonviolence to violence discussed briefly in "Critique on Violence," and which is stressed by Butler and Critchley, then Arendt's analysis of power, violence, and the revolutionary spirit is highly relevant. Before turning to this, I want to comment on the relation between Schmitt and Arendt. Arendt refers to Carl Schmitt in the *Origins of Totalitarianism*, but she doesn't mention him in *The Human Condition*, *On Revolution*, or in her essay *On Violence*. She was, however, a close reader of Schmitt. Many of his books – some extensively annotated – are in her library. It has become fashionable to draw comparisons between Schmitt and Arendt. Each sought to provide a distinctive characterization of what Schmitt calls "the political" and Arendt calls "politics." They both sharply distinguish between politics and morality. Some commentators emphasize the "political theological" references to miracles in both thinkers. Frankly, I think that these comparisons are superficial, because the spirit that breathes through Arendt's writings is antithetical to Schmitt. It is far more accurate to read Arendt as opposing and refuting Schmitt's characterization of "the political" and rejecting his conception of sovereignty. Schmitt scorns the political significance of debate and persuasion. But for Arendt this is the heart of politics (or what politics ought to be). Arendt's conception of politics, and especially her analysis of the revolutionary spirit, excludes any appeal to sovereign will and decision. Arendt relentlessly criticized the idea of sovereignty – the fundamental idea of Schmitt's political theology. Schmitt has little patience with the very idea of pluralism and plurality. Plurality, for Arendt, is not only the *condition sine qua non*, but the *conditio per quam* of all political life.[5] Politics for Arendt does not require any appeal to transcendence to explain or justify it. The polis is an *artificial* creation of a plurality of human beings who confront each other as political equals.[6]

I characterized Arendt's political thinking as an "exaggerated" thinking. She is acutely aware that in the "real world" power and violence are rarely separated from each other. (Nor does she underestimate the pervasiveness of the conception of power as "power over" – a conception of power that is intimately related to violence.) "Power and violence, though they are distinct phenomena, usually appear together" (Arendt 1970: 52). Nevertheless, they are antithetical concepts. Power is *essentially* nonviolent. It relies on opinion and requires persuasion and debate among human beings. Power for Arendt is not *power over*; it is *empowerment* that comes into existence when human beings act together. Violence – in contrast to power – is instrumental. Violence employs implements (including highly sophisticated deadly weapons) to enhance individual strength. And violent instruments can become a substitute for strength. Arendt's critique of means–end rationality is more nuanced than Benjamin's. She recognizes that means–end rationality is essential for fabrication – one of the three types of human activity. The making of artificial things – whether useful objects or works of art – involves a type of violence. But Arendt criticizes what happens when a *fabricating mentality* infects politics; it destroys politics. Revolutions are not made; they are not fabricated. Furthermore, power is not an isolated concept for Arendt. It is part of an interlocking network of concepts that include natality, spontaneity, public space, isonomy, and public tangible freedom. Collectively this network of concepts textures Arendt's vision of politics.

The language of "normativity" is not part of Arendt's vocabulary. Her project is one of retrieval – like Shakespeare's pearl diver. She seeks to make us aware of a "treasure" that is in danger of being lost through forgetfulness. Her phenomenological account of the space of appearances, in which a plurality of individuals share a common world and encounter each other as equals, retrieves the meaning of politics. Perhaps it is more accurate to say that she wants to recover those "privileged moments" of political freedom that can still serve as a standard and criterion for judging politics. In this sense, her phenomenological thick description of politics and power has a *normative* force. This becomes especially clear in her analysis of the modern revolutionary spirit that has its origins in the eighteenth century and has reappeared over and over again in the most diverse historical constellations. In *On Revolution* she presents a sustained argument to show that the American Revolution was essentially nonviolent. Of course, it was "preceded" by a war of liberation that involved violence. But liberation from the "tyranny" of British rule is not to be identified or confused with the aim of revolution – the creation of tangible public freedom. Her detailed examination of the American Revolution (and the contrast she draws with the French Revolution) is intended to refute the legendary claim that all beginnings and all revolutions are based on violence – "that no beginning could be made without using violence" (Arendt 1977: 20). The deliberation, argumentation, compromises, and debates that went into the writing and ratification of the Constitution signify the creation of a new revolutionary order – *novus ordo saecalorum*. And this acting together was itself based on a long tradition of covenants, compacts, and mutual promising. The true legacy of the revolutionary spirit is the council system that spontaneously arises in every genuine revolution.

> The councils, obviously, were spaces of freedom. As such, they invariably refused to regard themselves as temporary organs of revolution and, on the contrary, made all attempts at establishing themselves as permanent organs of government. Far from wishing to make the revolution permanent, their explicitly expressed goal was "to lay the foundations of a republic acclaimed in all its consequences, the only government which will close forever the era of invasions and civil war"; no paradise on earth, no classless society, no dream of socialist or communist fraternity, but the establishment of "the true Republic" was the "reward" hoped for as the end of the struggle. (Arendt 1977: 264)

This hope has been disappointed over and over again; the councils have been crushed by "professional revolutionaries." But Arendt does not subscribe to the thesis that "the establishment of 'the true Republic'" is a utopian ideal that must *necessarily* be defeated.[7]

Arendt, as I have indicated, never commented on Benjamin's "Critique of Violence," but if she had, she might have pointed out that nonviolence is not simply a matter of resolving private conflicts or diplomacy, but is what is most distinctive about the privileged moments of politics. She certainly did not think that all law involves or is based upon violence. She might have criticized Benjamin's appeal to divine violence. *Any* sort of violence that opposes violence perpetuates the cycle of violence. Violence is not creative – it is only destructive. For Benjamin divine violence is "law destroying."

But violence can never *create* power or achieve public freedom. The alternative she proposes to *sovereign* states is a federation of republican councils.[8] Arendt shows the limits of violence and why it must not be confused with nonviolent power. Violence by itself does not achieve power or public freedom. Violence stands ready to destroy this freedom. The concrete actualization of public freedom – the true aim of the revolutionary spirit – is one of the highest expressions of our humanity.

Despite the sharpness with which Arendt distinguishes the concepts of power and violence, there is a serious lacuna in her analysis. She admits that in certain exceptional circumstances violence may be justified, but she doesn't explore in any depth what these circumstances are and what it means to justify violence. I want to suggest an interpretation of Fanon's *The Wretched of the Earth* that supplements Arendt's reflections on violence. Although Fanon never mentions Arendt and was probably unaware of her existence, Arendt was definitely aware of Fanon and his widespread influence. One of the motivations for writing *On Violence* was the popularity that *The Wretched of the Earth* was enjoying among students throughout the world. *On Violence* has frequently been read as a critique of Fanon's "glorification of violence." Arendt (directly and indirectly) makes this accusation several times in the course of her essay. But in a footnote explaining why she discusses *The Wretched of the Earth*, she writes: "I am using this work because of its great influence on the present student generation. Fanon himself, however, is more doubtful about violence than his admirers. It seems that only the book's first chapter, Concerning Violence, has been widely read. Fanon knows of the 'unmixed and total brutality [which], if not immediately combated, invariably leads to the defeat of the movement within a few weeks'" (Arendt 1972: 116).[9]

Although Arendt quotes this critical passage, she does not explore its significance. On the contrary, when she mentions and quotes Fanon in the rest of her essay, she considers him to be one of the "glorifiers" of violence who confuses power and violence.[10] She even ridicules those passages in which Fanon revives "thoughts and emotions from which Marx had hoped to liberate the revolution once and for all" (122). Fanon, she declares, like Sorel and Pareto, is motivated by a deep hatred of bourgeois society. In the collective violence that Fanon celebrates, "its most dangerously attractive features come to the fore" (164).

It is perfectly true that in military as well as revolutionary action "individualism is the first [value] to disappear"; in its stead, we find a kind of group coherence which is more intensely felt and proves to be much stronger, though less lasting than all the varieties of friendship, civil or private. To be sure, in all illegal enterprises, criminal or political, the group, for the sake of its own safety, will require "that each individual perform an irrevocable action" in order to burn his bridges to respectable society before he is admitted into the community of violence. (Arendt 1972: 164)[11]

Much of "the present glorification of violence is caused by severe frustration of the faculty of action in the modern world" (180). She scorns the idea of "creative madness" in violent action, and mocks the very idea of the "Third World." "The Third World is not a reality but an ideology" (123).

Consequently, it certainly appears that the views of Arendt and Fanon are antithetical – and that if we accept Arendt's analysis of power and violence, then we have a strong, and perhaps definitive, refutation of Fanon. Yet, when we look more closely, things do not turn out to be quite so straightforward. Their respective analyses are not as incompatible as they may initially appear. They each provide a corrective to the deficiencies of the other's position. I do not want to "domesticate" Fanon's provocative rhetoric or to soften Arendt's criticism of "revolutionary violence." But by exploring their respective strengths and weaknesses, we can come to a better understanding of the complex dialectic of violence and nonviolent power.

Let me begin by citing some passages from Arendt that might have been written by Fanon. Fanon stresses the significance of the initial spontaneous rage and violence of the colonized, who have been abused and dehumanized by the colonists. In her discussion of rage and violence, Arendt writes:

> That violence often springs from rage is a commonplace, and rage can indeed be irrational and pathological, but so can every other human affect. . . . Only where there is reason to suspect that conditions could be changed and are not does rage arises. Only when our sense of justice is offended do we react with rage, and this reaction by no means necessarily reflects personal injury, as is demonstrated by the whole history of revolution. (Arendt 1972: 160)

Fanon might have written this passage, because Arendt describes the rage that Fanon describes when he writes about the spontaneous reactions of the colonized. Arendt makes a further point that is central to Fanon's argument.

> To resort to violence when confronted with outrageous events is enor-
> mously tempting because of its inherent immediacy and swiftness.
> To act with *deliberate speed* goes against the grain of rage and violence,
> but this does not make them irrational. On the contrary, in private as
> well as public life there are situations in which the very swiftness of a
> violent act may be the only appropriate remedy. . . . The point is that
> under certain circumstances violence – acting without argument or
> speech and without counting the consequences – is the only way to set
> the scales of justice right again. . . . In this sense, rage and the violence
> that sometimes – not always – goes with it belong among the "natural"
> human emotions, and to cure man of them would mean nothing less
> than to dehumanize or emasculate him. (Arendt 1972: 160–1)[12]

Fanon would certainly agree that to try to cure human beings of these "natural" emotions would be to dehumanize them.[13] Arendt was no pacifist. She admired Gandhi and his achievements in employing nonviolent strategies. But she also says: "In a head-on clash between violence and power, the outcome is hardly in doubt. If Gandhi's enormously powerful and successful strategy of nonviolent resistance had met with a different enemy – Stalin's Russia, Hitler's Germany, even prewar Japan, instead of England – the outcome would not have been decolonization, but massacre and submission" (Arendt 1970: 53).[14] Fanon argues that pacifist strategies (like Gandhi's) had no chance of success in African colonial societies – especially Algeria. The French were determined to use any and every means possible to keep Algeria a French colony.[15] The several attempts by Algerians to be "reasonable" succeeded only in reinforcing the colonial system. A key thesis of *The Wretched of the Earth* is that a colonial system (at least in Africa), when analyzed, shows that only armed resistance can destroy it.

Fanon might even turn Arendt's distinction between power and violence against her. In *On Violence* Arendt refers to the US involvement in the Vietnam War: "And as for actual warfare, we have seen in Vietnam how an enormous superiority in the means of violence can become helpless if confronted with an ill-equipped but well-organized opponent who is much more powerful. This lesson, to be sure, was there to be learned from the history of guerilla warfare, which is at least as old as the defeat in Spain of Napoleon's still unvanquished army" (Arendt 1970: 51). Fanon argues that the Algerian guerilla war teaches the same lesson – how the *power* of Algerian people defeated the French despite the latter's "enormous superiority in the means of violence." The events that followed Fanon's death are further confirmation of the triumph of power over violence. In the Battle of Algiers, the French succeeded in destroying the FLN in the Casbah. But this military success only furthered the power of the Algerians to achieve independence.

There are many more passages in Arendt that reveal a striking similarity with Fanon, but I do not want to limit myself to these comparisons. Rather, I want to show how the structures of their overall arguments complement each other. Although Arendt says that in some circumstances violence can be justified, her remarks about this are all too sketchy. The justification of violence "loses its plausibility the farther its intended end recedes into the future. No one questions the use of violence in self-defense, because the danger is not only clear but also present, and the end justifying the means is immediate" (Arendt 1970: 52).

Suppose we juxtapose her remarks about the justification of violence with the distinction she draws between liberty and freedom. If liberty is a *necessary* condition for public freedom, then the fight for liberty (which involves violence) can be justified – at least for those who seek to achieve freedom. Liberty is not limited to liberty from hunger or from being overburdened by the labor required to survive. It also includes liberty from *oppressors* – governments, tyrants, totalitarian regimes, and colonizers who seek to destroy the power of the oppressed. If we accept Arendt's claim that the aim of revolution is public freedom, then we must recognize that revolutions are "preceded" by wars of liberation. The American Revolution, Arendt's favored instance of a modern revolution, was preceded by a war of liberation, which like all wars involved violence.

The Wretched of the Earth presents a whole battery of arguments to demonstrate that liberation from the oppressive violent rule of the colonizers can be achieved only by armed struggle. This is the only way in which those who are oppressed could achieve the public freedom that Arendt celebrates – or at least have the possibility of achieving public freedom.

Arendt herself, in a very different historical situation, justified the violence of armed struggle. As we have seen, in the early 1940s, soon after her arrival in New York, Arendt called for the formation of an international Jewish army to fight Hitler and the Nazis.

Of course, there are vast differences between the fight against Hitler and the Nazis and the fight against the French in Algeria. But the *arguments* that each develops are strikingly similar. Both argue that armed resistance is necessary to fight the enemy. Once we see that both are arguing that there are concrete historical circumstances in which armed struggle – violence – is justified, then the issue between Arendt and Fanon appears in a very different light. Was Fanon right in his judgment that armed struggle was necessary for the Algerians to free themselves from the dehumanizing humiliation of colonial rule? On independent grounds, a strong case can be made that Fanon was essentially right.[16] There is overwhelming evidence that, without violent armed struggle, the French would never have granted independence to Algeria. Even after Fanon's death and the Évian Accords, the *pied-noirs* and their sympathizers in the French army sought to sabotage De Gaulle's decision to grant independence.

Still, it may be objected: Isn't Fanon guilty of "glorifying violence" and confusing power and violence? Fanon's rhetorical flourishes sound like an unrestrained celebration of violence. But remember that Fanon was primarily addressing his comrades – encouraging them to fight on and not to betray the liberation struggle. When he suggests that violence "cleanses" the people and creates a new humanity, many of Arendt's criticisms are apt. But we should distinguish the provocative performative role of *The Wretched* from the basic *argument* that runs through it. I have called this argument Fanon's critique of violence.

Violence is not the main concern of Fanon. Or rather, to the extent that he focuses on violence, it is the violence of the colonial system that he analyzes and damns. He describes how the violence of the colonists generates the violence of the colonized. *Fanon's main concern is liberation (libération)*. What he means by *libération* is close to what Arendt means by freedom. *Libération* is not the same as national independence. Independence of a nation is only the necessary condition for liberation. Most of *The Wretched of the Earth* deals with the obstacles that stand in the way of *libération* and with the ways in which the liberation struggle can be betrayed. This is why Fanon is so critical of a leadership that is out of touch with the people; a national bourgeoisie that he accuses of being useless and that adopts "the most despicable aspects of the colonial mentality" (Fanon 2004: 108). He condemns the "anti-racist racism" of the colonized. Fanon barely explains what he means by *libération*, but from the few hints he provides we can detect strong affinities with Arendt's horizontal conception of power and public freedom. Fanon stresses the need to educate the people, to involve them "in the management of public affairs" (124) and to encourage their active participation. A "genuine party" should be an "instrument in the hands of the people" (127). "For the people the party is not the authority but the organization whereby they, the people, exert their authority and will" (128). *Libération* requires the maximum active participation of the people. Fanon, like Arendt, wants to *break* the cycle of violence and counterviolence. Fanon doesn't spell out what the new society that he envisions might look like – the society that he hopes will emerge once the colonial system is destroyed, once the violence of the colonizers *and* the colonized is overcome. He speaks of a "new humanity" and a "new history of man."[17] In Arendtian terms, he is envisioning a society in which the power of the people triumphs. For both Arendt and Fanon the aim of revolution is freedom (*libération*).

Despite the ways in which Fanon and Arendt complement each other, I do not think their differences can be reconciled. But this tension is a productive one. Fanon is not concerned with developing a general argument about the relationship of power and violence. He shows concretely why armed struggle was necessary to overthrow the African colonial system. He is also acutely aware of the danger of perpetuating the cycle of violence. Initially, the colonized "dream" of replacing the colonists. But this is *not* the aim of the struggle. And even after a colonial country achieves independence, the greatest threat to *libération* comes from a colonized mentality that survives the colonial system. To the extent that this mentality prevails, the cycle of violence continues. Fanon's vision of *libération* begins to look very much like what Arendt calls the "revolutionary spirit" – the manifestation of "public freedom" where the people fully and actively participate.

Arendt, however, serves as a corrective to Fanon. She warns us about the excesses and severe limitations of violence. She warns against any suggestion that violence can achieve public tangible freedom. There is another respect in which Fanon and Arendt can illuminate each other. Even if it is conceded that there are circumstances in which violence can be justified, what constraints are there in determining when this is so? And who determines this? As we know from history – especially recent history – the abuse of attempts to "justify" violence is all too common. I do not think that there is any *abstract* way of answering the question of when violence can be justified. I am also skeptical about the appeal to guidelines. For this too can be (and has been) abused. Even the appeal to self-defense is not innocent. One of the arguments used by the United States administration for the military intervention in Iraq after 9/11 was that it was an "act of self-defense" against the potential use of weapons of mass destruction. The justification of violence will always depend on a judicious grasp of concrete circumstances and the specific reasons offered. Thus, for example, the justification in the 1940s for forming a Jewish army to fight Hitler was radically different from justifying armed struggles against colonizers. But a point that Arendt stresses in her understanding of politics can be helpful. Persuasion – rational persuasion in which there is an exchange and public testing of opinions – is what she takes to be the heart of politics. Consequently, when a risky decision is being contemplated to engage in violence, then what is required is serious engaged debate in which the pros and cons are set forth and evaluated by the participants involved. This is why the creation of public spaces and the empowerment that results from participants acting together is so vital. When there is no effective public, the "space" is left open for violent decision. From this perspective, we might say that what Fanon was doing in *The Wretched of the Earth* was developing a political argument for justifying armed struggle against the colonial system. A persuasive argument is not (and can never be) a knock-down demonstration; it always leaves open the possibility of it being challenged. This is not a deficiency of political argument, but rather an essential feature of serious political argument. There is no escape from the fallibility and uncertainty of political judgment. No matter how persuasive and solid a justification is provided, there are likely to be unforeseen consequences that may require revising our political judgments. Benjamin, we recall, tells us that there are exceptional cases where we may decide to ignore the commandment – the guideline – not to kill. Persons and communities must wrestle with this in "solitude" (*Einsamkeit*). They must take on themselves the responsibility for ignoring the commandment not to kill. But Arendt helps us to see that any such wrestling in solitude demands opening ourselves to public debate and political judgment. And she warns us that when politics (in her sense) and power wither, then there are no constraints on the appeal to, and employment of, violence.

When we turn to the work of Jan Assmann, initially we seem to be involved in a very different type of discourse. Schmitt, Benjamin, Arendt, and Fanon are all directly concerned with violence as it pertains to politics. But Assmann's analysis of revolutionary monotheism concerns the cultural memory of religious phenomena. He draws a sharp distinction between religious violence and political violence. The basic idea behind biblical monotheism, Assmann claims, is to erect a counter-power to the totality of politics and political violence. When he discusses the passages in the Hebrew Bible that deal with – or illustrate – violence, he argues that these are to be interpreted *symbolically*. They are primary warnings to the Hebrews not to slip back into idolatry.

In my chapter on Assmann, I have argued that Assmann's distinction between the religious violence of revolutionary monotheism and political violence is not convincing. There are too many passages in the Hebrew Bible where no distinction is made between religious and political violence. It is anachronistic to read these modern categories back into the Bible. This doesn't mean that revolutionary monotheism must necessarily lead to actual violence. This is why Assmann introduces the distinction between "propensities" and "consequences." Revolutionary monotheism is potentially violent, but this potential violence need not turn into actual political violence. Assmann makes an even stronger claim. The true "mission" of monotheism is to counter the totality claims of the political. I have argued that the logic of Assmann's argument about the cultural memory of revolutionary monotheism tells a different, darker story. As he reiterates over and over again, what is distinctive about revolutionary monotheism is its *exclusivity. No god but God!* There is but one true religion; all others are false. Once rigid exclusivity is introduced, then we have the *grounds* for justifying actual physical violence – the destruction of infidels. The history of exclusive monotheisms shows how, throughout the centuries, they have been used to justify physical violence against those who are taken to be infidels. Assmann himself declares that today religion can no longer be viewed as the "opium of the people"; it has become the "dynamite of the people" in some religious movements. I find it revealing that Assmann uses an expression that is so closely associated with physical killing – "dynamite."

Assmann, responding to his critics, now speaks about "monotheistic moments" that erupt in the course of history. Cultural memory is haunted by the *potential* violence – the return of the repressed – of the Mosaic distinction that can turn into physical violence. There is always the real possibility that these "monotheistic moments" erupt with new and harsh severity. Because this violent potential can *never* be finally put to rest, never finally overcome, we must be vigilant in opposing its dangerous consequences. We may agree with Freud (and Assmann) that monotheism has been a major source of *der Fortschritt in der Geistigkeit*, but the "price of monotheism" is the ever present danger of the eruption of real violence. That is why the Mosaic distinction must be at once affirmed and deconstructed.

I have also argued that Assmann's appropriation of the Freudian categories of latency and the return of the repressed in cultural memory has disruptive consequences for theories of modernity and progress. He is, in effect, challenging one of the most entrenched narratives of historical progress. This is the story that with the triumph of modernity and reason, not only will superstition and myth disappear, but there will also be the overcoming of political violence – the initiation of an era of perpetual peace. But it is an illusion to think that we can ever escape from the potential violence that is intrinsic to revolutionary monotheism. We must acknowledge the ever present danger of this potential violence and, at the same time, be alert to preventing this potential from turning into actual violence – physical killing. This is the practical consequence of Assmann's claim that both affirming and deconstructing the Mosaic distinction is a constant *Aufgabe*. Consequently, Assmann's study of the cultural memory of the Mosaic distinction and revolutionary monotheism is not limited to the discourse of religion. It has direct political consequences.

Finally I want to return to the general issue of the relation of violence and nonviolence. Speaking in my own voice, I want to address the lessons learned from the examination of these five thinkers. I will discuss three issues: (1) the endurance and protean quality of violence; (2) the limits of violence; (3) nonviolence, violence, and politics.

1.   *The endurance and protean quality of violence.* There are different types of violence and, depending on our analytical purposes, we can propose different schemas. For example, there is legal violence – the type of violence that Benjamin analyzes. There is structural violence – the type of violence that Fanon argues is intrinsic to the colonial system. His main objective is to explain how the colonial system functions – how it transforms an indigenous population into colonized subjects who are systematically and brutally dehumanized. There is symbolic violence, which is illustrated by the way in which Assmann interprets the violence in the Hebrew Bible. He argues

that the primary function of these passages is to warn against slipping back into paganism and idolatry. There is the distinctive form of totalitarian violence that Arendt describes that seeks to transform human nature and make human beings superfluous. This is what she calls radical evil. There are specific types of violence such as sexual and racial violence. My main concern throughout this study has been not with the classification of different types of violence, but rather with the ways in which these different types of violence easily turn into, or sanction, physical violence – bodily harm, torture, murder, and genocide. Throughout history violence has always been with us, and it continues to haunt us. Assmann has shown that no matter how much one stresses the universalistic legacy of monotheistic religions, one must also acknowledge that revolutionary monotheism is based on exclusion. There is one and only one God – one and only one true religion. Throughout history there have been eruptions of "monotheistic moments" when potential religious violence turns into actual violence. And cultural memory teaches us that "the past" is never simply past. Even after long periods of latency there can be a violent return of the repressed. To think that there is – or can be – some final enlightenment, some final way to put an end to violence, is an illusion. And it is a dangerous illusion because the true task (*Aufgabe*) of enlightenment is to be constantly vigilant in opposing or minimizing destructive forms of violence. Although I have been sharply critical of Schmitt for his failure to provide any adequate normative-moral framework for evaluating and limiting violence, he reminds us of how much of political history has focused on enmity. He graphically describes and warns us about how limited enmity turns into absolute enmity, where we don't seek to defeat an enemy but rather to annihilate a foe.

There is a protean quality about violence; it can take ever new forms. We cannot anticipate the ways in which violence will manifest itself in the course of history. Like Proteus, violence disguises and conceals itself. One of our most constant and difficult challenges is to become aware of new forms of violence, to understand their structure and dynamics, and to bring them to public self-consciousness. We can only seriously consider a proper response to violence when we analyze and understand it. For example, I have argued that this is what Fanon was doing in regard to colonial violence. There was a time when colonialism was not really seen and understood as violence, but rather as civilizing a backward native population. Exposing colonialism as a form of violence is not simply a matter of revealing overtly cruel practices, but requires becoming aware of how the complex system of colonialism works, how it institutes procedures that systematically humiliate and dehumanize an indigenous population.

Or we might focus on how Benjamin helps us to understand the ways in which state power manifests pernicious forms of legal violence. Normally we think of law and the rule of law as protecting citizens against gratuitous violence. But Benjamin helps us to see that there is a dark side of the rule of law – how law itself, especially in times of crisis, becomes an instrument of violence. Furthermore, Benjamin also teaches us how problematic it is to distinguish "legitimate" uses of violence from those that are "illegitimate." Derrida, in commenting on Benjamin, is insightful in exposing the illusion that there are (or can be) clear determinate criteria, rules, or principles, for distinguishing between acceptable and unacceptable violence.

Or consider a third example that I have discussed – Arendt's analysis of the violence of twentieth-century totalitarianism – especially Nazi totalitarianism. She seeks to comprehend what is distinctive about totalitarianism – what were the subterranean historical tendencies that crystallized into totalitarian regimes. She recognizes that many of the violent practices of these regimes were similar to those that have existed in the past and in other forms of government. There has been a long history of massacres, torture, and genocide. But she argues that with the event – the eruption of totalitarianism – a new form of violence emerged. The ultimate aim of this violence was to transform human beings – to make human beings into something less than human; to eliminate human plurality and spontaneity and to make human beings superfluous.

I have cited these examples to make a general point. We cannot anticipate how and when new forms of violence will emerge. Violence does not appear in the world "marked" as violence. Violence disguises itself. It presents itself as something innocent, necessary, justified, legitimate. This becomes especially alarming with the rapid development of new technological and robotic forms of warfare that have the effect of making violence almost invisible. So it is a complex and difficult task to expose violence, to clarify what sustains and perpetuates it, and what should be the response to violence. This is not just a theoretical task of comprehension, but a practical task. The task is to develop the concepts, the modes of description, and the types of analyses that enable us to perceive why a phenomenon that initially presents itself as neutral or acceptable is really a form of violence. But this intellectual work can be futile unless one also makes a serious attempt to educate and *motivate* the public to respond to the violent behavior.

It would be misleading to think that the problem of violence is restricted to the emergence of new varieties of violence. All too frequently we are blind to the violence that surrounds us. In some parts of the world there has been an increasing awareness and resistance to sexual violence, racial violence, violence against children, and violence against homosexuals. These are not new forms of violence, but in the past they have not been perceived as expressions of violence. The growing awareness and resistance to these forms of violence would never have been achieved had they not been exposed – showing how and why they have been ignored and concealed. But if there is to be an effective response to violence, there must be a change in a public that is motivated to take action. No one should underestimate how difficult this task can be, or how the attempts to limit and constrain violence are more often met with failure than with success.

2.   *The limits of violence.* Throughout history there has been a cycle – or what Benjamin calls an oscillation – between violence and counter-violence. This oscillation is portrayed dramatically in the Greek tragedies and has been played out over and over again in history. There is always the temptation to answer violence with violence. Arendt and Fanon are perceptive in recognizing the potential ethical and political significance of spontaneous immediate rage and violence. The rage of those who have been brutally victimized and humiliated can be irrational, but it can also be an expression of a personal or political sense of righteous indignation. Traditionally, resentment has been viewed as a negative emotion that needs to be overcome. But we should distinguish pathological forms of resentment from those that are elicited as a reaction to violent moral or political injury. To cure people of experiencing these "natural" emotions when they have been victimized is – as Arendt declares – to "dehumanize" them. But even if we acknowledge the function of spontaneous rage and violence, we need to make crucial discriminations. Without denying that individuals and groups experience the immediate emotional intensity of rage and violence, we must be wary of the temptation to celebrate and

glorify violence. Violence is not creative; it is essentially destructive. This is why Arendt is so sharp in condemning Sartre's claim that the "mad fury" and "irrepressible violence" of the victims of colonization "create" free men. I completely agree with her. But so does Fanon. Fanon is acutely aware of the limits of violence. He claims that the brutality of the colonial system provokes immediate spontaneous violence. Without this initial rage there would never be a revolutionary movement. But he knows full well that "mad fury" and "spontaneous violence" can quickly degenerate and destroy a revolutionary movement. This is why he places so much emphasis on a political leadership that listens and educates a people, and thereby transforms violence into a sustained armed struggle against colonialism. Spontaneous violence does *not* create free men. This irresponsible romanticism is self-defeating. It completely distorts the seriousness and temporality of the struggle for *libération*. Furthermore, Fanon is fully aware of the many threats to the success of a revolutionary movement. The most serious of these are not external; they are internal. He is skeptical about the role of native national parties and how national bourgeoisies are complicit with colonials. But most of all he is worried about the betrayal of the revolutionary movement after the achievement of national independence. The greatest danger is that a colonial mentality persists. New rulers use the rhetoric of *libération* but actually employ violence against their own people. Looking back over what has happened in many African countries in the fifty years since Fanon wrote *The Wretched of the Earth*, it is difficult to resist the conclusion that his anxieties and fears are more justified than his dreams and hopes for Third World *libération*.

There is a more general lesson to be learned from Fanon's own analysis of the failures of spontaneous violence. Whatever role violence and armed struggle may play in overthrowing repressive regimes, it is *never* sufficient to create what Fanon calls *libération* or what Arendt calls public freedom. Although I think that Arendt exaggerates the conceptual difference between liberty and freedom as well as between violence and power, she is making a vital point that must not be neglected. Violence can be a necessary and effective means to overthrow repressive regimes, dictators, and totalitarian rulers. But violence cannot create the type of power and the empowerment of a public that are required for the concrete manifestation of public freedom. This public tangible freedom requires human beings acting together, engaging in deliberation, forming and testing opinions, engaging in persuasion, not violent coercion. This is not a utopian ideal to be achieved in some remote unreal future. Nonviolent public freedom has been manifested in those privileged political moments that have arisen again and again in the most diverse historical conditions since the eighteenth century. This is what Arendt names "the revolutionary spirit." I also agree with Arendt that we should be suspicious of any overt or covert theory of historical necessity that claims that the bursting forth of the revolutionary spirit is either inevitable or impossible. Reckless optimism and reckless despair are two sides of the same coin. They are both articles of superstition. This is especially true when we are confronting violence. Perhaps what is even more important is that the very idea of public freedom – of nonviolent political power that arises when people act together – remains a critical standard for judging and evaluating current "political" practices. Arendt never succeeded in showing us how this revolutionary spirit and public freedom can be sustained and politically institutionalized. She was more successful in describing what Andreas Kalyvas calls "extraordinary" revolutionary politics rather than everyday ordinary politics. Phenomenologically, she captured the joy, the excitement, that emerges in those revolutionary situations in which there is the spontaneous creation of councils. But she left us with a paradox that still remains a theoretical and practical paradox for us – perhaps the most poignant and central paradox that confronts us today. The difficulty we confront today is how to keep alive the idea and the *practice* of nonviolent public tangible freedom in an increasingly globalized world where there is an enormous temptation to resort to violence.

3. *Nonviolence, violence, and politics.* There are strong arguments for a fundamental ethical and political commitment to nonviolence – although I have focused primarily on the politics of nonviolence. Most of the power that confronts us in the contemporary world is "power over." If we accept the "command-obedience" structure of power relationships as the hegemonic way of thinking about power, then it is difficult to resist C. Wright Mills's dictum that all politics is a struggle for power and the ultimate kind of power is violence. Even if we reject Arendt's categorical way of distinguishing violence and power, she enables us to grasp another way of understanding power. And it is not just a matter of conceiving of a different way of thinking

about power, but pointing to political and historical phenomena that are too frequently ignored or marginalized. She enables us to discern the ways in which people can be empowered – how power can grow and develop when human beings act together to oppose and overcome systematic violence. Without the emergence and growth of this type of power, no revolutionary movement or movement to achieve radical reform can be successful. The effectiveness of nonviolent power has been demonstrated by Gandhi in India, the civil rights movement in America, the Solidarity movement in Poland, as well as the nonviolent movements throughout Eastern Europe that resulted in the collapse of Communist regimes. Even in armed struggles, the growth of the power of the people can be more effective in confronting violence than military victories. In the Algerian war for independence the nonviolent general strike in Algiers was a decisive event in persuading the French that colonialism was a lost cause despite their military victories. I do not think it possible to predict when and where there will be an emergence and growth of this type of power – what events will catalyze such a movement. But when we carefully examine those nonviolent movements that have been successful in achieving empowerment of the people, we discover that there have always been those helping to prepare for it. Even in dark times, when opposing violence may seem hopeless, it is essential to keep alive the idea of what nonviolent power can achieve.

At the same time we have also to be aware of the limits of nonviolent power – how it can be undermined or crushed. So the question arises as to when and how violence can be justified. Even Arendt, who claims that power and violence are antithetical, acknowledges that there are circumstances in which violence can be justified. I have argued that one of the primary aims of Fanon's *The Wretched of the Earth* is to provide a justification of the necessity of armed resistance to colonial violence. And, of course, like all such justifications it is open to challenge and debate. I have also admitted that I am skeptical about the possibility of establishing universal principles or criteria that will enable us to decide when violence is (and is not) justified. Any general principle – even the appeal to self-defense – is open to abuse. But what, then, are the constraints on justifying violence?

I want to return for one final time to the passage in Benjamin's "Critique of Violence" that is crucial for both Judith Butler and Simon Critchley. After introducing divine violence as law-destroying, Benjamin raises the question "May I kill?" He immediately tells us that this question "meets its irreducible answer in the commandment 'Thou shalt not kill.'" The remark that follows is what is so intriguing and controversial. He tells us that the commandment precedes the deed and that no judgment can be derived from the commandment. "Those who base a condemnation of all violent killing of one person by another on the commandment are therefore mistaken. It exists not as a criterion of judgment, but as a guideline for actions of persons or communities who have to wrestle with it in solitude and, in exceptional cases, take upon themselves the responsibility for ignoring it" (Benjamin 1996: 250). Both Butler and Critchley interpret this commandment as an *ethical* demand that calls for an *ethical* response. One may refuse this ethical demand and take on the responsibility for this refusal. In their reading, this is why the commandment not to kill is only a guideline. More generally they understand an overarching commitment to nonviolence as an *ethical* demand that allows for the permissibility and the justification of violence in exceptional cases. I find the Butler/Critchley view unsatisfactory for several reasons. Although they stress that the commandment is an ethical demand calling for an ethical response, Benjamin's text doesn't say this. There is no mention of "ethical" (*Sittlich*) in this context. Their reading is one that makes it sound as if the decision to engage in violence is a personal existential decision. I don't want to deny that Benjamin's highly condensed elliptical style can invite such an interpretation (although we have also seen that others read Benjamin's text in a far more political manner). But, regardless of the interpretive issue, I think it is wrong and potentially dangerous to think of the permissibility or justification of violence in exceptional cases as an exclusively ethical issue that one wrestles with in solitude.

It essentially is (or ought to be) a public political issue in the Arendtian sense of politics. Considering the dangers of any justification of the use of violence and the ways in which such "justifications" have been – and continue to be – abused, the only viable constraint on such abuses is engaged public critical discussion in which there is vigorous debate about the pros and cons of any proposed justification. This is not a matter "to wrestle with in solitude" but demands opening oneself to sharing and evaluating conflicting opinions and arguments that address the concrete situation. Any justification of the use of violence is a matter of political judgment. There are no algorithms for making such judgments. Political judgment is always risky, but its proper exercise depends on keeping alive – or creating new – publics (local, national, and global) committed to debate and persuasion, publics that take account of the specific concrete circumstances, publics that are acutely aware of their own fallibility. When such publics are manipulated and distorted by outside interests, when engaged public debate dies or withers away, there is nothing left to prevent the triumph of violence.

Notes

Chapter 1   The Aporias of Carl Schmitt

1   In this essay I am not primarily concerned with discussing Schmitt's
    Nazi period or the significance of his anti-Semitism. For a discussion of
    these issues see Rüthers 1990, Koenen 1995, Gross 2000, Bendersky
    2005, and Mehring 2009.

2   Ironically, in 1987 Ellen Kennedy published an extremely controversial
    article arguing that there was a subterranean influence of Schmitt on
    the Frankfurt School. She singled out the "Schmittianism" of Habermas's
    early writings. She provoked fierce rebuttals by Martin Jay, Alfons
    Söllner, and Ulrich K. Preuss. More recently Schmitt has been used as
    a "weapon" to attack Habermas and the Kantian turn in political theory.
    For Kennedy's article and the rebuttals, see the special section on "Carl
    Schmitt and the Frankfurt School," *Telos*, 71:11 (Spring 1987).

3   For a full discussion of the "hidden dialogue" between Schmitt and
    Morgenthau see ch. 9 of Scheuerman 1999. Scheuerman also explores
    the influence of Schmitt on Joseph Schumpeter and Friedrich Hayek.

4   The English translation (as the translator George Schwab informs us)
    omits some material included in the 1932 German edition. Problems of
    interpreting *The Concept of the Political* become even more complex when
    we take into account Schmitt's own comments in the 1963 Foreword to
    the German edition where he voices his concern about taking his friend/
    enemy distinction as a slogan and claims that the nuances and complex-
    ity of his theory have been distorted. Although he never repudiated his
    original discussion, he also sought to clarify and supplement it in his
    Theory of the Partisan, which he subtitled *Intermediate Commentary on the
    Concept of the Political*.

5   It is clear from this and similar passages that Schmitt uses the adjective
    "political" to refer to phenomena that are normally called political (e.g.

political parties); but the nominative expression "the political" refers exclusively to the friend/enemy distinction.

6   Meier argues: "One of the most widespread errors in the literature on Schmitt is the supposition that Schmitt's concern is the defense of the 'autonomy of the political.' One could not possibly miss the thrust of Schmitt's conception of the political more fundamentally than this supposition does, and in particular it ignores the significance of the sentence *The political is the total*" (Meier 1998: 75, n. 24).

7   Meier and Scheuerman offer different explanations for this shift. Meier thinks it is related to Schmitt's political theology, whereas Scheuerman suggests that it is a response to the implicit critique of Schmitt by Hans Morgenthau. (See Meier 1998: 30–1 and Scheuerman 1999: 229.)

8   Schmitt notes that the famous expression of Clausewitz "is generally incorrectly cited." See Schmitt 1996a: 34, n. 14. For an illuminating discussion of the relation between Clausewitz and Schmitt, see Dodd 2009.

9   In *The Concept of the Political*, Schmitt does not systematically explain what groupings qualify as exemplifying "the political." He focuses primarily on nations and states although he acknowledges that the political can be manifested within a state or a nation.

10   Schmitt does not clarify the precise meaning of "existential" when he declares that the friend and enemy concepts are to be understood in their concrete and existential sense (*in ihren konkreten, existenziellen Sinn*). Herbert Marcuse points this out in his sharp critique of Schmitt's political existentialism. Consider his comments on the following statement by Schmitt: "There is no rational end, no norm however correct, no program however exemplary, no social ideal however beautiful, and no legitimacy or legality that could justify man's killing one another."

> It must be stressed right from the start that in political existentialism there is not even an attempt to define the "existential" conceptually. The only thing we have to go on in elucidating the intended meaning of the existential is the passage by Carl Schmitt cited above. There the existential appears essentially as a contrast to the "normative," i.e. as something that cannot be placed under any norm lying outside it. From this it follows that one absolutely cannot think, judge, or decide about an existential condition as a "nonpartisan third [party]." "The possibility of correct knowledge and understanding and therewith also competence to participate in speaking and to judge is given here only by existential partaking and participation." There is no fundamental or general criterion in existentialism for determining which facts and conditions are to be considered existential. (Marcuse 1968: 30–1)

11   In *Carl Schmitt and the Politics of Hostility, Violence and Terror*, Gabriella Slomp introduces the distinction between the *function* and the *essence* of "the political." Insofar as the friend/enemy principle describes the function of the political, "it simply makes explicit a basic assumption that

has always been implicit in western theorizing, namely that in order to provide security and protection a political entity must be able to detect an enemy." Schmitt's significant innovation, she tells us, is that the friend/enemy principle is meant to capture not only the function of the political but its essence. "Schmitt's break from the mainstream does not follow from his claim that distinguishing friends and enemies is what politics does, but from the claim that that is what politics is" (Slomp 2009: 7–8). If we accept this distinction between *function* and *essence*, then the question arises of what is Schmitt's justification for claiming that this is the *essence* of politics. Emphatic assertion is not the same as justification.

12 In the German text, Schmitt places pessimism and pessimistic in quotation marks: *"Pessimismus"* and *"pessimistische."* He does this in order to distinguish his use of the expression "pessimism" from the common understanding of it. The *American Heritage Dictionary* defines pessimism as "a tendency to stress the negative or unfavorable or to take the gloomiest possible view." This is *not* what Schmitt means. Rather, he wants to call attention to the "realism" of Hobbes, Machiavelli, and Fichte, insofar as they acknowledge "the reality or possibility of the distinction of friend and enemy" – the reality or possibility of political enmity.

13 In his "Notes on Carl Schmitt" (included in the 1996 English translation of *The Concept of the Political*) Leo Strauss restricts himself primarily to a discussion of the problems and aporias in Schmitt's text. Many of his critical points are useful for my own critique of Schmitt. Unlike Heinrich Meier, I am not appealing to Strauss to draw a sharp contrast between political theology and political philosophy.

14 The close meanings of "enemy" and "enmity" are even clearer in German: *Feind* and *Feindschaft.*

15 In his notorious 1938 book on Hobbes's *Leviathan* – sprinkled with deeply offensive anti-Semitic innuendoes – Schmitt emphasizes the role of reason in Hobbes's theory of the state: "But the more dangerously this asocial 'individualism' asserts itself, the stronger becomes the *rational necessity* for reaching a general peace. The difficult problem of fitting the rebellious and self-seeking man into a social commonwealth is finally solved, but only with the help of *human intelligence.*" "With admirable clarity in the seventeenth century, he [Hobbes] had thought through the idea of a commonwealth brought about by human reason" (Schmitt 1996a: 36, 37, emphasis added). See David Dyzenhaus's perceptive analysis of Schmitt's complex relation to Hobbes (Dyzenhaus 1997: 85–98).

The following passage illustrates Schmitt's admiration for Hobbes's *Leviathan*, his utter contempt for the era of liberal constitutionalism, which he virtually blames on the Jews, and his vicious anti-Semitism (with its sexual overtones).

Stahl-Jolson, in accordance with the line developed by his people [the Jews – RJB], used a deceitful manner to mask his motivations, which became all the more horrible the more desperate he became to be somebody other than he actually was. . . . But in the great historical continuum that leads from Spinoza by way of Moses Mendelssohn into the century of "constitutionalism," Stahl-Jolson did his work as a Jewish thinker – that is, he did his part in *castrating a leviathan that had been full of vitality*. (Schmitt 1996a: 70, emphasis added)

16 When discussing the counter-revolutionary philosophy of the state in *Political Theology*, Schmitt writes: "Every political idea in one way or another takes a position on the 'nature' of man and presupposes that he is either 'by nature good' or 'by nature evil'" (Schmitt 2007: 56).

17 Slomp claims that "the political does not coincide with enmity: the two concepts are not co-extensive. Indeed, for Schmitt, the Hobbesian position that viewed enmity and politics as mutually exclusive concepts is as objectionable as the opposite stance that takes politics and enmity to coincide" (Slomp 2009: 9). Slomp introduces the concept of "limited enmity" to clarify Schmitt's stance. Later, I will consider the rationale for this qualification.

18 If we trace liberalism back to Hobbes (as Strauss does), then liberalism is itself based on a pessimistic conception of man. This is one reason why Strauss claims that Schmitt doesn't get beyond the "horizon of liberalism" (Schmitt 1996a: 107).

19 The page numbers in this passage refer to the 1963 edition of *Der Begriff des Politischen*.

20 At times, Schmitt writes as if we are now living in an epoch when politics, in his demanding sense, no longer exists. This is because the core of the political idea, the exacting moral decision, is evaded.

21 The passage from *Political Theology* that Meier quotes occurs in the context of Schmitt's passionate discussion of Donoso Cortés. There is little doubt that Schmitt is endorsing Cortés's linkage of the theological, the moral, and the political. Consider Schmitt's phrasing: "Donoso Cortés always had in mind the final consequences of the dissolution of the family resting on the authority of the father, because *he saw that the moral vanished with the theological, the political idea with the moral, and all moral and political decisions are thus paralysed in a paradisiacal worldliness of immediate natural life and unproblematic concreteness*" (Schmitt 2005: 65, emphasis added). Meier claims that "Politics needs theology. . . . The theological is the *conditio sine qua non*" (Meier 1995: 54). And he adds:

The connection between political theories and theological dogmas of sin "is explained" in the new edition of 1933 "first in terms of the ontological-existential mentality that conforms to the essence of a theological, as well as political, line of thought. But then [the connection is explained] also in terms of kinship of these methodological intellectual presuppositions." In each case Schmitt is ultimately concerned not with instances of kinship, with parallels, or with analogies of structure, but solely with what constitutes the agreements between theology and politics. (Meier 1995: 55)

22 Schmitt traces the beginnings of the age of technology back to Hobbes's *Leviathan* and the seventeenth-century state. "The state that came into being in the seventeenth century and prevailed on the continent of Europe is in fact a product of men and differs from all earlier kinds of political units. It may even be regarded as the first product of the age of technology, the first modern mechanism in a grand style, as a *machina machinarum*. . . . With that state was created not only an essential intellectual or sociological precondition for the technical-industrial age that followed but also the typical, even the prototypical, work of the new technological era – the development of the state itself" (Schmitt 1996a: 34). Schmitt associates this "technical-industrial age" with modern humanistic liberalism. For an examination of Schmitt's critique of liberalism in the age of politics as technology, see McCormick 1997.

23 I use the expression "normative-moral" deliberately. The concept of norms has a broad significance and takes on different meanings in different contexts. We can speak of rational norms, social norms, legal norms, morals norms, etc. A common thread in these different uses is the appeal to implicit or explicit criteria of correctness and incorrectness, standards for what counts (and does not count) as a deviation or rejection of a norm. When Schmitt criticizes norms, he is frequently attacking the appeal to legal norms – or more specifically, the precise role that legal positivists assign to legal norms. But he does not distinguish between the several types of norms. When I use the expression "normative-moral" I am referring to those norms that are specially related to moral behavior and evaluation, where robust issues of right and wrong, good and bad, are the primary issue.

24 I have used Slomp's translation of this passage because the Ulmen translation of *Theory of the Partisan* does not mention "*Gestalt*." The German passage reads: "Der Feind is unsere eigene Frage als Gestalt. Wenn die eigene Gestalt eindeutig bestimmt ist, woher kommt dann die Doppelheit der Feind? Feind ist nicht etwas, was aus irgendeinem Grunde beseitigt und wegen seines Unwertes venichtet werden muss. Der Feind steht auf meiner eigen Ebene. Aus diesem Grunde muss ich mich mit ihm kämpfend auseinandersetzen, um das eigene Mass, die eigene Grenze, die eigene Gestalt zu gewinnen" (Schmitt 2006: 87–8).

25 I have followed Schmitt's use of masculine pronouns. Derrida notes that the Schmittian individual and the Schmittian political group are *aggressively* masculine:

> Not a woman in sight. An inhabited desert, to be sure, an absolutely full absolute desert, some might even say a desert teeming with people. Yes, but men, men and more men, over centuries of war, and costumes, hats,

uniforms, soutanes, warriors, colonels, generals, partisans, strategists, politicians, professors, political theoreticians, theologians. In vain would you look for a figure of a woman, a feminine silhouette, and the slightest allusion to sexual difference.

At any rate, this seems to be the case in the texts that deal with the political as such (*The Concept of the Political* and the *Theory of the Partisan*). (Derrida 1997: 155–6)

26 Schmitt claims that, according to De Maistre, sovereignty essentially means decision and that "any government is good once it is established." The reason why decision is so valuable is "precisely because, as far as the most essential issues are concerned, *making a decision is more important than how a decision is made*" (Schmitt 2005: 55–6, emphasis added). Although he attributes this view to De Maistre, Schmitt appears to hold the same view. Indeed, this helps to explain why (at least initially) Schmitt was so enthusiastic about Hitler's decisiveness.

27 See Jacques Derrida's discussion of the enemy in the figure of the "brother" in Derrida 1997: 161–7.

28 The story of Cain and Abel doesn't "fit" Schmitt's account of the friend/ enemy distinction for another reason. The Lord not only curses Cain and compels him to be a "wanderer," he also promises to protect Cain against those who threaten to slay him. The mark of Cain is a mark of the Lord's protection. "And the Lord said unto him, 'Therefore whoever kills Cain shall suffer sevenfold vengeance.' And the Lord set a mark upon Cain so that whoever found him would not slay him" (Gen. 4:15).

Commenting on Schmitt's interpretation of the story of Cain and Abel, Heinrich Meier writes: "When Schmitt calls Cain's fratricide to mind, he reminds us that the enemy who is my brother is bound to me by a common link that transcends all human recognition: the enemy becomes a *just enemy* by means of my recognition, but he is my brother by virtue of his and my being, thanks to a destiny of which we are not master" (Meier 1998: 56).

29 During his Nazi years, Schmitt defended the *right* of the Führer to murder in "exceptional circumstances." Shortly after Hitler purged Röhm and the SA, Schmitt wrote an article entitled "The Führer Protects the Law." Bendersky notes that Schmitt argues that "the Führer had the right, in moments of extreme danger to the nation, to act as the supreme judge, distinguish friend from enemy, and take appropriate measures" (Bendersky 1983: 216). The Führer has the *right* to decide who the enemy is and who is to be killed. And the Führer has the *right* to decide what counts as "extreme danger to the nation." Whatever Schmitt's motivation for writing this article, it is a perverse justification for the *right* to murder – one that is unfortunately still used today.

30 I have used Slomp's textual sorting out of the three different types of enemy and enmity in the following discussion, but I do not agree with her interpretation of this triad of enmity. She doesn't explain why one

ought to favor "limited enmity." See her chapter "Hostility: Historical and Conceptual Forms" in Slomp 2009: 79–91.

31   A number of historians have criticized the historical accuracy of Schmitt's idealized account of the character of war after the Westphalia Treaty. (See Slomp 2009: 81.) Slomp gives a lucid summary of the meaning of conventional enmity (hostility): "[C]onventional hostility implies limited and regulated enmity: its limitation is imposed by the classical distinctions assumed by *jus publicum europaeum* between war and peace, criminal and enemy, civilian and combatant. The protagonist of conventional enmity is the nation-state. The circumstances under which it materializes are inter-state wars. Schmitt claims that the practice of conventional enmity was dominant in Europe from the Westphalia treaty of 1649 to the First World War" (Slomp 2009: 82).

32   Slomp notes: "Whilst blaming the just war tradition, Marxism, Leninism and Liberalism for the revival of absolute enmity, Schmitt never acknowledges that the most striking carrier of absolute enmity in the twentieth century was Nazism. In the Foreword [to *The Concept of the Political*] of 1963, Schmitt does list 'race' as a type of abstraction that, like class, can provide the foundation for abstract absolute hostility, and yet he makes no comment about Nazism" (Slomp 2009: 88).

33   For further discussion of the distinction between enemy and foe see Ulmen 1987 and Schwab 1987.

34   According to the *Oxford English Dictionary*, the word *foe* was frequently used as a name for the Devil.

35   To see how vividly Schmitt anticipated current developments, consider the following passage: "The partisan also participates in the development, in the progress of modern technology and its science. The old partisan, who wanted to take his pitchfork in hand after the 1813 Prussian *Landsturm* edict, today appears comical. The modern partisan fights with automatic pistols, hand grenades, plastic bombs, and perhaps soon also with tactical atomic weapons. He is motorized, and linked to an information network with clandestine transmitters and radar gadgetry" (Schmitt 2007: 76).

36   For an extremely perceptive interpretation and development of Schmitt's reflections on the new type of partisan – the sacrificial partisan – see Bargu 2010.

37   I have omitted Bargu's footnote references in this passage.

38   Derrida discusses these Hegelian overtones in Derrida 1997: 161–7.

39   G. L. Ulmen, the English translator of the *Theory of the Partisan*, quotes the following remark from Schmitt's post-Second World War notebooks. "*Historia in nuce* [history in a nutshell], Friend and Enemy. The friend is he who affirms and confirms me. The enemy is he who challenges me (Nuremburg 1947). Who can challenge me? Basically, only myself. The enemy is he who defines me. This means *in concreto*: only my brother can challenge me and only my brother can be my enemy" (Schmitt 2007: 85, n. 89).

40   Slomp claims that although Schmitt distinguishes three historical forms of enmity, his major conceptual distinction is between limited and unlimited enmity.

> Although Schmitt praises *jus publicum europaeum* for limiting enmity, he also holds the belief that a limitation of hostility based on the classical distinctions of combatant and noncombatant made sense during the Westphalian period (when wars were inter-state wars) but was not applicable to the twentieth century. Rather in times when most wars are civil or colonial or revolutionary, a new foundation for limiting enmity was required. Schmitt believed that a new *nomos* of the earth could limit hostility in a way that was more appropriate to the twentieth century. (Slomp 2009: 93)

But the question that demands an answer is: What is the *justification* for advocating such a limitation? This is a question that Schmitt neither honestly raises nor answers. It is an evasion to say that it is obvious that enmity ought to be limited because absolute enmity leads to unlimited violence and dehumanizes both friend and enemy. This only underscores the need to make fully explicit and justify the normative-moral standard for evaluating the different types of enemy and enmity.

Chapter 2   Walter Benjamin: Divine Violence?

1   The literal translation of the German title is "On the Critique of Violence." Many commentators have noted that the German word *Gewalt* can be translated in a variety of ways, including "violence," "force," "power," "authority." In his essay, Benjamin does not systematically distinguish among these various meanings of *Gewalt*. In light of the centrality of Sorel's *Réflexions sur la violence* for Benjamin, the most appropriate translation of *Gewalt* is "violence." Sorel, however, introduces a distinction between "*la violence prolétarienne*" and "*la force bourgeoise*" (Sorel 1908: 160). When Benjamin critiques law-making (*rechtsetzend*) and law-preserving (*rechtserhaltend*) *Gewalt*, he is critiquing what Sorel calls "*la force bourgeois*."

2   See Rogowski 1994 for the biographical details. See also the discussions by Beatrice Hanssen (2000) and Axel Honneth (2009) on the political and intellectual context of Benjamin's essay.

3   One of the few significant thinkers who took note of Benjamin's article was Carl Schmitt. Benjamin's article appeared before the publication of Schmitt's *Political Theology*.

4   The Suhrkamp edition included five German texts of Benjamin: "The Political Agenda of the Coming Philosophy," "A Critique of Violence," "Character and Destiny," "Principles of a Philosophy of History," and "A Political-Theological Fragment." Marcuse's German Afterword has

not been translated. My citations are from a provisional English translation by Charles Reitz. My page references are to the German text.
When Hannah Arendt published the first English collection of Benjamin
texts, *Illuminations*, in 1968, she did not include "Critique of Violence."
The English translation was published in *Reflections*, edited by Peter
Demetz, in 1978. This translation has been slightly modified in Benjamin
1996.

5 See also Negt 1968: 168–85.

6 Marcuse's "Afterword" is about the five essays he selected. Both the title
   of his collection and the above remarks make clear that Marcuse assigns
   central importance to "Critique of Violence."

7 Page numbers in the text refer to the English translation, *"Critique of
   Violence"* in Benjamin 1996.

8 See Honneth's discussion of how violence "in the precise sense" bears
   on *sittliche* issues: Honneth 2009: 95–6.

9 Judith Butler clarifies this mutual interdependence of law-making and
   law-preserving violence, thus:

> The fact that law can only be preserved by reiterating its binding character
> suggests that the law is "preserved" only by being asserted again and
> again as binding. In the end, it would seem, the model of law-instating
> violence, understood as fate, a declaration by fiat, is the mechanism by
> which law-preserving violence operates, as well. . . . For a law to be
> preserved is for its binding status to be reasserted. That reassertion binds
> the law again, and so repeats the founding act in a regulated way. (Butler
> 2006: 202)

10 Jacques Derrida, in his "deconstructive" reading of Benjamin's essay,
    emphasizes this mutual dependency of law-making and law-preserving
    violence. He writes:

> I shall propose the interpretation according to which the very violence of
> the foundation or position of the law (*Rechtsetzende Gewalt*) must envelop
> the violence of conservation (*Rechtserhaltende Gewalt*) and cannot break
> with it. It belongs to the structure of fundamental violence that it calls
> for the repetition of itself and founds what ought to be conserved,
> conservable, promised to heritage and tradition, to be shared . . . there is
> no more a pure foundation or a pure position of law, and so a pure
> founding violence, than there is a purely conservative violence. Position
> is already iterability, a call for self-conserving repetition. Conservation in
> its turn refounds, so that it can conserve what it claims to found. Thus
> there can be no rigorous operation between positioning and conservation.
> (Derrida 1990: 997)

He calls this a *"différantielle* contamination between the two." I agree
with Derrida's characterization of the interdependence of *Rechtsetzende*
and *Rechtserhaltende Gewalt*. But where I differ from Derrida is that he
thinks Benjamin is presupposing the possibility of a pure uncontaminated

relation between these two forms of legal violence, whereas I think Benjamin is fully aware of this "contamination." It is precisely the point he is emphasizing.

11   See his essays collected in Cover 1993, especially "Violence and the Word" and "Nomos and Narrative." Cover also notes how the violent side of law and its connection with legal interpretation has been ignored by prominent liberal legal theorists. See Cover 1993: 204, n. 2.

12   Benjamin also draws an analogy between the nonviolence of conflict resolution among private persons and among diplomats. "Fundamentally they must, entirely on the analogy of agreement between private persons to resolve conflicts case by case, in the names of their states, peacefully without contracts. . . . Accordingly, like the intercourse of private persons, that of diplomats has engendered its own forms and virtues, which were not always mere formalities, even though they have become so" (247).

13   In a parenthetical remark, Benjamin makes clear that the abortive German revolution was not a *genuine* revolutionary general strike but only a political general strike that reinforced the power of the state (246).

14   Although, as I have suggested above, Benjamin's text is marked by the immediate historical events of post-First World War Germany, we gain a deeper appreciation of the force of his essay when we realize that he, like many thinkers of his time, is reacting against the growing dominance of means–end rationality (*Zweckrationalität*) that has been shaping and infecting all aspects of modern life – including law, politics, culture, and language. He is searching for an alternative to this mode of thinking and acting. Viewed from this perspective, we can relate his project to the deep worries of Weber, Bloch, Lukács, Adorno (and the other Frankfurt thinkers), as well as Schmitt, Heidegger, Gadamer, and Arendt. Of course, the difference that makes a *real* difference among these thinkers is *precisely* how they conceive of this alternative.

15   Earlier (see n. 1), I indicated that although Benjamin praises Sorel, he deviates from Sorel. Benjamin uses the term *Gewalt* to refer to *both* "*la violence*" and "*la force*." But there is another significant departure from Sorel. Sorel defends the idea that the proletarian general strike is a myth. "[Men] who are participating in a great social movement always picture their coming action as a battle in which their cause is certain to triumph. These constructions . . . I propose to call myths." Sorel defends the choice of "myth" as a happy one, "because I thus put myself in a position to refuse any discussion whatever with the people who wish to submit the idea of a general strike to a detailed criticism, and who accumulate objections against its practical possibility" (Sorel 1908: 41, 43). What Sorel calls a "myth" is closer to what Benjamin calls "divine." For Benjamin divine violence and mythic violence are antithetical.

16   This is further evidence of how, for all his appropriation and praise for Sorel, Benjamin departs from Sorel in a fundamental way. For Sorel, the revolutionary general strike is a myth – indeed, a myth that resists analysis.

17   Marcuse, in his brief Afterword, does not claim to give a detailed reading of "Critique of Violence," but he does make clear how he reads this essay.

18   Although Butler proposes an interpretation of divine violence as non-violent, she warns her readers about its tentativeness.

> Is there a kind of violence that is not only waged against coercion, but is itself noncoercive and, in that sense if not some others, fundamentally nonviolent? He refers to such noncoercive violence as "bloodless," and this would seem to imply that it is not waged against human bodies and human lives. As we will see, it is not finally clear whether he can make good on this promise. If he could make good on it, he would espouse a violence that is destructive of coercion, shedding no blood in the process. This would constitute the paradoxical possibility of a nonviolent violence, and in what follows I hope to consider that possibility in Benjamin's essay. (Butler 2006: 201–2)

19   Axel Honneth claims that Benjamin must have been fully engaged with the two-volume *Der Zweck in Recht* (*The End in Law*) by Rudolf von Jhering published in a first edition in 1877 and a second edition in 1884. Many of Benjamin's legal distinctions seem to rely on this classic text. Jhering "anticipates the idea that would be decisive for Benjamin's purposes, that a domination-free alternative to the coercive institution of law can be found built into the voluntary altruism and intersubjectivity of 'ethical life'." Honneth suggests that the contrast that Jhering draws between egoism, which is connected with law, and the moral power of ethical life, reinforces "Benjamin's thoroughly negative conception of law. The idea that he took from Sorel that law is merely an instrumental institution for the maintenance of social order was further sharpened by its connection to the egoistic nature of human beings" (Honneth 2009: 103–4).

20   Many readers of Benjamin's essay (including Derrida and Habermas) are critical of the sharp contrast between mythic legal violence and divine violence, because Benjamin seems to call for the destruction of *all* law. Although Butler concedes this difficulty, she wants to leave open the possibility that Benjamin's critique is directed to the violence of *particular* legal systems.

> Quite abruptly toward the end of the essay, Benjamin resolves that the *destruction* of all legal violence becomes obligatory (249). But we do not understand whether this is a violence that is exercised by particular legal systems, or a violence that corresponds to law more generally. His discussion remains at a level of generality that leads the reader to assume

that it is law in general that poses a problem for him. When he writes that the destruction of all legal violence is obligatory, it would appear that he writes at a moment and in a certain context that remains undelineated within the essay. (Butler 2006: 209)

21   Butler suggests that Benjamin's essay "offers in a fragmented and potential form the possibility of countering a misconception of Jewish law that associates it with revenge, punitiveness, and the induction of guilt. Over and against the idea of coercive and guilt-inducing law, Benjamin invokes the commandment in mandating only that an individual struggle with the ethical edict communicated by the imperative. This is an imperative that does *not* dictate, but *leaves open* the modes of its applicability, the possibilities of its interpretation, including the conditions under which it can be refused" (Butler 2006: 204–5).

22   Benjamin does not restrict this wresting to individuals; he speaks of "persons and communities." "[The commandment] exists not as a criterion of judgment, but as a guideline for the actions of *persons or communities* who have to wrestle with it in solitude and, in exceptional cases, to take on themselves the responsibility of ignoring it" (250, emphasis added).

23   Butler also offers an illuminating interpretation of Benjamin's claim that the commandment is not based on the sanctity of what Benjamin calls "mere life." See her discussion of the contrast between "mere life" and "sacred transience" (Butler 2006: 216–17). See also Agamben's discussion of mere or bare life (*blosses Leben*) in Agamben 1998: 63.

24   Peg Birmingham, developing a different line of thought, argues that Hannah Arendt's "work on violence, especially her insistence on the distinction between violence and power, is an attempt to think further and to clarify Benjamin's understanding of divine violence" (Birmingham 2010: 8). Insofar as she identifies Arendt's concept of power (the antithesis of violence) with Benjamin's divine violence, she is, in effect, claiming that divine violence is nonviolent.

25   Even though Butler and Critchley, following Benjamin, speak about "exceptional cases," we must not identify what they are saying with Carl Schmitt's decisionism. Neither is speaking about a decision that arises out of nothingness. On the contrary, both emphasize that the commandment – the ethical guideline of nonviolence – is a demanding constraint on what we do. Both stress the importance of wrestling with this ethical imperative of nonviolence.

26   Both Butler and Critchley stress how the *individual* must struggle with the commandment in solitude. But Benjamin's wording is different. He speaks of the commandment "as a guideline for the actions of persons or *communities* who have to wrestle with it in solitude" (250, emphasis added). Furthermore, neither Butler nor Critchley deal directly with the theological (or non-theological) status of the commandment "Thou

shalt not kill." They do not clarify what *they* take to be the justification for this commandment – especially for a nonbeliever.

27 Critchley declares that Žižek is a "crypto-Bismarckian" authoritarian – "the only choice in politics is all or nothing: state power or no power" (Critchley 2012: 19).

28 Each chapter is preceded by a musical notation. The title of this chapter is *"Allegro*: Divine Violence," perhaps because of the rapidity of its rhythm.

29 Derrida sums up the paradox that he explores in three claims: "1. The deconstructibility of law (*droit*), of legality, legitimacy or legitimation (for example) makes deconstruction possible. 2. The undeconstructibility of justice also makes deconstruction possible, indeed is inseparable from it. 3. The result: deconstruction takes place in the interval that separates the undeconstructibility of justice from the deconstructibility of *droit* (authority, legitimacy, and so on)" (Derrida 1990: 945).

30 Throughout his essay, Derrida associates mythic violence with the Greek world and divine violence with Judaism.

31 Although Benjamin uses the word *Dasein*, which in the English text is translated as "existence," Derrida's reiterated use of German *Dasein* is clearly intended to suggest a comparison with Heidegger. Derrida explicitly says that Benjamin's "critique of vitalism or biologism" resembles Heidegger's critique (Derrida 1990: 1029).

32 For an alternative interpretation of this conditional, see La Capra 1990: 1074–5.

33 In Part I of "Force of Law," Derrida writes: "Deconstruction is generally practiced in two ways or two styles, although it most often grafts one on to the other. One takes on the demonstrative and apparently ahistorical allure of logico-formal paradoxes. The other, more historical or more anamnesic, seems to proceed through reading of texts, meticulous interpretations and genealogies. I will devote my attention to these two practices in turn" (Derrida 1990: 957–9).

34 See also the debates about Derrida's deconstructive interpretation in *Cardozo Law Review*, 13/4 (1991), and in Haverkamp 1994.

35 Rose takes this to be a criticism of Derrida, but I believe that Derrida would say that this is precisely his point. No *discourse* can exclude this possibility.

36 Honneth perceptively notes that Benjamin's frequent references to Sorel "should make it clear that what is at stake here is a kind of social protest whose violence is not a means to achieving an anticipated end but, rather, the expression of moral outrage. Benjamin seems to want to generalize this so far merely outlined thought in order to be able to bring a concept of violence into play that is free of all instrumental connotations" (Honneth 2009: 118).

37 This "nervousness" has been incisively noted by my student Patricia de Vries.

38   La Capra also criticizes Benjamin for postulating a divine violence that is "inaugural," foundational, as "beyond good and evil" (La Capra 2009: 98).
39   I have slightly altered the standard English translation. I have translated *erweisen* as "shows" rather than "furnishes proof."
40   Butler makes a similar point when she writes:

> I would suggest that the anarchism or destruction that Benjamin refers to here is to be understood neither as another kind of political state nor as an alternative to positive law. Rather, it constantly recurs as the condition of positive law and as its necessary limit. It does not portend an epoch yet to come, but underlies legal violence of all kinds, constituting the potential for destruction that underwrites every act by which the subject is bound to law. For Benjamin, violence outside positive law is figured as at once revolutionary and divine – it is, in his terms, pure, immediate, unalloyed. It borrows from the language in which Benjamin describes the general strike, the strike that brings an entire legal system to its knees. (Butler 2006: 214)

41   Benjamin anticipates his later concept of the *jetzzeit*. In the "Theses on the Philosophy of History," written shortly before his death, he says: "History is the object of a construction whose site forms not homogeneous, empty time, but time filled by the 'presence of the now' (*jetzzeit, nunc stans*)" (Arendt 1968b: 263).

Chapter 3   Hannah Arendt: On Violence and Power

1   *On Violence* is an expanded version of "Reflections on Violence," originally published in 1969 in the *Journal of International Affairs* and reprinted in the *New York Review of Books* (Feb. 17, 1969).
2   For a description of the panel discussion, the interventions of Sontag and Hayden, and Arendt's reactions to the student movement, see Young-Bruehl 1982: 412–21.
3   Her remarks about the Black Power movement occur early in her text, where she is providing the background of experiences that are the occasion for raising "the question of political violence in the political realm" (Arendt 1970: 35). But later, when she explicitly discusses racism, she writes: "Racism, as distinguished from race, is not a fact of life, but an ideology, and the deeds it leads to are not reflex actions, but deliberate acts based on pseudo-scientific theories. Violence in interracial struggle is always murderous, but it is not 'irrational'; it is the logical and rational consequence of racism, by which I do not mean some rather vague prejudices on either side, but an explicit ideological system" (Arendt 1970: 76).

4 See Shlomo Avineri's perceptive discussion of Marx's views on violence in Avineri 1968: 185–201.

5 For an illuminating comparison of Sartre's and Arendt's views on violence see Dodd 2009: 46–76.

6 Although recent events were the occasion for Arendt's essay, she was deeply concerned about how the technical development of violence in the twentieth century had reached a point where "no conceivable goal could conceivably correspond to their destructive potential." This is a point that she frequently emphasized. She makes this point emphatically in the opening of *On Violence*.

> These reflections were provoked by events and debates of the last few years as seen against the background of the twentieth century, which has become indeed, as Lenin predicted, a century of wars and revolutions, hence a century of violence which is currently believed to be their common denominator. There is, however, another factor in the present situation which, though predicted by nobody, is of at least equal importance. The technical development of the implements of violence has now reached the point where no political goal could conceivably correspond to their destructive potential or justify their actual use in armed conflict. (Arendt 1970: 3)

7 Arendt notes that Voltaire had already stated that power "consists in making others act as I choose" (Arendt 1970: 36).

8 For a fuller account of authority see her essay "What is Authority," in Arendt 2006.

9 Arendt frequently characterizes beginning and initiating as a "miracle." But one should be careful about drawing misleading inferences about political theology from the use of her talk about the "miracle" of beginnings. The following passage states clearly what she means:

> To ask in all seriousness what such a miracle might look like, and to dispel the suspicion that hoping for or, more accurately, counting on miracles is utterly foolish and frivolous, we first have to forget the role miracles have always played in faith and superstition – that is, in religions and pseudoreligions. In order to free ourselves from the prejudice that a miracle is solely a genuinely religious phenomenon by which something supernatural breaks into natural events or the natural course of human affairs, it might be useful to remind ourselves briefly that the entire framework of our physical existence – the existence of the earth, of organic life on earth, of the human species itself – rests upon a sort of miracle. For, from the standpoint of universal occurrences and the statistically calculable probabilities controlling them, the formation of the earth is an "infinite improbability." And the same holds for the genesis of organic life from the processes of inorganic nature, or the origin of the human species out of evolutionary processes of organic life. It is clear from these examples that whenever something new occurs, it bursts into the context of predictable processes as something unexpected, unpredictable,

and ultimately causally inexplicable – just like a miracle. In other words every new beginning is by nature a miracle when seen and experienced from the standpoint of the processes it necessarily interrupts. In this sense – that is, within the context of processes into which it bursts – the demonstrably real transcendence of each beginning corresponds to the religious transcendence of believing in miracles. (Arendt 2005: 111–12)

10 Many critics of Arendt (mistakenly) think that her conception of politics is based exclusively on her understanding of the Greek polis. But Arendt was fully aware of the limitations of the Greek polis. Indeed, in her "Introduction *into* Politics," she sharply distinguished the Greek and Roman conception of politics. She attributes to the Romans a politics of foreign policy, a politics based on treaties and alliances and a new conception of *lex*. She claims that "the idea of a political order beyond the borders of one's own nation or city, is solely of Roman origin. The Roman politicization of the space between peoples marks the beginning of the Western world – indeed, it first created the Western world as *world*" (Arendt 2005: 189).

11 The specter that haunts Arendt's reflections on violence and power is not only twentieth-century totalitarianism, but the new threat of total annihilation in the nuclear age. This unprecedented threat and the belief that politics now is both "dangerous" and "meaningless" urgently demands a rethinking of the meaning of violence and power. See the Introduction to *On Revolution* (Arendt 1977) and the opening of her "Introduction *into* Politics" (Arendt 2005).

12 See my discussion of radical evil in Bernstein 1996: 137–53.

13 Although I agree with Lefort that there is a strong connection between Arendt's reading of totalitarianism and her understanding of politics, I would emphasize that it was by "dwelling on horrors" that Arendt came to appreciate the plurality and spontaneity that are the conditions for action and politics. For it was precisely this plurality (and consequently men's humanity) that totalitarianism sought to destroy. Consequently, I reject the idea that Arendt's conception of politics is based upon an (idealized) conception of the Greek polis. On the contrary, her appeal to the Greeks (and Romans) is intended to help elucidate what she takes to be at the core of men's humanity – plurality, action, power, and public freedom.

14 On the cover of the 2006 Penguin edition of *Between Past and Future*, there is a representation of the double-faced Roman god, Janus. This is directly related to the gap between past and future. But the double-faced Janus has symbolic significance for Arendt. Action, natality, and new beginnings are double-faced. New beginnings do not necessarily result in favorable outcomes. The emergence of totalitarianism in the twentieth century is also rooted in the human capacity to act and initiate something new; it was an unprecedented event, a dark "new beginning."

15 Although Arendt thinks that there is a distinctive manifestation of power in the "privileged moments" that exemplify the revolutionary spirit, her concept of power has a broader significance. All governments, even totalitarian and tyrannical governments, "rest" on power insofar as the authority of the government is accepted by the people who are governed. No government can survive on violence alone. "No government exclusively based on the means of violence has ever existed. Even the totalitarian ruler, whose chief instrument of rule is torture, needs a power basis – the secret police and its net of informers.... Even the most despotic domination we know of, the rule of master over slaves, who always outnumbered him, did not rest on superior means of coercion as such, but on a superior organization of power – that is the organized solidarity of the masters" (Arendt 1970: 50).

16 For a discussion of the meaning of revolution and how it differs from rebellion, see Arendt 1977: 21–58.

17 Arendt is emphatic in distinguishing liberation from revolution.

> There is perhaps nothing more detrimental to an understanding of revolution than the common assumption that the revolutionary process has come to an end when liberation is achieved and the turmoil and the violence, inherent in all wars of independence, have come to an end. This view is not new. In 1787, Benjamin Rush complained that "there is nothing more common, than to confound the term of American Revolution with those of the late American war. The American war is over: On the contrary, nothing but the first act of the great drama is closed. It remains yet to establish and perfect our new forms of government.".... We may add that there still is nothing more common than to confound the travail of liberation with the foundation of freedom. (Arendt 1977: 299)

18 Arendt has been criticized for the historical inaccuracy of her portrayal of the American and French Revolutions. And she has a tendency to overemphasize the contrast by presenting an "ideal" account of the founding of the American Republic. But ever since the path-breaking historical study of Gordon S. Wood, *The Creation of the American Republic*, historians have come to appreciate those elements of the founding of the Republic that Arendt highlights – and at times exaggerates.

19 This passage, the final paragraph of the penultimate chapter of *On Revolution*: "Foundation II: *Novus Ordo Saeculorum*," sums up what is distinctive about the revolutionary spirit as exemplified by the American Revolution. It takes on special significance in light of Arendt's opening remarks in *On Revolution* about the long and deeply embedded tradition that all politics – and especially revolutions – are based on an original violent crime.

> The relevance of the problem of beginning to the phenomenon of revolution is obvious. That such a beginning must be intimately connected with violence seems to be vouched for by the legendary beginnings of our

history as both biblical and classical antiquity report it: Cain slew Abel, and Romulus slew Remus; violence was the beginning and, by the same token, no beginning could be made without using violence, without violating. The first recorded deeds in our biblical and our secular traditions, whether known to be legendary or believed in as historical fact, have traveled through the centuries with the force which human thought achieves in rare instances when it produces cogent metaphors or universally applicable tales. The tale spoke clearly: whatever brotherhood human beings may be capable of has grown out of fratricide, whatever political organization men may have achieved has its origin in crime. (Arendt 1977: 20)

Although Arendt was skeptical about Freud and psychoanalysis, she might have drawn upon Freud's *Totem and Taboo* for support that the "legendary beginnings of our history" are founded on violence. For Freud, however, the "beginning" of politics and morality is patricide, not fratricide. The brothers in the "primal horde" kill the father. And this "event" is repeated throughout history.

Arendt's reflections on the revolutionary spirit can be read as a radical challenge to, and refutation of, the long tradition that sees *all* politics as having its "origin" in violent crime. Her basic argument is that a proper understanding of the "problem of beginning" and the "revolutionary spirit" reveals a politics that is not based upon violence; it is a beginning based on "the combined power of the many" and is antithetical to violence. Furthermore, her sharp distinction of power and violence helps to explain her profound skepticism about the concept of sovereignty, which has been associated with "legitimate" violence. Indeed, she claims that "the greatest American innovation in politics as such was the consistent abolishment of sovereignty within the body politic of the republic, the insight that in the realm of human affairs sovereignty and tyranny are the same" (Arendt 1977: 153).

20   When Arendt praises the politics of the early stages of the worldwide student movement in the 1960s, she explicitly relates this to the tradition of the revolutionary spirit. "The one positive slogan the new movement has put forth, the claim for "participatory democracy" that has echoed around the globe and constitutes the most significant common denominator of the rebellions in the East and the West, derives from the best in the revolutionary tradition – the council system, the always defeated but only authentic outgrowth of every revolution from the eighteenth century" (Arendt 1970: 22).

21   In her essay "Lying in Politics: Reflections on the Pentagon Papers," Arendt argues that the mentality of *homo faber* shaped American foreign policy and led to the disastrous escalation of the Vietnam War (Arendt 1972: 3–43).

22   Arendt's quotations in this passage are from Henri Bergson's *Creative Evolution*.

23 Before (and sometimes after) Arendt sharply distinguished power and violence, she frequently uses "power" in the more conventional sense of "power over" – the power by one individual or group to control other individuals and groups. For example, in chapter 12 of *The Origins*, "Totalitarianism in Power," she describes how totalitarian regimes acquire, maintain, and use their power over their subjects.

24 For a discussion of what Arendt means by "radical evil" and how it is related to her better-known phrase "the banality of evil," see Bernstein 1996: 137–78.

25 Arendt made changes in the various editions of *The Origins*, sometimes adding and sometimes deleting material. "Ideology and Terror: A Novel Form of Government," the final chapter of *The Origins*, is based on a paper that she wrote in 1953. She added it to the 1958 edition of *The Origins*, and it is included in all subsequent editions.

26 In 1939, Hans Jonas, a close friend of Arendt from her student days in Germany who was then living in Palestine, also wrote an open letter calling for a Jewish army to fight "our war." Jonas subsequently fought against the Nazis in the famous Jewish Brigade, wearing the Star of David. His open letter is included as an appendix in Wiese 2007: 167–75.

27 In her interview with Günter Gaus, when he describes her as a philosopher, she replies: "I am afraid I have to protest. I do not belong to the circle of philosophers. My profession, if one can even speak of it at all, is political theory. I neither feel like a philosopher, nor do I believe that I have been accepted in the circle of philosophers, as you so kindly suppose" (Arendt 1994: 1).

28 I have criticized her interpretation of Hegel and Marx in Bernstein 1977.

29 She also writes: "To expect people, who have not the slightest notion of what the *res publica*, the public thing is, to behave nonviolently and argue rationally in matters of interest is neither realistic nor reasonable" (Arendt 1970: 78).

30 See the perceptive discussion of the council system in Kalyvas 2008: 254–91.

31 In my chapter on Fanon, I show that he, in effect, advances this argument for the colonized who are violently oppressed by a colonial system.

32 For further reflections on the meaning and role of thinking, see Bernstein 2000.

Chapter 4   Frantz Fanon's Critique of Violence

1 Richard Philcox, who published a new English translation in 2004, mentions that he had listened to a tape of an address by Fanon. "Knowing that *Les Damnés de la Terre* had been dictated to his wife during his final year, I used the oral tone I had captured over the tape in my translation

of *The Wretched of the Earth* and endeavored to make it read more like an oral presentation with that earnestness of voice he was known for" (245). All page references in the text are to Fanon 2004.

2   For a perceptive analysis and critique of Sartre's preface see Butler 2006.

3   Richard Philcox, the second English translator of *Les Damnés*, notes the difficulty of translating *colon*. "One of the translation problems I had to settle, which came up time and time again throughout the text, was the translation of 'colon,' the European inhabitant of a colony once the colonization process has got under way. I was tempted to use the word colonizer since it sounded right pitted against the word colonized. But a colonizer composes the original force that colonized the country and does not convey the meaning of the European who settled, lived, worked, and was born in the colony" (246–7). Philcox translates *colon* as "colonist" and *colonisé* as "colonized subject." I have generally followed Philcox in using the expression "colonist" when referring specifically to *colon*. Occasionally, I use the term "colonizer" in opposition to the "colonized," especially when discussing the dynamics of the colonial system.

In *The Wretched of the Earth*, Fanon analyzes the general structure of the colonial system – primarily as it existed in Africa. Algeria was, strictly speaking, not a French colony but part of French territory. The Constitution of 1848 divided Algeria into three French departments. This distinctive political and legal structure exacerbated the colonial situation in Algeria because it was at once French and not French.

4   Fanon's main point calls to mind a wonderful scene in the 1966 film *The Battle of Algiers* – a brief dialogue between Ali and Ben M'Hidi, one of the four members of the Central Executive Committee of FLN. They are discussing the general strike that is taking place in Algiers. Ben M'Hidi speaks: "Wars aren't won with terrorism, neither wars nor revolutions. Terrorism is a beginning but afterward, all the people must act. . . . This is the reason for the strike, and its necessity: to mobilize all Algerians, count them and measure their strength." He then continues: "Do you know something Ali? Starting a revolution is hard, and it's even harder to continue it. Winning is hardest of all. But only afterward, when we have won, will the real hardships begin."

5   The following sentences are typical: "Pratiquement *il y aura* au moins un membre du bureau politique dans chaque region et on évitera de le nommer chef de région. *Il n'aura pas* entre ses mains les pouvoirs administratifs. Le membre du bureau politique régional n'est pas tenu d'occuper le plus haut rang dans l'appareil asmistratif régional. *Il ne doit pas* obligatoirement faire corps avec le pouvoir" (Fanon 1991: 227, my emphasis). "Nous pensons au contraire que l'intérieur, l'arrière-pays *devrait être* privilégié" (ibid. 228, my emphasis). "Les fonctionnaires et les techniciens autochtones *doivent* s'enfoncer non dans les diagrammes et les statistiques, mais dans le corps du peuple" (ibid. 229, my emphasis).

Fanon wrote *Les Damnés* before Algeria was granted independence. Consequently, his sharp critique of the national bourgeoisie is based on his observation of what was happening in other African countries – and perhaps his anxiety about what might yet happen in Algeria.

6   Fanon perceptively describes these changes in his phenomenologically descriptive essays included in *A Dying Colonialism*. In "Algeria Unveiled" he traces the stages – the actions and reactions – of Algerian women in veiling and unveiling themselves. In "This is the Voice of Algeria" he describes the initial skepticism of Algerians about the radio because they associated it with the occupier. Gradually the rural population bought battery radios and attentively listened to the "Voice of Fighting Algeria" (despite French attempts to jam the frequency). This form of communication came to play a key role in the struggle for liberation. See Fanon 1994.

7   In the Introduction to *Black Skin, White Masks*, Fanon writes: "The structure of the present work is grounded in temporality. Every human problem cries out to be considered on the basis of time, the ideal being that the present always serves to build the future" (Fanon 2008: p. xvi). This statement is even more applicable to *The Wretched of the Earth*.

8   One of the major differences between Fanon's first book, *Black Skin, White Masks* (written when he was living in France and before he moved to Algeria), and *The Wretched of the Earth* is that in the former book Fanon is almost exclusively concerned with Black–White relations. In the latter book he focuses on the colonized oppressed (including Africans and Arabs).

9   It is well known that in the Algerian war there were acts of extreme brutality and torture by both the French and the Algerians. In the Preface to *A Dying Colonialism*, Fanon addresses this issue:

> Because we want a democratic and a renovated Algeria, because we believe one cannot rise and liberate oneself in one area and sink in another, we condemn, with pain in our hearts, those brothers who have flung themselves into revolutionary action with the almost physiological brutality that centuries of oppression give rise to and feed.
>
> The people who condemn us or blame us for these dark aspects of the Revolution know nothing of the terrible problem faced by the chief who must take disciplinary action against a patriot guilty, for example, of having killed a notorious traitor – or, worse, a woman or child – without having received orders to do so. This man who must be judged in the absence of a code, of any law, only by the conscience that each one has of what is allowable and what is forbidden, may not be a new man in the combat group. He may have given, over a period of months, unmistakable proofs of abnegation, of patriotism, of courage. Yet he must be judged. . . .
>
> It is not easy to conduct, with a minimum of errors, the struggle of a people, sorely tried by a hundred and thirty years of domination, against an enemy as determined and as ferocious as French colonialism. (Fanon 1994: 25–6)

10   I believe that the reason why Richard Philcox translates *colonisé* as "colonized subject" is to make clear that the colonized are *fabricated* by the colonizers. *"C'est le colon qui a fait et qui continue à faire le colonisé."*

11   Fanon consistently uses masculine pronouns and frequently refers to the "muscular" reactions of the colonized. Some feminists have criticized Fanon's masculine bias. In fairness to Fanon, his appreciative description of the role of women in the revolutionary struggle should be emphasized. See his "Algeria Unveiled" in Fanon 1994.

12   There is another scene in *The Battle of Algiers* (based on a real incident) that illustrates Fanon's point about the role of leadership in restraining spontaneous violence. This is the scene in which the French authorities covertly explode a bomb in the Casbah. The native Algerians are so enraged that they begin to descend into the French Quarter shouting "Murderers, Murderers." But the mob scene is stopped by leaders of the FLN who warn that the Algerians will be massacred. They promise that the FLN will retaliate. Eventually the FLN does bomb several French sites, killing French civilians.

13   One should remember, however, that the seven-day nonviolent general strike that was organized in the Casbah in 1957 proved to be one of the most dramatic and effective events in changing world opinion in favor of Algerian independence.

Chapter 5   Jan Assmann: The Mosaic Distinction and Religious Violence

1   Assmann distinguishes different types and functions of memory. The most important type of memory for mnemohistory is *cultural memory*. In *Religion and Cultural Memory* he explains what he and Aleida Assmann mean by cultural memory:

> In her book *Time and Tradition*, Aleida Assmann has contrasted communication and tradition: "Tradition can be understood as a special case of communication in which information is not exchanged reciprocally and horizontally, but is transmitted vertically through the generations." In this way, cultural memory can be considered to be a special case of communicative memory. It has a different temporal structure. If we think of the typical three-generation cycle of communicative memory as a synchronic memory space, then cultural memory, with its traditions reaching far back into the past, forms the diachronic axis. (Assmann 2006: 8)

For a fuller account of cultural memory and its relation to other types of memory, see Assmann 2006.

2   "Polytheism" and "monotheism" are terms that were invented in the eighteenth century. Assmann frequently prefers to speak of

"cosmotheism" rather than "polytheism." For his detailed understanding of polytheism, see Assmann 2008.

3 For details of the variations of this early extra-biblical mnemohistory of Moses the Egyptian, see "Suppressed History, Repressed Memory: Moses and Akhenaten," in Assmann 1997: 23–54.

4 Assmann is quoting from John Toland, *Origines Judaicae* (London, 1709).

5 One of the most fascinating subplots in Assmann's reconstruction of these ancient memories is the story of the lepers. In Manetho's account, Moses was a rebellious Egyptian priest who made himself a leader of a colony of lepers. Assmann argues that the story of the lepers originally referred to Akhenaten. But after Akhenaten's death "the traumatic memories of his revolution were encrypted and dislocated; eventually they came to be fixed on the Jews" (Assmann 1997: 5). This encrypted and distorted memory trace lives on in anti-Semitism right up to the twentieth century – the anti-Semitic portrayal of the Jews as epitomizing a highly contagious disease. Assmann explicitly states that his mnemohistory of the symbolic antagonism between Israel and Egypt is intended "to contribute to a historical analysis of anti-Semitism" (Assmann 1997: 6).

6 Assmann uses the term "discourse" and "discourse history" in a distinctive way. "By 'discourse' I understand something much more specific than what this term has come to refer to in the wake of Michel Foucault and others. I am referring to a concatenation of texts which are based on each other and treat or negotiate a common subject matter. In this view, discourse is a kind of textual conversation or debate which might extend over generations and centuries, even millennia, depending on institutionalizations of permanence such as writing, canonization and clerical institutions, and so forth" (Assmann 1997: 15–16).

7 For a fuller discussion of the narrative of this deconstruction, see my review of *Moses the Egyptian* (Bernstein 1999).

8 Assmann briefly discusses two early periods of Egyptian "revival" or "Egyptomania" in Europe, the Renaissance and Napoleon's expedition to Egypt, but his main focus is on the Moses/Egypt discourse that anticipates and is influenced by the Enlightenment.

9 Although the principle of normative inversion is elaborated by Maimonides, it was already used by Manetho in the contrast he draws between Egypt and Israel. Israel is the inversion of everything that is true and desirable in Egypt.

10 Assmann distinguishes between a historical and a mnemohistorical approach to thinkers:

> The approach of mnemohistory is highly selective. A historical – either Egyptological or Biblical – investigation of the traditions about Moses and Egypt would be far more comprehensive. It would certainly take account of the considerable amount of available epigraphical, archaeological, and philological evidence. . . . I am reading Maimonides

only in light of Spencer, John Spencer in the light of William Warburton, Warburton in the light of Reinhold and Schiller, and Freud insofar as he partakes in this discourse and reflects on its issues. (Assmann 1997: 10)

11   The title in German is *Die Hebräischen Mysterien oder die ältese religiöse Freymaurerey*. For details of Reinhold's contribution to the discourse history of Moses the Egyptian, see Assmann 1997: 115–25.

12   Freud was a great admirer of Schiller, and there is strong evidence that he was familiar with *Die Sendung Moses*, although he doesn't cite it in *Moses and Monotheism*. I have followed the convention of referring to Freud's book as *Moses and Monotheism*, which is the English title of both translations of *Der Mann Moses und die monotheistische Religion: Drei Abhandlungen*. I have argued, however that a more perspicacious translation (the literal title in German) would be "The Man Moses and the Monotheistic Religion." See Bernstein 1998: 122, n. 2. See also Assmann 1997: 149.

13   Assmann has changed his mind about Freud. He no longer thinks that Freud was trying to abolish the Mosaic distinction between the true and false religion. For Assmann's revised understanding of Freud, see his chapter "Sigmund Freud and Progress in Intellectuality" in Assmann 2010: 87–103. For my own critique of Assmann's original interpretation of Freud's *Moses and Monotheism*, see Bernstein 1999: 246–52.

14   See Bernstein 1998 and 1999 where I argue for this thesis. Assmann now agrees with me. In *The Price of Monotheism*, he writes:

> In the Freud chapter of my book *Moses the Egyptian*, I misunderstood the connection between the Mosaic distinction and Freud's notion of "progress in intellectuality." I advanced there a view that I no longer believe tenable today, especially since reading Richard Bernstein's *Freud and the Legacy of Moses*. My claim was that, in depicting Moses as an Egyptian, Freud was trying to abolish the Mosaic distinction between the true and false religion. I could receive this impression because I came to Freud's book on Moses immediately after reading Spencer, Reinhold, and Schiller and while still under their influence. . . . I now think that Freud was trying, on the contrary, to present the Mosaic distinction (in the form of the ban on graven images) as a seminal, immensely valuable, and profoundly Jewish achievement, which ought on no account to be relinquished, and that his own psychoanalysis could credit itself precisely with taking this specifically Jewish type of progress a step further. (Assmann 2010: 86)

15   The target of most of these severe critiques has *not* been Assmann's account of the seventeenth- and eighteenth-century Moses/Egypt discourse – what Assmann takes to be his scholarly discovery – but rather the way in which he frames this discourse as a response to the Mosaic distinction. "The book was almost universally understood as a contribution to the critique of religion, if not a frontal attack on monotheism in general and/or Christianity in particular" (Assmann 2010: 4).

16 Assmann is quoting the critic Erich Zenger. See Assmann's summary of the objections of his critics in Assmann 2010: 5–6.

17 Assmann explains what he means by a "revolution" in this monotheistic context. "[O]ne is dealing here with the phenomenon of retrospection (*Nachträglichkeit*), to use the Freudian term, a revolution a posteriori, after the fact; and a feat not of history but of memory. . . . [I]n the Hebrew Bible, the codified cultural memory of the Jewish people, successful realization of monotheism, is represented as a leap and a revolutionary break as radical as one can possibly imagine" (Assmann 2008: 108).

18 Assmann makes clear that "there is no such thing as 'the' biblical monotheism" and that "the Bible contains many different traditions and correspondingly, many varieties of monotheism or monolatry," but he nevertheless claims that "Deuteronomism, or covenant theology, has proven enormously influential in the course not only of Jewish but also Christian – especially Protestant – history" (Assmann 2008: 114). Assmann distinguishes between primary and secondary religions. Exclusive monotheism is a secondary religion.

> Primary religions evolve historically over hundreds and thousands of years within a single culture, society, and generally also language, with all of which they are inextricably entwined. Religions of this kind include the cultic and divine worlds of Egyptian, Babylonian and Greco-Roman antiquity, among many others. Secondary religions, by contrast, are those that owe their existence to an act of revelation and foundation, build on primary religions, and typically differentiate themselves from the latter by denouncing them as paganism, idolatry and superstition. (Assmann 2010: 1)

19 Assmann distinguishes four simple or original kinds of truth: truths of experience, mathematical or geometrical truths, historical truths, and truths conducive to life. But with the Mosaic distinction a new "fifth truth enters the world along with it: *Credo in unum Deum*" (Assmann 2010: 15).

20 Compare this passage with the concluding paragraph of *The Price of Monotheism*:

> I am thus endeavoring to undertake a labor of remembrance that brings the repressed to light so that it may then be worked through or "sublimated," to borrow Freud's expression. I want to sublimate the Mosaic distinction, not revoke it. I firmly believe . . . that we can no longer rely on "absolute" truths, only on relative, pragmatic truths, which will constantly need to be renegotiated. The Mosaic distinction stands, as Freud taught us, not just for trauma, repression, and neurosis, but equally for "progress in intellectuality," which ought not to be relinquished, no matter how dearly it may have been purchased. We need to hold fast to the distinction of true and false, to clear concepts of what we feel to be irreconcilable with our convictions, if these convictions are to retain their

strength and depth. But we will no longer be able to ground this distinction in revelations that have been given once and for all. In this way, we must make the Mosaic distinction the object of incessant reflection and redefinition, subjecting it to a "discursive fluidification" (Jürgen Habermas), if it is to remain, for us, the indispensable basis for an advance in humanity. (Assmann 2010: 120)

21　See Assmann 2008: 106–26 for his analysis of other examples of the language of violence in the Hebrew Bible.

22　See also "Monotheism, Memory, and Trauma: Reflections on Freud's Book on Moses" (Assmann 2006: 46–62), where Assmann argues that the themes of trauma, guilt, and memory "have nothing at all to do with that phylogenetic dimension of depth that Freud believes he must explore. Instead, they form an explicit part of the surface reality of the history of religion and its documents" (Assmann 2006: 47).

23　Freud speaks of the "Jews" in this context, not the "Hebrews" or "Israelites." This is consistent with his key claim that the man Moses created the Jewish people.

24　Freud doesn't simply *assume* that concepts applicable to individuals are applicable to cultural memory and repression. He argues for the plausibility of drawing this analogy. See my discussion in Bernstein 1998: 40–4.

25　For the text of Freud's letter and Andreas-Salomé's reply see Bernstein 1998: 117–20.

26　See my discussion of the interplay of conscious and unconscious memory traces in Bernstein 1998: 58–64.

27　See Bernstein 1998: esp. 30–5; 83–9, and 114.

28　Assmann says that this violence is what "Benjamin for some obscure reason calls 'divine violence'" (Assmann 2008: 142). This is a highly dubious interpretation of "divine violence." See my discussion of Benjamin's concept of divine violence in Chapter 2.

29　See his discussion of ritual violence in Assmann 2008: 28–52.

30　See Girard 1972. See also Charles Taylor's discussion of the traces and transformation of ritual violence in Christianity in Taylor 2007: 638–75.

31　Assmann is referring to Schmitt's famous friend and enemy (*Freund und Feind*) distinction, which is the antithesis that defines "the political." In some of his later writings, Schmitt distinguishes "enemy" and "foe." The "foe" is someone that we attempt to annihilate, not simply defeat.

32　See my discussion of ambivalence in Bernstein 2002: 138–40.

Chapter 6　Reflections on Nonviolence and Violence

1　Critchley comments that "'guideline' doesn't quite render the provisional – indeed artisanal – idea of a plumb line or thumb-line suggested by *Richtschnur*, where the latter is that piece of string or *Schnur* used by a builder to mark out an intended direction or *Richtung* for construction. Such a *Richtschnur* – I take it this is Benjamin's point – is not an exact measure, but an approximation, a guess, a rule of thumb rather than an absolute, categorical law" (Critchley 2012: 218).

2   In *On Violence* Arendt also cites self-defense as an example of when violence may be justified.

3   See Goldoni and McCorkindale 2012 for a collection of perceptive essays that discuss Arendt's varied and complex understanding of *nomos* and *lex*.

4   Peg Birmingham claims that Arendt's "distinction between instrumental violence, on the one hand, and the living spirit of power, is extremely close to Benjamin's distinction between mythical and divine violence." I am not persuaded by Birmingham's claim that Arendt's essay on violence, especially her insistence on the distinction between violence and power, is an attempt to think further and clarify Benjamin's understanding of "divine violence" (Birmingham 2010: 5). Benjamin's brief remarks about divine violence bear little resemblance to Arendt's characterization of power.

5   The antithesis between Schmitt and Arendt is epitomized in their different conceptions of the act of constituting a new government. Schmitt understands the *pouvoir constuant* in a collectivist and plebiscite manner. The "people" consist of an organic unity. For Arendt "the people" consist of a *plurality* of individuals who share a common world. Democratic participation for Schmitt is by acclamation. For Arendt, democratic participation involves debate, deliberation, and the mutual testing of opinions. See Kalyvas 2008 for a critical discussion of Schmitt's plebiscitary conception of democracy.

6   See Kalyvas 2008 for an analysis of the similarities and differences between Schmitt and Arendt concerning "extraordinary" politics.

7   In an interview that Arendt gave in 1970, she was asked about her alternative to the modern concept of the sovereign state. In her reply she gave a brief description of the council system and said: "A council-state of this sort, to which the principle of sovereignty would be wholly alien, would be admirably suited to federations of the most various kinds, especially because in it power would be constituted horizontally and not vertically. But if you ask me now what prospect it has of being realized, then I must say to you: Very slight, if at all. And yet perhaps, after all – in the wake of the next revolution" (Arendt 1972: 233).

8   Although Arendt's sketch of a federation of councils as an alternative to the idea of a sovereign state is barely developed, her *critique* of sovereignty takes on a new relevance in light of recent debates concerning the need to move beyond the sovereignty of "autonomous" nation-states.

9   Arendt's Fanon quotations are from the first English translation by Constance Farrington of *The Wretched of the Earth*, published by Grove Press in 1968.

10   Arendt shows her sensitivity to the complexity of Fanon's reflections on violence when, later in her essay, she writes: "Fanon, who had an infinitely greater intimacy with the practice of violence than either [Sorel or Pareto], was greatly influenced by Sorel and used his categories even when his own experiences spoke clearly against them." Arendt adds a fascinating footnote to this sentence. She quotes a passage from Deming 1968: "It is my conviction that [Fanon] can be quoted as well to plead for nonviolence.... Every time you find the word 'violence' in his pages, substitute for it the phrase 'radical and uncompromising action.' I contend that with the exception of a very few passages this substitution can be made, and that the action he calls for could just as well be nonviolent action." (See Arendt 1970: 71.)

11   The quotations in this passage are from *The Wretched of the Earth*.

12   The classic example of this violence, for Arendt, is Billy Budd who strikes "dead the man who bore false witness against him" (Arendt 1970: 64).

13   The similarity between Fanon and Arendt goes even deeper. Fanon agrees with Arendt that rage can also be irrational and pathological. He shows this in his analysis of mental disorders of *both* Algerians and Frenchmen caused by the colonial war. ("Colonial War and Mental Disorders," in Fanon 2004)

14   In the sentence that follows this passage, Arendt writes: "However, England in India and France in Algeria had good reasons for their restraint" (Arendt 1970: 53). I find this claim – especially about the French in Algeria – baffling. Given what was well known at the time about the severity of the French reaction to the Algerian uprising – the systematic use of torture, imprisonment, and massacres – I can't imagine what she has in mind when she speaks about the restraint of the French in Algeria.

15   On November 12, 1954, Pierre Mendès France, who, only a few months before, had completed the liquidation of France in Indochina, declared before the French National Assembly: "One does not compromise when it comes to defending the internal peace of the nation, the unity and integrity of the Republic. The Algerian departments are part of the French Republic. They have been French for a long time, and they are irrevocably French.... Between them and metropolitan France there can be no conceivable secession."

16   This does *not* mean – as Fanon himself notes – that everything that the FLN did in the name of their struggle was justified.

17   Here we see another common theme in Fanon and Arendt. For Arendt, revolution institutes a new beginning, a new worldly order – although she would not describe this as a "new humanity."

References

Agamben, G. (1998) *Homo Sacer: Sovereign Power and Bare Life*. Stanford: Stanford University Press.

Arendt, H. (1958a) *The Human Condition*. Chicago: University of Chicago Press.

—— (1958b) *The Origins of Totalitarianism*, 2nd edn. New York: Median Books.

—— (1965) *Eichmann in Jerusalem: A Report on the Banality of Evil*, 2nd edn. New York: Viking Press.

—— (1968a) *Men in Dark Times*. Harcourt Brace & World.

—— (1968b) *Illuminations*. New York: Harcourt, Brace & World.

—— (1970) *On Violence*. New York: Harcourt, Inc.

—— (1972) *Crises of the Republic*. New York: Harcourt Brace Jovanovich.

—— (1976) *The Origins of Totalitarianism*, 3rd edn. New York: Harcourt, Inc.

—— (1977) *On Revolution*. New York: Penguin Books.

—— (1978) *The Life of the Mind*. New York: Harcourt Brace & Co.

—— (1994) *Essays in Understanding*. New York: Harcourt Brace & Co.

—— (2005) "Introduction *into* Politics," in *The Promise of Politics*, pp. 93–200. New York: Schocken Books.

—— (2006) *Between Past and Future*. New York: Penguin Books.

—— (2007) *The Jewish Writings*. New York: Schocken Books.

—— and Jaspers, K. (1992) *Correspondence 1926–1979*. New York: Harcourt Brace Jovanovich.

Assmann, J. (1997) *Moses the Egyptian: The Memory of Egypt in Western Monotheism*. Cambridge, Mass.: Harvard University Press.

—— (2006) *Religion and Cultural Memory*. Stanford: Stanford University Press.

—— (2008) *Of God and Gods: Egypt, Israel, and the Rise of Monotheism*. Madison: University of Wisconsin Press.

—— (2010) *The Price of Monotheism*. Stanford: Stanford University Press.

Avineri, S. (1968) *The Social and Political Thought of Karl Marx*. Cambridge: Cambridge University Press.

Bargu, B. (2010) "Unleashing the Acheron: Sacrificial Partisanship, Sovereignty, and History," *Theory & Event*, 13/1: 1–23.

Bendersky, J. (1983) *Carl Schmitt: Theorist for the Reich*. Princeton: Princeton University Press.

—— (2005) "Schmitt and the Jewish Question," *Telos*, 132: 64–82.

Benjamin, W. (1996) *Walter Benjamin: Selected Writings*, vol. 1: *1913–1926*. Cambridge, Mass.: Harvard University Press.

Bernstein, R. J. (1977) "Hannah Arendt: The Ambiguities of Theory and Practice," in *Political Theory and Praxis: New Perspectives*, ed. Terrence Ball, pp. 141–58. Minneapolis: University of Minnesota Press.

—— (1983) *Beyond Objectivism and Relativism: Science, Hermeneutics, and Praxis*. Philadelphia: University of Pennsylvania Press.

—— (1996) *Hannah Arendt and the Jewish Question*. Cambridge: Polity.

—— (1998) *Freud and the Legacy of Moses*. Cambridge: Cambridge University Press.

—— (1999) "Review of Jan Assmann's *Moses the Egyptian*," *Graduate Faculty Philosophy Journal*, 21/2: 233–53.

—— (2000) "Arendt on Thinking," in *The Cambridge Companion to Hannah Arendt*, ed. Dana Villa, pp. 277–92. Cambridge: Cambridge University Press.

—— (2002) *Radical Evil: A Philosophical Interrogation*. Cambridge: Polity.

—— (2005) *The Abuse of Evil: The Corruption of Politics and Religion since 9/11*. Cambridge: Polity.

Birmingham, P. (2010) "On Violence, Politics, and the Law," *Journal of Speculative Philosophy*, new series, 24/1: 1–20.

Butler, J. (2006) "Critique, Coercion, and Sacred Life in Benjamin's 'Critique of Violence'," in *Political Theologies: Public Religions in a Post-Secular World*, pp. 201–19. New York: Fordham University Press.

Cover, R. (1993) *Narrative, Violence and the Law*, ed. M. Minow, M. Ryan, and A Sarat, pp. 203–38. Ann Arbor: University of Michigan Press.

Critchley, S. (2012) *The Faith of the Faithless: Experiments in Political Theology*. New York: Verso.

Deming, Barbara (1968) "On Revolution and Equilibrium," *Liberation*, 12/2: 10–21.

Derrida, J. (1990) "Force of Law: The Mystical Foundation of Authority," *Cardozo Law Review*, 11: 921–1045.

—— (1997) *Politics of Friendship*. London: Verso.

Dodd, J. (2009) *Violence and Phenomenology*. New York: Routledge.

Dyzenhaus, D. (1997) *Legality and Legitimacy*. Oxford: Oxford University Press.

Fanon, F. (1991) *Les Damnés de la terre*. Paris: Editions Gallimard.

—— (1994) *A Dying Colonialism*, trans. Haakon Chevalier. New York: Grove Press.

—— (2004) *The Wretched of the Earth*, trans. Richard Philcox. New York: Grove Press.

—— (2008) *Black Skin, White Masks*, trans. Richard Philcox. New York: Grove Press.

Freud, S. (1964) *Moses and Monotheism*, in *The Standard Edition of the Complete Works of Sigmund Freud*, vol. 23. London: Hogarth Press.

Girard, René (1972) *Violence and the Sacred*. Baltimore: Johns Hopkins University Press.

Goldoni, M., and McCorkindale, C. (eds) (2012) *Hannah Arendt and the Law*. Oxford: Hart Publishing.

Gross, R. (2000) *Carl Schmitt und die Juden*. Frankfurt: Suhrkamp Verlag.

Habermas, J. (1979) "Consciousness-Raising or Redemptive Criticism: The Contemporaneity of Walter Benjamin," *New German Critique*, no. 17: 30–59.

Hanssen, B. (2000) *Critique of Violence: Between Poststructuralism and Critical Theory*. London: Routledge.

Haverkamp, A. (ed.) (1994) *Gewalt und Gerechtigkeit*. Frankfurt: Suhrkamp Verlag.

Hegel, G. W. F. (1977) *The Phenomenology of Spirit*. Oxford: Clarendon Press.

Hill, M. A. (ed.) (1977) *Hannah Arendt: The Recovery of the Public World*. New York: St Martin's Press.

Honneth, A. (2009) "Saving the Sacred with a Philosophy of History," in *Pathologies of Reason*, pp. 88–121. New York: Columbia University Press.

Jay, M. (1987) "Reconciling the Irreconcilable? A Rejoinder to Kennedy," *Telos*, 71: 67–80.

—— (2003) *Refractions of Violence*. New York: Routledge.

Kalyvas, A. (2008) *Democracy and the Politics of the Extraordinary: Max Weber, Carl Schmitt, and Hannah Arendt*. Cambridge: Cambridge University Press.

Kennedy, E. (1987) "Carl Schmitt and the Frankfurt School," *Telos*, 71: 37–66.

Koenen, A. (1995) *Der Fall Carl Schmitt: Sein Aufsteig zum "Kronjuristen des Dritten Reiches."* Darmstadt: Wissenschaftliche Buchgesellschaft.

La Capra, D. (1990) "Violence, Justice, and the Force of Law," *Cardozo Law Review*, 11: 1065–78.

—— (2009) "Toward a Critique of Violence," in *History and its Limits*, pp. 90–122. Ithaca: Cornell University Press.

Lefort, C. (1988) "Hannah Arendt and the Question of the Political," in *Democracy and Political Theory*, pp. 45–55. Minneapolis: University of Minnesota Press.

Marcuse, H. (1965) "Afterword," in *Walter Benjamin: Zur Kritik der Gewalt und andere Aufsätze*, pp. 99–106. Frankfurt: Suhrkamp Verlag.

—— (1968) "The Struggle Against Liberalism in the Totalitarian View of the State," in *Negations*, pp. 3–42. Boston: Beacon Press.

McCormick, J. P. (1997) *Carl Schmitt's Critique of Liberalism: Against Politics as Technology*. Chicago: University of Chicago Press.

Mehring, R. (2009). *Carl Schmitt: Aufsteig und Fall*. Munich: C. H. Beck.

Meier, H. (1995) *Carl Schmitt & Leo Strauss: The Hidden Dialogue*. Chicago: University of Chicago Press.

—— (1998) *The Lesson of Carl Schmitt: Four Chapters on the Distinction between Political Theology and Political Philosophy*. Chicago: University of Chicago Press.

Mills, C. W. (1956) *The Power Elite*. New York: Oxford University Press.

Morgan, B. (2007) "Undoing Legal Violence: Walter Benjamin's and Giorgio Agamben's Aesthetics of Pure Means," *Journal of Law and Society*, 34/1: 46–64.

Negt, O. (1968) *Rechtsordung, Öffenlichkeit und Gewalt*, in *Der Auferstehung der Gewalt*, pp. 168–85. Frankfurt: Europäische Verlagsansalt.

Preuss, U. K. (1987) "The Critique of German Liberalism: A Reply to Kennedy," *Telos*, 71: 97–110.

Rogowski, R. (1994) "The Paradox of Law and Violence: Modern and Postmodern Readings of Benjamin's 'Critique of Violence'," *New Comparison*, 18: 131–51.

Rose, G. (1993) "Of Derrida's Spirit," in *Judaism & Modernity: Philosophical Essays*, pp. 65–87. Oxford: Blackwell.

Rüthers, B. (1990) *Carl Schmitt im Dritten Reich*. Munich: C. H. Beck.

Scheuerman, W. (1991) "Carl Schmitt and the Nazis," *German Politics and Society*, 23: 71–9.

—— (1999) *Carl Schmitt: The End of Law*. Lanham, Md.: Rowman & Littlefield.

Schmitt, C. (1927) "Der Begriff des Politischen," in *Archiv für Sozialwissenschaft und Sozialpolitik, Band* 58, pp. 1–33. Tübingen: Verlag von J. C. B. Mohr (Paul Siebeck).

—— (1996a) *The Concept of the Political*, trans. G. Schwab (with Leo Strauss's Notes on Schmitt's Essay). Chicago: University of Chicago Press.

—— (1996b) [1938] *The Leviathan in the State Theory of Thomas Hobbes: Meaning and Failure of a Political Symbol*, trans. G. Schwab and E. Hilfstein. Westport, Conn.: Greenwood Press.

—— (2002a) [1932] *Der Begriff des Politischen. Text von 1932 mit einem Vorwort und drei Corollarien*, 7th edn. Berlin: Duncker & Humblot.

—— (2002b) [1950] *Ex captivitate salus*. Berlin: Duncker & Humblot.

—— (2005) *Political Theology: Four Chapters on the Concept of Sovereignty*. Chicago: University of Chicago Press.

—— (2006) [1963] *Theorie des Partisanen. Zwischenbemerkung zum Begriff des Politischen*. Berlin: Duncker & Humblot.

—— (2007) *Theory of the Partisan: Intermediate Commentary on the Concept of the Political*, trans. G. L. Ulmen. New York: Telos Press.

Schwab, G. (1987) "Enemy or Foe: A Conflict of Modern Politics," *Telos*, 72: 194–201.

Slomp, G. (2009) *Carl Schmitt and the Politics of Hostility, Violence and Terror*. London: Palgrave Macmillan.

Sorel, G. (1908) *Réflexions sur la violence*. Paris: Librairie de "Pages libres."

Taylor, C. (2007) *The Secular Age*. Cambridge, Mass.: Harvard University Press.

Ulmen, G. I. (1987) "Return of the Foe," *Telos*, 72: 187–93.

Wiese, C. (2007) *The Life and Thought of Hans Jonas: Jewish Dimensions*. Waltham, Mass.: Brandeis University Press.

Wood, Gordon S. (1969) *The Creation of the American Republic*. Chapel Hill: University of North Carolina Press.

Yerushalmi, Y. (1991) *Freud's Moses: Judaism Terminable and Interminable*. New Haven: Yale University Press.

Young-Bruehl, E. (1982) *Hannah Arendt: For Love of the World*. New Haven: Yale University Press.

Žižek, S. (2008) *Violence*. New York: Picador.

Name Index

Subject Index